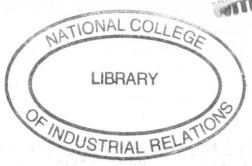
In the Footsteps of Big Jim

A Family Biography

Jim Larkin

BLACKWATER PRESS

Blackwater Press would like to thank the following for permission to use copyright material: Tom Connolly, Tommy Clancy, SIPTU, *Irish Press* Newspapers Ltd., *The Irish Times* , and the *Irish Worker.*

Editor
Susannah Gee

Design & Layout
Edward Callan

ISBN
0-86121-702-0

© – Jim Larkin

Produced in Ireland by
Blackwater Press
c/o Folens Publishers
8 Broomhill Business Park,
Tallaght, Dublin 24.

Contents

Acknowledgements v

Forewords
Dick Spring T.D. (Leader, of the Irish Labour Party, Tanaiste
and Minister for Foreign Affairs). vii
Peter Cassells (General Sec. ICTU) viii

Introduction ix

Family Tree x

The Early Years

Big Jim's Grandparents & Parents. 3

Childhood in Liverpool. 10

Work in Liverpool 12

Jim Larkin — Leader of Men 15

Big Jim Through Others' Eyes. 17

Belfast & Dublin

Jim Larkin in Belfast, 1907 21

Dublin 1909-1914 and the 'Lock-Out'. 24

Statements to the Commission of Inquiry 35

Reports of Police Officers (August 1913) 51

Public Opinion 56

British TUC and Labour Party View of 1913. 70

Two Continents Apart

Big Jim in America 79

Peter, and Australia 90

Delia 100

Jim's Return from America and the Formation of
The Workers' Union of Ireland .103

Big Jim — More Quotes 107

Continuation of the Larkin Tradition

Jim Jnr and Denis Larkin 113

Political Beliefs 116

Public Representation 122

Big Jim's Last Weeks 128

Jim Jnr and Denis as Others Viewed Them 130

My Father Denis 150

My Family Life

My Mother's Parents 157

My Arrival, Childhood and Youth 161

Starting Work 179

Working for the WUI 186

The Labour Court 197

Retirement 203

Life After Retirement 211

A Changing World 217

The ICTU 226

The Future 230

Acknowledgements

My first acknowledgement has to recognise the invaluable assistance I received from my wife, Brenda and daughter Miriam.

John O'Connor of Blackwater Press, and Editor, Susannah Gee, Senior Editor, Anna O'Donovan, have been of tremendous help and encouragement.

So many people are entitled to thanks for their kindness that I am sure that I have been the beneficiary of the affection with which my late grandfather, his family and his sons, are held in the memory of working people internationally. The numbers of organisations and people who responded positively to my request for information and anecdotes has been so large as to necessitate the division of acknowledgement. The responses have come from as far afield as Ireland, North and South, England, America and Australia (including Tasmania). When I started my research I never, for a moment, thought that so many people would be so kind and helpful.

Organisations in Ireland

Dail Eireann — Dick Spring T.D.; Dublin Corporation — William Soffe; Dublin Public Libraries; Dublin Diocesan Archives — David Sheehy (Archivist); National Archives — Catriona Crowe; National Gallery — D. Brian Kennedy; National Library — Patricia Donlon (Director) Kevin Brown (Archivist); Office of Public Works — Jim Phillips & John King (Personnel), Michael Breathnach — St Enda's Rathfarnham; John Toolin — Kilmainham Jail, Dept. of Environment (N.I.) — Dr. Chris Lynn; Hugh Lane Municipal Gallery; Public Registry Office; Garda Siochana Museum; University College Dublin Folklore Archives — Dr Fergus Darcy; Trinity College Dublin Library — Jack McGinley; Irish Labour History Society — Teresa Moriarty, Francis Devine, Charlie Callan; ICTU — Peter Cassells; SIPTU — Billy Attley, Brendan Hayes, Tom Crean, Manus O'Riordan, John Swift and all my other colleagues; BBC Radio Ulster — Pat Loughrey, George Jones, Siobhan Kane.

Newspapers

Irish Independent — Dr Tony O'Reilly, David McGrath, Paddy McMahon, Paul Dunne, Michael Daly; *Fingal Independent* — Ciara Ryan, Isobel Hurley; *Irish Press* — Tony Tormey (Features Editor), Tom Hanahoe (Photographs), Louise Ni Criaodan; *The Irish Times, RTE* — Gay Byrne, Joe Duffy.

Individuals

Dr John de Courcey Ireland, James Plunkett Kelly, Stella McConnon, Joe Ready (President ILHS), Bishop James Kavanagh, Martin King, Eddie Cassidy, ALT, Ben Briscoe T.D., Brian Fitzgerald T.D., Jean and Maureen McGrane, Jack Harte, Paddy and Breda Cardiff, Ger O'Leary, Jim Sheridan, Peter Sheridan, Patrick Joseph Ryan, Donal Nevin, Matt Merrigan Snr, Betty Hughes,

Barney and Molly McAvoy, Kathleen McAvoy, Margaret, Pat Gallagher, Pat and Jean O'Connor, Michael Boner, Verona Ni Bhroinn, Emily Barr, Tim Pat Coogan, Helen Carrish, Joan Carmichael, Seamus and Ann Fay, Michael & Bernie Gogarty, Betty Grant, Joe & Sylvia Harford, Brian Hoey, Pat and Margaret Keane, Kim Jenkinson, Bill McCamley, Liam Fitzsimons, Michael Cox (former Gen. Sec. NATE), Richard Kelly (photographer), Mrs Elders, (Killester Ave), Peter A. Keenan, Ken Devitt (printer).

England

Liverpool Public Libraries, Walker Museum — Teresa Doyle; Public Records Office (London); Liverpool Maritime Museum — Mariji Van Helmond; British Newspaper Library; Foreign Office; TUC — Christine Coates, Librarian; T & GWU (Liverpool) — E.J. Roberts; T & GWU (London) — Regan Scott; National Museum of Labour History (Manchester) — Nicholas Mansfield, Dr Stephen Bird (Archivist); Brian and Hilary Larkin; Bill and Marilyn Barber (Manchester); Tony Birtils (Liverpool), Alan O'Toole, Eileen and Cathy White; Ken Coates M.E.P.; Eric Taplin; Bob Parry M.P.; John Nettleton; Sheila Coleman; Sheila Graham; Margaret and John Helyer C.I.; J.E. Mortimer (Former Sec. British Labour Party). Many newspapers in Britain were most helpful.

America

AFL/CIO and Affiliates; Rebecca Larkin; Brian Larkin; Denis Larkin; Bill Lenahan (Asst. Director, Irish American Coalition); Terri Gallagher. Many American newspaper assisted.

Australia

As with America many Australian newspapers helped in my research.

Also Sonia and Brian Birks, George and Sheila Russell, Jack Tucker, Dr Frank Caine, Dr Verity Burgman.

I wish to acknowledge the following traders who have been most helpful. SWORDS; Clarke's, Camera Cabin, Peter Marks, Bank of Ireland, Michael Savage, Superquinn, Roy McCabe, Village Coffee Shop, J.C. Savage. MALAHIDE; The Buttery, Village Bookshop. SANTRY; Photo-on, John Adam.

As you can appreciate, a failure to acknowledge assistance, in my part, is purely due to an oversight as a result of the overwhelming response.

Special acknowledgement is due to my wife Brenda, Staff at Ty Mawr holiday camp, ambulance staff, medical, nursing and general staff at Glan Clwyd Hospital, Bodelwyddan, North Wales; Dr Brendan Dempsey, Swords; and medical, nursing and general staff at Beaumont Hospital, Dublin without whose care and attention I might not have survived my two heart attacks and been able to finish this book.

Foreword

Big Jim Larkin and his sons Denis and Jim Jnr. were giants of the Irish Labour Movement. They were three totally different characters, of course — Big Jim was a charismatic, impatient and dynamic man, young Jim was an innovator, and Denis was a conciliator. As someone said of them, if Big Jim Larkin was designed to create a revolution, his sons were designed to consolidate it.

They share a number of things in common — tremendous organising skills, a life-long commitment to the cause of social justice, and the same burning desire to "close the gap between what ought to be and what is".

Between them, they have left an indeliable mark on the Irish Labour Movement. Big Jim helped to found the Labour Party, and occupies today an honoured place in our history as one whose dedication and passion underpins everything we believe in. The new Constitution of the Party makes it clear that the inspiration of Larkin and Connolly has been and will remain our fundamental goal as long as poverty, deprivation, and oppression exist.

In their own way, each of the members of the Larkin family including Big Jim's sister, Delia Larkin — left behind monuments to that continuing aspiration. The two Jims served together as Labour Deputies in the short-lived Dáil of 1943, and I hope they would be proud today of the central role played by the Party in every aspect of Irish public life, and of strength and unity of the Party in the Dáil. For as long as the Labour Party exists, it will draw strength and inspiration from the name of Larkin.

Dick Spring — Leader of the Labour Party

Foreword

The Larkins as Trade Unionists

The Larkin Family have given us not only great trade union leaders, but also a form of trade unionism known as Larkinism. In the early days of this century the unskilled workers of this country were exploited, downtrodden, without hope and without organisation. They needed, as Christy Ferguson has pointed out, a giant figure, a man with the courage of a lion and the voice of a trumpet to rouse them... the Larkin Family gave us Big Jim.

In the fifties, when we needed, to again quote Christy Ferguson, a skilled negotiator rather than a fiery orator, a polished advocate, an intellectual with a brain as keen as a butcher's knife... the Larkin Family gave us young Jim.

In the seventies, when we needed someone to consolidate the National Wage Agreements, to give a larger and more vital role to Congress, to broaden the trade union negotiating agenda beyond wages, to include employment, taxation and the social wage, — the Larkin Family gave us Denis Larkin.

All three men had the unique distinction in their time of being General Secretary of the Workers' Union of Ireland and President of Congress.

Many key questions, of concern to workers and their unions, were addressed by the Larkins and their answers are as relevant now as they were then.

Involvement in Wealth Creation

"Not only do we work in industry, but live in the community.... If our people are to have more schools, more houses, more factories and more public facilities, increased wealth has got to come and our people must produce it... We are no longer, going to be told that industry is the private concern of the employer".

Beyond Wages

Whether the rank and file trade unionist realises or not, ever rising wages will not of themselves fulfil his needs, which have multiplied and taken on new forms. It is this many-sided aspect of today's trade unionist which is increasingly giving rise to conflict between the interest of the trade union as a producer and as a consumer.

A Strong Congress

Any union is free to be a lone wolf and hunt alone, but if it does, it cannot expect the rest of us to catch its prey and hold it down while it feeds upon it... No Union, whether it is the Electrical Trade Union or the biggest union in Congress, is powerful enough today to hunt on its own.... We all gain by our mutual association and our mutual support.

Peter Cassells, General Secretary, Congress

Introduction

No biography of any family would be complete without some reference to the social and economic background which influenced the philosophies of members of that family. I was fortunate enough to be able to secure information on my grandfather's parents and both his paternal and maternal grandparents. Both these families, the Larkins and the McAvoys, came from a Southern Ulster farming background. Like the majority of Irish people they were directly affected by the Great Famine and, from 1840 to 1870, many family members were compelled by force of circumstances to seek sustenance as widely afield as England, America, and Australia. It was this forced emigration that moulded my grandfather's vision of a better life and this was supported by the attitudes of his forebears. On the course of the book I am attempting to demonstrate that the same philosophy has been passed down through the subsequent generations.

Amongst the purposes I have in writing this book is to show the commitment of many members of the family to the Labour Movement – politically and industrially. You will see that our family has much in common with a large number of Irish families, in that its development was greatly affected by the Irish diaspora.

I have also tried to show the variety in our family life. We have had the same joys and sorrows as everyone else — the difference being that a number of members of my family took an active interest in attempting to balance the scales in favour of those in greatest need.

In the course of writing, I have tried to include some pointers that could well be of help. Some of these are taken directly from my grandfather's own words and those of others of the family. Despite the views of some people, I am well aware that my grandfather and those who came after him were human enough to enjoy life, including its humorous side. Every public figure is affected by family considerations.

Finally, working on this book has given me great joy and I trust that you will enjoy reading it.

Jim Larkin
September 1995

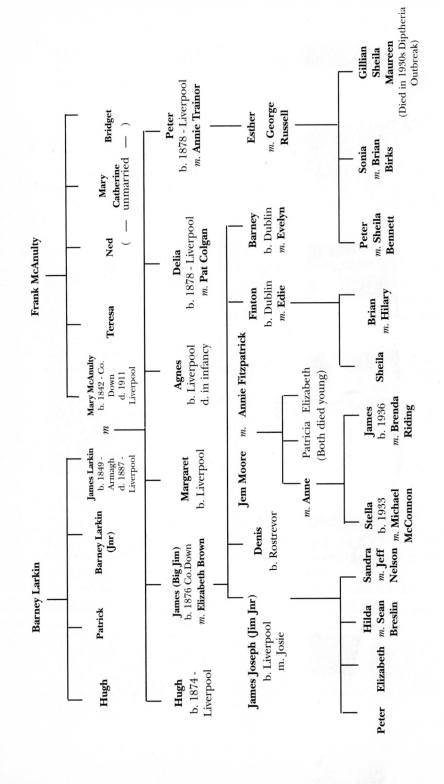

Back Row: Michael McConnon, Sean Breslin, Peter Larkin, Jim Larkin, Finton Larkin, Denis Larkin, Brian Larkin, Graham Larkin.
Middle Row: Hilda Breslin, Brenda Larkin, Stella Larkin, Evelyn Larkin, Josie Larkin, Hillary Larkin, Betty Larkin.
Front Row: Neil McConnon, Eoin McConnon, James Breslin, Hilda Breslin, Maeve McConnon, Blathin Breslin, Aoife Breslin,.

The Early Years

Mary McAnulty, Jim Larkin's mother,
Newry 1863

Big Jim's Grandparents & Parents

My great-great-grandfather, Barney Larkin and his wife lived in Lower Killeavy, a small townland in South Armagh, in the early 1820s. Like much of the area, Lower Killeavy was mainly devoted to small farming. Barney himself, though physically strong and imposing was subjected to the difficult life of being a tenant farmer with a small holding and no security of tenure. He was totally dependant on the whim of his landlord, as were so many others of his calling throughout Ireland at that time.

They had four sons — Barney, Hugh, James and Patrick. As their father believed in education the sons were taught more than was usual at that time. Barney, the eldest, started a hedge-school, teaching youngsters who would have faced a future without knowledge but for his help. The police regarded hedge-schoolmasters as dangerous and it was said that Barney was breeding seditious ideas. He consequently left his home and country at night and his two brothers Hugh and Patrick were also forced to leave. They disappeared without a trace.

James was born in Lower Killeavy in 1845 and he had suffered from a respiratory illness since childhood. As a result of this condition, his father Barney and his brothers had ensured that he became literate at an early age. He acquired an interest in both prose and poetry, as well as in politics and social problems, influencing his own son, Jim, in his early years. Whilst he was tall, as was his father, he was also thin and his features were quite gaunt. He was not strong. I am certain that the respiratory complaint he suffered from was asthma as a number of his descendants developed this complaint, including my own sister Stella and relatives in America and England.

Finally, the third son, James, Big Jim's father, had to leave — he went to Liverpool and the family was broken up. James sailed from Warrenpoint, to Liverpool with no prospect of ever returning to Ireland. The vessels that carried emigrants at that time were rather primitive and far from comfortable or sanitary. The duration of the crossing would have been three or four times longer than the slowest present crossing and much more hazardous.

Thomas Treanor of Burren, Co. Down, in an interview with Michael J. Murphy, some years ago, spoke about the house in which he was born. It was at 'Larkin's Bridge' at Aghyallgue. It was bought by his grandfather from Barney Larkin and was Larkin's Farm.

Apparently, there had been an older house there with a thatched roof which was burned down after being ignited by sparks from a train. The railway authorities built the house Thomas Treanor was born in. It was near Killeavy. (Main Manuscript 1803, pp40-41 in the Dept. of Irish Folklore, University College, Dublin). During the same period, another family lived in Burren in South Down. Frank and Cathy McAnulty had several children and a far larger holding of land. Of the two families who were to be ultimately united, the McAnulty's were by far the most well-off.

The photograph of my great-great-grandfather, Frank McAnulty was taken in the early 1830s beside the Burren dolmen, which at that time had not been excavated. It stood in the ground of the family home, close to the house. Dr Chris Lynn, of the Historic Monuments Division, Dept. of the Environment, Northern Ireland, provided me with technical information for this dolmen, but I have been unable to ascertain whether there were traces of any ancient ancestors of mine interred here.

Frank McAnulty

Jim Larkin, Burren, 1995

In 1842 a daughter was born, Mary. One of her sponsors was her aunt, Bridget McAnulty. As she grew up she came to be a most attractive and determined young lady. Her father arranged a marriage for her to a wealthy businessman in Newry but fate was to intervene.

In 1863 Mary was invited to the christening of a relative's child in Liverpool. She took the boat from Warrenpoint and during the course of the journey she met Jim Larkin, who was in the process of emigrating. He was 18 and she was 21. By coincidence they were both invited to the same christening and met again a few days later. Afterwards Mary returned to Burren. By this time she and Jim had decided to get married, against her family's wishes. For a farmer's daughter in the 1860s to go against her father in respect of marriage shows how strong-willed and single-minded a person my great-grandmother was.

Mary was unable to travel back to Liverpool immediately and I have been told by older family members in Burren, that she had her photograph taken to send to Jim as a keepsake until they could be together at last, and that the photograph at the beginning of this section is the actual one. Three years later, after a breach with her father, Mary did go to Liverpool and married Jim. He was 21 and she was 24. There is no doubt that the love between Jim and Mary was very strong and with the difficult future that faced them both, it had to be. Mary herself sacrificed a life of comfort and respect for a life of toil and sorrow. She received no assistance from her parents.

5

In 1874 their first son, Hugh, was born and in early 1876, when Mary was heavily pregnant with Jim, she received a message to say her father was dying. She set sail from Liverpool to Warrenpoint through a terrible storm. My relatives in South County Down have informed me that on her arrival there Mary was seriously ill and subsequently gave birth to Jim in a townland beside Burren called Tamnaharry probably in a relative's house or possibly in the convent there. My grandfather referred to this in the course of his trial in the 1920s in New York.

I have always regarded the controversy over my grandfather's birthplace to be somewhat of an unnecessary mystery. It was merely an attempt by Big Jim's adversaries to discredit him. In the course of my research I have what I believe to be an accurate picture of the time and place of his birth. What I believe to be factual is as follows:

(a)   My grandfather's conception took place in Toxteth in Liverpool.

(b)   His mother travelled in early 1876 to see her dying father. Being very pregnant at the time and having suffered a very rough crossing, she gave birth to him in a small townland called Tamnaharry near Burren in South County Down. That townland is also near Newry.

(c)   My grandfather, in his trial in New York in the 1920s, stated that his birthplace was Tamnaharry.

(d)   W.P. Ryan, a contemporary of his, confirmed that Jim was born near Newry in 1876.

(e)   My sister, Stella, has in her possession an identity card for my grandfather that states his place of birth as Tamnaharry.

(f)   His passport application also includes the same location for his birth.

(g)   My own relatives from County Down confirmed all of these points as included above directly to me.

(h)   Others have denied the above date and place without the production of a full birth certificate, which I have sought for myself both in Britain and in Ireland, North and South. The World War II Blitz of Liverpool and London and the fire in the Customs House in Dublin destroyed many valuable records. The parish records I examined both in the National Libraries in Dublin and in Liverpool proved to be largely illegible.

(i)   My uncle, Jim Larkin Jnr, son of Big Jim, in his Presidential address to the 55th Annual meeting of Irish Trades Union Congress held in Belfast, 27-29th July 1949, stated in the first paragraph of his speech:

6

"Today, however, tradition is broken insofar that I, unlike the Presidents of previous congresses held in Belfast, am not a native of this city, but at least I am the son of an Ulsterman who had a close association with the working people of Belfast".

Anyone who knew my late Uncle Jim would not dare to impune a statement of his. He was always punctilious about statements that he made, particularly at such important gatherings.

(j) The Chief Superintendent of the Detective Branch, Dublin Castle, wrote to the Minister for Justice, on 18th December 1924 about a meeting he had with Colonel Carter of Scotland Yard who enclosed a history of the Irish Workers' League and its founder, James Larkin. He included the following statement:

"James Larkin, about whose birthplace there is some difference of opinion, was born near Newry, County Down in 1876".

(k) The date of 1876 for Jim's birth is confirmed by his Certificate of Marriage to Elizabeth Brown of which I have a copy.

(l) James Plunkett Kelly in writing a series of articles for the Daily Express, confirmed that Jim was born near Newry.

(m) Thomas Treanor of Burren, Co. Down, in an interview some years ago with Michael J. Murphy regarding the Burren area said, "Jim Larkin, the famous Labour leader was born in Tamnaharry, Burren". (Ref. Main manuscript 1470 in the Dept. of Irish Folklore UC.)

(n) Dr John de Courcey Ireland, in discussing the situation with me, commented that the view I expressed was consistent with his knowledge of my grandfather's particular affection for South County Down.

Finally, on this matter, I would believe my late grandfather's statement of his place of birth above all others.

Jim was looked after by his grandmother, Cathy McAnulty, for a period of time whilst Mary stayed with her sister to recover from her ordeal. She later returned to Liverpool and the family was completed with the births of Delia, Peter, and Margaret. Their last child Agnes died at birth. Young Jim stayed with Cathy from around 1878-1882 and attended school in Burren.

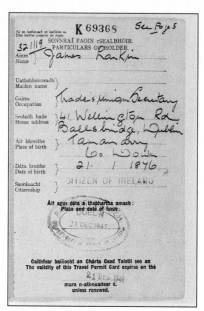

Travel Permit

Catherine McAnulty

The poor living conditions and the associated problems that the family had to endure were horrendous — overcrowding, endemic sickness, poverty, high infant mortality. The slums in Liverpool were as awful and unappealing as the slums in any city, Dublin included. In spite of the poverty on small farms, real grinding poverty was, and always will be, an urban condition. These conditions frequently led to the breakdown of families either through necessity to ensure that individuals would survive (for example, Hugh emigrated to America as a young man) or unavoidably. Jim had to start work at an early age due to the serious illness of his father who died when he was eleven.

The conditions they had to face, together with their genetic inheritance from Barney Larkin and Jim and Mary, without doubt motivated Jim, Delia and Peter to strive for better conditions for working people and for those in need, both nationally and internationally. I am certain that the initial faltering footsteps taken in the interests of workers, were taken without having the slightest idea of the direction the path would lead. Nor did they realise how far they would travel or how much they would change life for the better for workers of the world. They were certainly could not anticipate the enormous opposition they would face from employers and establishment figures as well as some bureaucrats from the Labour Movement.

Childhood in Liverpool

Hugh, Jim, Delia, Peter and Margaret grew up in Toxteth, in Liverpool with their father Jim and mother Mary. Their life was difficult, all the more so, as their father Jim suffered from a respiratory complaint, probably asthma, which made it harder to find employment as he was unable to undertake heavy physical work. As a result of this, Jim and Hugh had to find work at an early age to help supplement the family income. Jim worked at delivering papers at the age of 6 and also worked for a butcher as a delivery boy. When he was about 9 years old Jim's father took him to a meeting where Michael Davitt was speaking — he was deeply impressed.

In the late 1880s the family was enlarged with the arrival of Jim's grandfather Barney who, now he was older, found the struggle to survive on his small tenancy in Lower Killeavy beyond his ability. Shortly after he arrived his son Jim died prematurely and left Mary a widow. In 1892 Jim joined the Independent Labour Party. The pressure on Hugh and Jim to work increased and Jim stowed away on a ship leaving Liverpool for Montevideo in South America, returning in 1894. The conditions on board were harsh and the voyage was a long and hazardous one. As a precursor to what was to become his life's work, Jim organised the other stowaways on the vessel in order to secure better food and conditions. He felt degraded by having little employment especially after seeing the slums of Montevideo. On his return from South America, Jim and his siblings had to undertake strenuous work in order to survive. Jim and Peter worked on the docks, Hugh emigrated to America and Delia worked in a hospital. I know nothing of Margaret's life unfortunately.

When he was quite young, Big Jim had an accident at work and his employer, unlike many in those days, paid him his £1 a week wages while he was off sick for many months. He also advised him to study while he was recuperating, supplied him with books and suggested he use the public library. With little in the way of formal education behind him these habits stood Jim in good stead for the rest of his life.

Visualise if you can, life towards at the turn of the century — a life without television, computers and few cars. Most public transport consisted of horse or mechanically drawn trams. Whilst life was hard for very many people it was also simpler in many ways. They were not subjected to incessant advertising of goods and services which may be beyond their reach and whose value was dubious. The pressure on parents at birthdays and Christmas was not what it is today. In cases of extreme poverty or need, neighbours, friends and family who lived in similar conditions, were much more supportive. The only other support forthcoming for those in need was charity at the Workhouse. Social Welfare payments had not been dreamt of and there was no family or children's allowance. Search as you will, in historical records, you will not find a child murdering another for the sake of stealing a pair of branded sports shoes or for sweatshirts. Theft was more likely to take place because of hunger alone.

Children in those days were an integral part of family life who helped with the support of the family. They were not subjected to the massive peer-pressure experienced by youngsters today. Boys and girls of today are not truly aware of their own value and talents.

The Victorian age was the period so vaunted recently by leading Conservatives whose blinkered approach to so-called 'Victorian Values' ensured that they were unable to see all the social ills and hypocrisies that existed at that time. There was widespread disease, exploitation of tenants and workers and the existence of tens of thousands of child prostitutes in cities throughout the British Empire. These values were never those of my family, who have consistently opposed all attempts to degrade workers and their families.

Work in Liverpool

Jim was strongly built and a good and conscientious worker. He was taken on by the firm of T & J Harrison, a large shipping company whose vessels used the south end of the Liverpool docks. His brother Peter worked regularly at the north end of the docks.

At the time that Jim Larkin became regular with T.J. Harrison's my wife's great-uncle, Jack Sargeant was, by coincidence, a stevedore, on the Liverpool docks. He like many others in the area came across my grandfather in the course of his work.

Jim joined the National Union of Dock Labourers (NUDL) in 1901. He was also active in the ILP and other Socialist organisations. He was a regular speaker on behalf of these organisations and became well versed in social problems and their resolution. It appears that his initial concern was for political remedial action to resolve these issues. As he became more involved with the Labour Movement his attentions were more firmly fixed on the use of industrial, rather than political, action.

Jim, by 1903, had been promoted to foreman dock porter. Compared to most positions on the docks, there was a degree of security and a regular income and on that basis Jim started to look to the future. He was a big, imposing, and charismatic figure who impressed all he came in contact with.

Early in 1903, he patronised a temperance café that was managed by Robert Brown who was also a Baptist lay preacher. Later in the year Robert Brown became his father-in-law as Jim married his daughter Elizabeth.

Elizabeth Brown

The marriage between Jim and Elizabeth was a uniting of opposites. Jim was a man who expressed himself publicly and forcefully on any and all Trades Union, labour and political topics. Elizabeth, on the other hand, had been brought up in an atmosphere of religious evangelism where a young lady of the family, when there was sufficient money, was not required to work for a living but rather to spend her time sewing, knitting, keeping house and reading acceptable literature including the Bible. Any remaining time she had she spent carrying out good works. It can be seen from the brief picture of the partners they were as alike as chalk and cheese. My grandmother told me, in her later years, that Jim's courtship of her consisted of him taking her to meetings at the Liverpool dock gates, as well as to ILP and Socialist meetings. Elizabeth was such a gentle person, and being so different in personality, I can only believe that she was mesmerised by the force of his personality.

By the age of 27 he had developed the skills of an orator that remained his strong point throughout his working life. This skill, together with his integrity, won him many supporters during his career. Many people have said that he frequently shouted in the course of speaking. My own memories of him speaking at public meetings are that he spoke deliberately, loudly and had excellent voice projection. His themes of speech mainly covered working class degradation, social revolution and the evils of capitalism. One of the ways he used to symbolise the latter was: "The largest swine with the biggest snout gets the most from the trough."

This idea of his brings us to privatisation, which in England, and in Ireland to a lesser extent, has led to wholesale redundancies in public industries, and the heads of the replacement private companies achieving in many cases obscene and astronomical pay rises. This is tantamount to robbing a lot of Peters (and their families) to pay a very few Pauls. It begs the questions — how many meals can one person eat in one day? How many suits of clothes can be worn at the one time? How many men, women and children have sufficient to eat and sufficient clothing? My grandfather would have been more critical of this state of things.

When I was young I remember hearing Jim speaking at a number of public meetings. I particularly recall a very large meeting at election time in 1943. It was held at the corner of Griffith Avenue, Malahide Road and Brian Road. There was a crowd of about 20,000 closing off the three roads. I was sitting up on the edge of the lorry from which the speeches were being made. The Chairman introduced my grandfather

13

to the crowd and he offered him a microphone. Jim refused the offer saying, "The day I have to use one of those things is the day I'll retire."

He spoke for almost an hour, without notes, on such matters as housing, unemployment and poverty. The response from the crowd clearly showed that they had heard, understood and supported his speech.

Painting by Elizabeth Brown

Jim Larkin – Leader of Men

In 1905 a dispute broke out in T.J. Harrison's over the employment of non-union foremen and with this came the first opportunity for Jim to demonstrate his leadership qualities. These included his powers of oration, his clarity in expressing the views of his members, and his integrity. The dispute in Harrison's lasted about three months. His activities during this period helped germinate the seed of the Utopian vision of society which had been planted in his childhood. Out of conflict he saw a world developing which was free of strife, suffering, and want.

With that dispute, he was metamorphosed from being a model foreman to being an extremely militant leader of men. He saw the necessity of industrial solidarity for the progress of the underclass. This vision stayed with him throughout his life, whether in Liverpool, Dublin, Belfast, Cork or the USA.

Jim's Trade Union activities in Harrison & Co. led to a position where, despite having been an excellent worker and a foreman himself, he was no longer acceptable as an employee. The next phase of his life began with his employment as a temporary official of the National Union of Dock Labourers. This period of his life, whilst developing his organisational skills, strengthened his dislike for administrators and bureaucracy in general. As you will see from the ensuing section, those feelings intensified, rather than lessened, over the years. His life from then on became a battle not only with employers, certain Trade Unions and Labour functionaries, but also with State Parliaments in Ireland, England, America and Australia, and what would be considered the forces of law and order, together with representatives of the Establishment in all its forms, including the churches. Consistently, however, throughout most of his working life he had the total support of the leading writers, poets, social thinkers and dreamers.

He was then appointed permanent organiser of the NUDL. The 1906 report of the NUDL, written by James Sexton, was full of praise for Jim Larkin. The next task allocated to Jim was the organisation of the Scottish ports — Glasgow, Aberdeen and others. The executive of the NUDL complimented him on the work that he had done and the Branches he had developed. After that he was assigned to Ireland. He found that the living and working conditions in the Irish cities were far worse than those existing in Britain at the time. However, he never failed to meet a challenge. 1907 saw the commencement of a major dispute on the docks of Belfast. This occasion was the first, but far from the last, that my grandfather had to face the united forces of the opposition, the State and its forces, the employers and the rest of the establishment. It was also the first time he was to come across the State supporting the widespread importation of scabs from England to do the work of those on strike.

His concern for the resolution of social problems became the driving force that motivated him throughout his life. It sustained him through many difficult times, including terms of imprisonment. As with many people who are driven by an ideal he was intolerant of and impatient with others who did not share his vision. There is little doubt that he was deeply influenced by his paternal grandfather, Barney Larkin, who lived with them when Jim was young. Barney had enlightened views of the rights of working people and of education for the masses.

Belfast Strike: labour leaders (Boyd, Larkin, Murray, McKessock) addressing the strikers at Queen's Square, Belfast.

Big Jim Through Others' Eyes

Although during his entire working life he had to face many powerful and bitter opponents, through the same period he had the support of very many thousands of working men and women and the help of authors and poets was consistent. A small number of committed labour activists were indefatigable in supporting Jim throughout his life. I believe it is necessary to view my grandfather through the eyes of others in order to see him more clearly.

W.P. Ryan in *The Irish Labour Movement* wrote:

> While still a young man, he (Jim) became a leader of his class and people. By the hostile he was deemed rude, domineering, turbulent, prone to passion and exaggeration; to the detached he seemed vigorous, reckless, racy; to the sympathetic he was often somewhat distressing, and by no means definite and conclusive in his social and industrial philosophy.
>
> What were his ideals, and where lay his goal? His harangues and exhortations suggested different conclusions. He advised, exhorted, struggled and struck from instinct, from an intense pity for the slave class amongst whom he had grown; yet from a feeling of pride in his manhood, depressed and distorted though it may be; and from a stern determination to secure fair play. He did not come with any shapely social scheme, he had not leaning or leisure in the way of Utopias; but he had a burning desire to right the immediate wrong and to go battling against the next. He called ugly things by their names, his more than child-like simplicity in this regard being mistaken for calculated daring and the desire to give offence. He said rude blunt things when he and his were cheated and hurt. Through all this two of his most decided characteristics were liable to be obscured; his genuine kindliness of heart and — although he was not easy to work with — his faculty of conciliation.

Jim Larkin Jnr, son of Big Jim, and my uncle, was reported as having said, in reply to a query about working for his father.

"It is difficult working for someone who is always right."

In his earlier years in the Union, my father Denis, big Jim's second son, was subjected to being dismissed out of hand from work frequently by his father, mainly at weekends. When he failed to get up the following Monday, his father would deny his earlier dismissal and demand that he immediately proceed to work!

James Sexton, General Secretary of the NUDL, said of Jim Larkin:

> Jim Larkin crashed upon the public with the devastating roar of a volcano, exploding without even a preliminary wisp of smoke. I have myself been called an agitator and not resented it. Believe me, however, in my earliest and hottest days of agitating, I was more frigid than a frozen millpond compared to Larkin. I was feeble, tongue-tied, almost dumb".

Constance Markievicz attended a meeting to welcome my grandfather after his early release from jail in 1910. She was invited in to the platform and later said:

> Sitting there listening to Larkin, I realised that I was in the presence of something that I had never come across before; some great primeval force rather than a man. A tornado, a storm-driven wave, the rush into life of Spring, and the blasting breath of Sutunin, all seemed to emanate from the power that spoke. It seemed as if his personality caught up, assimilated and threw back to that vast crowd that surrounded him every emotion that swayed them, every pain and joy that they had ever felt, made articulate and sanctified. Only the great elemental force that is in all crowds had passed into his nature forever.

In the early years of the century Lenin, in Russia, said:

> The Irish proletariat that is awakening to class consciousness has found a talented leader in the person of comrade Larkin, the Secretary of the Irish Transport Workers' Union. Possessing remarkable oratorical talent, a man of seething Irish energy, Larkin has performed miracles among the unskilled.

John Swift, a socialist, trade unionist and drafter, who was active in the late 1960s, in drafting the Labour Party's 'Workers Democracy' document said:

> James Larkin was a very impressive speaker. In fact, I have never heard an orator to equal or surpass Larkin. It is not very often you hear oratory that impresses you with its sincerity. It is very often forced, a kind of falseness, theatrical if you like, but with Larkin, it would be quite natural and spontaneous. When he would appear to be annoyed, he would really be annoyed. He had a great sense of social justice, and injustice, of course, and it was very easy for him to get annoyed and it was most convincing.

Belfast & Dublin

Jim Larkin, 1903

Charles McMullen

Funeral of Charles McMullen and Margaret Lennon

Jim Larkin in Belfast, 1907

After a period organising in English and Irish ports my grandfather arrived in Belfast in January 1907. The city was in a very depressed state, in that, the wage slaves from both the Falls and Shankill Road, were treated with contempt by their employers. These men, not only used the normal tools of their trade to keep workers from effectively combining, as had happened in Liverpool and elsewhere (i.e. paying labourers in public houses and using the principle of casual labour) which destroyed any security employees might have, but they also used to their advantage the so-called differences between different religious denominations, the main ones being Catholic and Protestant. Looking back at this distance in time it is clear how unchristian that approach was and how divisive.

At the time Jim arrived there was widespread dissatisfaction amongst the workers over the intolerable load they had to bear. Jim Larkin who has been called an agitator, with some good reason, tried to resolve some of the existing problems by negotiation and conciliation. The main groups of members who were involved in disputation included dockers, carters, and labourers.

Writing in the *Irish Worker* to men of the North Jim Larkin said: "Workers of Belfast, stop your damned nonsense... Let not what masquerades as religion in this country divide you... Not as Catholics and Protestants, as Nationalists or Unionists, but as Belfast men and workers stand together and don't be misled by the employers game of dividing the Catholic and Protestant".

The employers, however, were deaf to his blandishments and decided to take on the Union. One of the larger groups of employers was the Shipping Federation. This august body decided to take a hand in smashing the Union. They imported shiploads of scabs from Liverpool to do the work of dockers who were on strike. There was a period of very serious conflict and two people who were not connected with the dispute at all, were shot and killed by the forces who, like in other disputes, were virtually operating under the control of the employers. These two people were Charles McMullen and Margaret Lennon.

In the course of the dispute in Belfast there were also attempts to organise members in Derry and a colleague of my grandfather's, James Fearon, organised the dockers in Newry. James Fearon was my father Denis's godfather and he was totally committed to the battle to improve the lot of the unskilled.

When I was young I asked my grandfather if there was anything in his life he particularly remembered. He told me that for a brief time he had been able to help break down the barriers between Catholic and Protestant workers in Belfast. James Sexton, who was General Secretary of the NUDL, said that Jim Larkin had succeeded in calling out members of the R/C and having a strike meeting in their own barracks yard. He said he was present at the meeting which, "was surely unparalleled in all the history of labour effort and I still marvel at the power Larkin then revealed, however rife its duration may have been".

The dispute in Belfast did not end with a victory, but there were many people involved on the Union side who found they were no longer slaves. From Belfast, as a centre, Larkin opened up a campaign in other parts of Ireland, and, as the result of a strike in Cork in 1908 the Irish Transport and General Workers' Union was formed.

Belfast Strike: Goods being delivered

About Jim's achievements in Belfast, John Gray says in his book *City in Revolt, James Larkin and the Belfast Dock strike of 1907*:

> The Belfast Strike Movement of 1907 failed to achieve most of its immediate objectives . . . . that in no way detracts from the importance of the events in the summer of 1907 as a turning point in the fortunes of the Northern working class and of the Irish Labour Movement as a whole.... In so far as there is an heroic and revolutionary mythology associated with the events of 1907, it quite legitimately revolves around James Larkin.

Professor Emmet Larkin in his biography of Jim Larkin wrote: "In the long run Larkin achieved little of tangible nature in Belfast, not because he was something less than what he should have been, but because his enemies were too powerful and circumstances too adverse. In the short run he shook Belfast to its roots."

Dublin 1909 – 1914 and the 'Lock-Out'

In 1909 the Irish Transport General Workers' Union was founded by my late grandfather. It appears that this movement was generated to a large extent by the vacillation of James Sexton, who was General Secretary of the NUDL. Sexton was prepared to accept into membership the very many new members recruited by Jim. However he did not have the vision to recognise the immense discontent of workers throughout these islands.

The part Sexton played in the "settlement" of the Belfast dispute was known throughout Ireland as being less than satisfactory to working people. At a later date Mr Sexton's career was crowned by the receipt of a knighthood from the King. Sexton was prepared to accept members but not to recognise official strikes and finally dismissed Jim Larkin in 1908. This move took place because Jim was not prepared to sell-out workers and so he set up the ITGWU. The period between 1909 and 1912 was a time of great flux. There was competition for members between the NUDL and the ITGWU. It was a period of significant advance for the concept of the Irish union both in terms of membership and organisation. Whilst there were a number of disputes in different parts of Ireland the effectiveness of the union became apparent to very many employers and quite a number of problems were resolved through negotiation.

Jim and his family were by this time living in Dublin. Elizabeth had borne him four sons. My uncle, Jim Jnr, was born in Liverpool in 1904; my father Denis was born in Rostrevor in 1908; and Finton and Barney were subsequently born in Dublin.

Jim Larkin's insight into the personalities of his new recruits was far-reaching to the point of being remarkable. Speaking at a meeting of workers in the Faythe, Wexford on Sept. 9th, 1911, he pointed to "Young Dick Corish" and marked him out as a future Mayor of Wexford.

At a victory meeting in the Faythe on Feb. 1st 1920, after his election as Mayor of Wexford, Dick Corish said:

> The work that the Labour Party set out to accomplish in Wexford started in the foundries in 1911. In that fight the workers lighted the flame of Larkinism which would never be quenched. I am an

apostle of Larkin, and am proud of being so seeing the work accomplished by him for the workers. As long as I have breath I will preach Larkinism, because I recognise that Larkin first taught the workers how to live and how to make life worth living. People at last recognised that teaching, by returning representatives of their own class in the recent local elections.

Recruitment of members for the Union in Dublin had been developing during this time and these approached employers. Amongst those with a direct interest was William Martin Murphy who employed workers in a wide range of occupations in Dublin although initially his family came from Cork. Mr Murphy, by all accounts, was a hard but fair employer though some of the employment practices which were used would be looked at askance today. Mr Murphy's employees included: staff of the Imperial Hotel, Sackville Street, now Clery's department store; employees of the Dublin United Tramway Company and also of Independent Newspapers Ltd.

One of the forms of employment used by Mr Murphy, as well as by other employers, was the creation of two grades of workers — a permanent panel and a temporary panel. This approach very simply meant that those who were on the permanent panel remained in situ provided they behaved themselves with propriety, did exactly as they were told when they were told, were honest, sober and industrious, and did not have the temerity to become seriously ill causing inconvenience to their employer by missing some days at work. Offences against any of these rules would mean for a member of the permanent panel, immediate demotion to the bottom of the casual list, if not dismissal. This whole approach was an anathema to Jim whose entire aim in life was the betterment of workers' lives and security.

William Martin Murphy

It appears that, looking at current employment practices, there is a parallel that now exists. There is a threat to employment security by the use of fixed-term contract employment rather than permanent, pensionable positions. In the 1990s this means that too many people who are lucky enough to secure employment find it almost impossible to receive Bank finance to deal with such matters as mortgages and other loans, together with the problem of not having occupational pensions to look forward to in the future after a full working life. It is my view, after twenty-five years as a Union official, that this approach is short-sighted, leads to a serious reduction in morale, and is counter-productive in that men and women working who have no security have no interest in the success or otherwise of the enterprise. On the other hand, where there is a degree of security of employment, I believe this to be more financially rewarding to the enterprise as people who believe they are being treated fairly and with respect work better and to better effect. I am positive that my grandfather would agree wholeheartedly with these sentiments.

As the year 1913 commenced it was clear that a number of employers were becoming jittery. They had seen what had happened in Belfast and, to a lesser extent, in the rest of Ireland. They were nervous of the power Jim Larkin had to motivate workers who had previously been obedient and malleable and who would tolerate starvation wages for fear of getting nothing at all.

Jim Larkin at work in Liberty Hall

In looking at these developments in hind-sight, it is relatively easy to see that Jim was the catalyst for the dis-satisfaction of the men and women who comprised, what has been called, the "under-class" in Dublin as well as in other cities in Ireland and Britain.

At this stage of his life's work it might be appropriate to compare Jim to the prophet Moses, leading the Hebrews out of slavery. This analogy is only possible because of the willingness of both groups, the Dubliners of 1913 and the Hebrews of the Old Testament, to rebel against oppression and to follow the leaders who were capable of taking them both towards their Promised Lands. In neither case was their ultimate goal achieved — Moses did not live to lead his followers into the Promised Land. Similarly, with Jim, the 1913Lock-Out was not concluded totally successfully, but it can be said that with the solidarity of the men and women of Dublin, employers from then on had to concede that workers had rights and were entitled to human dignity.

The following open letter written by A.E. (George Russell) serves to illustrate the viewpoints held by the most famous thinkers and poets of the time regarding the conditions that the workers and their families continued to struggle against.

To the Masters of Dublin

Sirs,

I address this warning to you, the aristocracy of industry in this city, because, like all aristocracies, you tend to go blind among authority and to be unaware that you and your class and its every action are being considered and judged day by day by those who have power to shake or overturn the whole Social Order, and whose relentlessness in poverty today is making our industrial civilisation stir like a quaking bog. You do not seem to realise that your assumption that you are answerable to yourselves alone for your actions in the industries you control is one that becomes less and less tolerable in a world so crowded with necessitous life.

Some of you have helped Irish farmers to upset a landed aristocracy in this island, an aristocracy richer and more powerful in its sphere than you are in yours, with its roots deep in history. They, too, as a class, though not all of them, were scornful or neglectful of the workers in the industry by which they profited; and to many who knew them in their pride of place and thought them all-powerful, they are already becoming a memory, the good disappearing together with the bad. If they had done their duty by those from whose labour came their wealth they might have continued unquestioned in power and prestige for centuries to come.

The relation of landlord and tenant is not an ideal one, but any relations in a social order will endure if there is infused into

George Russell

them some of that spirit of human sympathy which qualifies life for immortality. Despotisms endure while they are benevolent and aristocracies while *noblesse oblige* is not a phrase to be referred to with a cynical smile. Even an oligarchy might be permanent if the spirit of human kindness, which harmonises all things otherwise incomparable, is present.

You do not seem to read history so as to learn its lessons. That you are an uncultivated class was obvious from recent utterances of some of you upon art. That you are incompetent men in the sphere in which you arrogate imperial powers is certain, because for many years, long before the present uprising of labour your enterprises have been dwindling in the regard of investors, and this while you carried them on in the cheapest labour market in these islands, with a labour reserve always hungry and ready to a accept any pittance. You are bad citizens, for we rarely, if ever, hear of the wealthy among you endowing your city with the magnificent gifts which it is the pride of merchant princes in other cities to offer, and Irishmen not of your city who offer to supply the wants left by your lack of generosity are met with derision and abuse. Those who have economic powers have civil powers also, yet you have not used the power that was yours to right what was wrong in the evil administration of this city.

You have allowed the poor to be herded together so that one thinks of certain places in Dublin as of a pestilence. There are twenty thousand rooms, in each of which live entire families, and sometimes more, where no functions of the body can be concealed and delicacy and modesty are creatures that are stifled ere they are born. The obvious duty of you in regard to these things you might have left undone, and it be imputed to ignorance or forgetfulness; but your collective and conscious action as a class in the present labour dispute has revealed you to the world in so malign an aspect that the mirror must be held up to you, so that you may see yourself as every humane person sees you.

The conception of yourselves as altogether virtuous and wronged is, I assure you, not at all the one which onlookers hold of you. No doubt, some of you suffered without just cause. But nothing which has been done to you cries aloud to heaven for condemnation as your own actions. Let me show you how it seems to those who have followed critically the dispute, trying to weigh in a balance the rights and wrongs. You were within the rights society allows when you locked out your men and insisted on the fixing of some principle to adjust your future relations with labour, when the policy of labour made it impossible for some of you to carry on your enterprises Labour desired the fixing of some such principle as much as you did. But, having once decided on such a step, knowing how many thousands of men, women and children, nearly one-third of the population of this city, would be affected, you should not have let one day to have passed without unremitting endeavours to find a solution of the problem.

What did you do? The representatives of labour unions in Great Britain met you, and you made of them a preposterous, an impossible demand, and because they would not accede to it you closed the conference; you refused to meet them further; you assumed that no other guarantees than those you asked were possible, and you determined deliberately in cold anger, to starve out one-third of the population of this city, to break the manhood of the men by the sight of the suffering of their wives and the hunger of their children. We read in the Dark Ages of the rack and thumb screw. But these iniquities were hidden and concealed from the knowledge of man in dungeons and torture chambers. Even in the Dark Ages humanity could not endure the sight of such suffering, and it learnt of such misuses of power by slow degrees, through rumour, and when it was certain it razed its Bastilles to their foundations.

It remained for the twentieth century and the capital city of Ireland to see an oligarchy of four hundred masters deciding openly upon starving one hundred thousand people, and refusing to consider any solution except that fixed by their pride. You, masters, asked men to do that which masters of labour in any other city in these islands had not dared to do. You insolently demanded of those men who were members of a trade union that they should resign from that union; and from those who were not members you insisted on a vow that they would never join it.

Your insolence and ignorance of the rights conceded to workers universally in the modern world were incredible, and as great as your inhumanity. If you had between you collectively a portion of human soul as large as a threepenny bit, you would have sat night and day with the representatives of labour, trying this or that solution of the trouble, mindful of the women and children, who at least were innocent of wrong against you. But No! You reminded labour you could always have your three square meals a day while it went hungry. You went into conference again with representatives of the State, because dull as you are, you know public opinion would not stand your holding out. You chose as your spokesman the bitterest tongue that ever wagged in this island, and then, when an award was made by men who have an experience in industrial matters a thousand times transcending yours, who have settled disputes in industries so great that the sum of your petty enterprises would not equal them, you withdraw again, and will not agree to accept their solution, and fall back again upon your devilish policy of starvation. Cry aloud to Heaven for new souls! The souls you have got cast upon the screen of publicity appear like the horrid and writhing creatures enlarged from the insect world, and revealed to us by the cinematography.

You may succeed in your policy and ensure your own damnation by your victory. The men whose manhood you have broken will loathe you, and will always be brooding and scheming to strike a fresh blow. The children will be taught to curse you. The infant being moulded in the womb will have breathed into its starved body the vitality of hate. It is not they — it is you who are blind Samsons pulling down the pillars of the social order. You are sounding the death knell of autocracy in industry. There was autocracy in political life, and it was superseded by democracy. So surely will democratic power wrest from you the control of industry. The fate of you, the aristocracy of industry, will be as the fate of the aristocracy of land if you do not show that you have some humanity still among you. Humanity abhors, above all things, a vacuum in itself, and your class will be cut off from humanity as the surgeon cuts the cancer and alien growth from the body. Be warned, ere it is too late. – Yours, etc.

A.E.

I believe that many aspects of improvement in relationships between employers and employees can be traced back directly, for 80 years, to the time of the Lock-Out. There is equally no doubt in my mind that my grandfather would be to the forefront today in saying that gains that had been made over the last century in improvements in conditions of employment — pay, security for workers — had been won at great cost and also great hardship to many thousands of people. Many of these gains are currently under attack and should be defended wholeheartedly by the labour movement.

The first strike action took place on the August Bank Holiday Monday of 1913, with staff from the Dublin United Tramway Company stopping work. Very rapidly the employers combined against the workers and the Lock-Out began. The employers used their influence to get support in opposition to the workers from the Government, magistrates, police, army and the established churches. The protagonists on the other side were the working people of Dublin, their unions, the writers, poets and literati of the time, a significant number of Order clergy together with a number of influential people with a social conscience. At a later stage, in the course of the Lock-Out, practical help was sent by the Co-operative Society in Britain as well as funds from a number of unions there and many thousands of individual Trade Unionists and Socialists.

On 29th August 1913, it was published in the newspapers that the Union was going to hold a meeting in O'Connell Street on the 31st which the magistrate, a Mr Swifte, had proclaimed an illegal assembly. There was a meeting held at Liberty Hall in Beresford Place on the following day, Saturday 30th August, when my grandfather confirmed that he would attend the meeting in O'Connell St. Before that meeting ended he publicly burned the proclamation written by Mr Swifte, declaring it to be illegal as it used the name Sackville Street instead of O'Connell Street. On that day two members of the Union lost their lives —James Nolan was batoned to death in Lower Abbey St .and James Byrne was killed in similar circumstances.

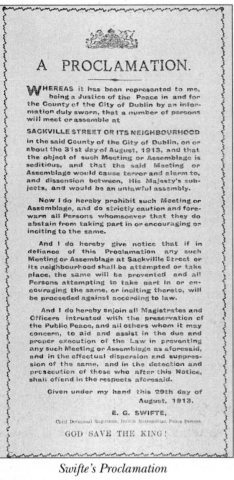

Swifte's Proclamation

The text of the proclamation reads:

A PROCLAMATION.

WHEREAS it has been represented to me, being a Justice of the Peace in and for the County of the City of Dublin by an information duly sworn, that a number of persons will meet or assemble at

SACKVILLE STREET OR ITS NEIGHBOURHOOD in the said County of the City of Dublin, on or about the 31st day of August, 1913, and that the object of such Meeting or Assemblage is seditious, and that the said Meeting or Assemblage would cause terror and alarm to, and dissension between, His Majesty's subjects, and would be an unlawful assembly.

Now I do hereby prohibit such Meeting or Assemblage, and do strictly caution and forewarn all Persons whomsoever that they do abstain from taking part in or encouraging or inciting to the same.

And I do hereby give notice that if in defiance of this Proclamation any such Meeting or Assemblage at Sackville Street or its neighbourhood shall be attempted or take place, the same will be prevented and all Persons attempting to take part in or encouraging the same, or inciting thereto, will be proceeded against according to law.

And I do hereby enjoin all Magistrates and Officers intrusted with the preservation of the Public Peace, and all others whom it may concern, to aid and assist in the due and proper execution of the Law in preventing any such Meeting or Assemblage as aforesaid, and in the effectual dispersion and suppression of the same, and in the detection and prosecution of those who after this Notice, shall offend in the respects aforesaid.

Given under my hand this 29th day of August, 1913.

E. G. SWIFTE,

Chief Divisional Magistrate, Dublin Metropolitan Police District.

GOD SAVE THE KING!

He was aware that efforts would be made to stop him attending the meeting. Countess Markievicz and her husband provided him with accommodation for that night. He was a great believer in dramatic gestures, he had informed no one where he intended to speak from. He was brought in a wheelchair disguised as an old man to the Imperial Hotel (now Clery's Stores). The premises were owned by William Martin Murphy, Jim's main protagonist on the Employer's side. Once inside the Hotel he proceeded upstairs in the lift with Helena Maloney, who was later to become the Secretary of the Irish Women Workers' Union. When they got to the room Jim got out of the wheelchair and went to the window of the hotel which is now almost exactly under the clock outside Clery's. He opened the window and started to speak to the crowd who had spontaneously gathered below. The police, of whom there were many in the street, acted promptly, rushed into the hotel and arrested him immediately. They took him to 5A College Street, which was then the headquarters of the Detective Division, Dublin Metropolitan Police, prior to transferring him to Mountjoy Jail the following day.

The events of the next hour or two reflected no credit on the behaviour of the Dublin Metropolitan Police. Many eye witnesses on that day claimed, with much justification, that the police rioted. Many people, including visitors and passersby were batoned and charged by police on horseback. Sunday 31st August 1913 is enshrined in Labour History as "Bloody Sunday".

In recent times, when SIPTU was created, the Irish Transport and the Federated Workers' Union, decided to locate and re-inter the remains of these three labour martyrs of 1913. It was not until this event that it brought home to me how hard life was in 1913. When the Union sought the three remains they could only locate those of James Nolan. I understand that the family graves of the other two who lost their lives were sold in 1914. Many people will understand the significance of this action, as it shows clearly the depth of poverty that affected the city then. Many thousands of people who had nothing in the material sense, would put 3d or 6 pence on the mantelpiece each week to pay the Insurance man for their burial policy. That money was sacrosanct and families would go without food rather than spend it because the worst degradation of all, in most people's minds, was to be buried in a pauper's grave.

The following statements illustrate vividly the events of that August Sunday and demonstrate the shock and revulsion people, from titled lady to ordinary man in the street, had for the rash and unjustified actions taken by the police on that day.

The Lord Mayor of Dublin instituted a public enquiry into the activities of the police and the reports that follow are some of the many statements made to that enquiry. Of course, nothing was done about it.

Jim Larkin and his followers, people seeking justice, gave no reason for the police to react so violently. What had been an orderly, good humoured public meeting was turned into a shambles and an afternoon of fear by rioting police.

No view of the dramatic events for the Lock-Out would be complete without some personal assessment of employer's leader William Martin Murphy. Like all of us Mr Murphy was a product of genetics, family and environment. It is necessary to take into account the age in which he lived, his family's status in society and the values that were prevalent the time. Mr Murphy was brought up at the end of the Victorian era which was a time when working conditions were harsh, where children were employed to do the work of adults and the greatest fear was unemployment and the workhouse. In this environment employers held the balance of power and the workers accepted whatever work they could get. As a result they gave up hope of retaining many of the rights that were due to them under natural law of human dignity. There was in that age quite a hypocritical attitude to people with major social problems and needs. I have no doubt, however, that William Martin Murphy, as a learned man, was not part of this. I believe that he was convinced that he was right in his attitudes in respect to employment practices. His philosophy regarding work was a product of his upbringing. Out of the background of the Victorian era came many social reformers who made many changes. One of these was Robert Owen, who though from the employing class, was of the view that employees be treated with understanding and respect. There were many other advancements in technology, with great engineers such as Stevenson, Brunel, Treford; explorers such as Livingstone, Stanley and Burton and archaeologists such as Hinders Petrie and Heinrich Schleimann. The fact that so many reforms were made as a result of the oppression of the Victorian era in some way indicates how socially backward attitudes in general actually were.

On the other hand Jim Larkin grew up in poverty, but learned from an early age that the conditions that existed had to be overturned. He saw that his sole aim in life should be to help workers to what the Victorians saw as the "New Jerusalem". In this he was not a typical product of his age and class.

Statements to the Commission of Inquiry

Draft of portion of evidence to be submitted to properly constituted Commission of Inquiry by The Dublin Civic League

The evidence covered by this preliminary statement was collected and arranged in order to be briefed to Counsel who were to represent the Dublin Civic League at the recent Police Inquiry. Owing, however, to the whitewashing nature of the Inquiry Commission appointed by Dublin Castle, the Civic League decided that they would not be represented there at nor would they in any way recognise it.

The Castle Counsel at the Inquiry in their apologia for the Police, traced the more serious disturbances to the action of Mr Larkin in attempting to address a meeting which had been proclaimed by a ukase of a Police Magistrate — which the Irish Attorney General subsequently admitted had no legal binding force. As a matter of fact the disturbances began on the previous day, Saturday, August 30th. On the afternoon of that day disturbances commenced in the vicinity of a football match in one of the Dublin suburbs. The police fomented the disorders — as Mr Handel–Booth, M.P. has testified — until they reached the heart of the city, and that night 250 citizens of Dublin were treated in the Hospitals for injuries sustained at the hands of the police; one of them, James Nolan, lay dead in Jervis St. Hospital: another, James Byrne, crept to his home and died a few days after, from the brutal injuries he received.

At the Inquest on the body of the unfortunate man, Nolan, three witnesses swore positively to the identity of the policemen who murdered him with their batons — bludgeoning him again and again as he tried to rise from the ground. Their direct evidence of identification established a clear *prima facie* case against these two constables, but nothing in the nature of criminal proceedings for murder was initiated by the Crown. At the present moment three men, against whom not one iota of direct evidence is tendered, lie in Mountjoy Prison on a charge of murdering a Free Labourer. Thus is the impartial administration of the law conducted in Dublin and thus is the King's Justice vindicated.

The sum total of the evidence enclosed is that for three days the Dublin Metropolitan Police and the Royal Irish Constabulary ran amok in the city of Dublin. Men and women coming out of Church on the Sunday were brutally beaten and batoned: the police, many of whom appear from the subjoined evidence to have been under the influence of drink, burst into the homes of the poor, broke and destroyed every little article of comfort which years of thrifty earning had secured for their owners, batoned old women and little girls and in some cases, of which evidence is enclosed, assaulted women who were about to become mothers or who had just been confined. Prematurely born infants — children crippled and weakly from birth — wrecked and shattered homes; those are the mementoes left to the poor of Dublin by the officers of Law and Order.

The subsequent proceedings in the Criminal Courts of Dublin were on a par with the conduct of the police, but these circumstances cannot be reopened owing to the absence of a Court of Criminal Appeal in Ireland.

The bulk of the evidence enclosed speaks for itself and needs no comment. But after all their sufferings the Citizens of Dublin, 700 of whom were treated in Hospitals as a result of police brutality, were promised an impartial inquiry into the conduct of the police. The Chief Secretary made a definite promise which he broke and an Inquiry composed of two Castle Lawyers heard ex-parte police evidence (which was not even tendered on oath) for some three weeks at a cost to the Citizens of Dublin of close on £1,000.

Charles S. Power,
Barrister at Law.

Statement by F. Sheehy Skeffington, MA.

The worst displays of police brutality and indiscipline in Dublin took place on August 30th and 31st. But it is necessary to touch on the circumstances of the days previous. Every evening during that week, Mr Larkin held huge meetings in Beresford Place; every evening the crowd dispersed quietly, but were treated with the utmost insolence by the police, who acted as if they wanted to provoke a row. On the Thursday and the Friday evenings (August 28th and 29th) I was in the streets at the hour when the meetings were dispersing, and I saw the attitude of the police. They appeared to be in a state of high excitement; fussy is the mildest word that could be applied to their conduct. Every group of half-a-dozen that stood on the streets was immediately approached by them and broken up. I saw them rushing at and breaking up such groups on both evenings, in O'Connell Street and on O'Connell Bridge, without the smallest provocation. Batons were not used so far as I saw, but the members of these standing groups, if they showed the smallest inclination to resent the action of the police in hustling them, were struck and cuffed. Those who were fairly well dressed, as a rule, escaped these attentions.

On those evenings, then, the attitude of the police was clearly provocative. If their intention had been to provoke a riot, so as to get an excuse for such a thorough batoning of the people as would cow them, they could not have acted otherwise than they did. These were the proceedings, repeated all through the week, that led to the attacks on the police on Saturday, which have been alleged as excuses for subsequent brutalities.

On the Saturday, too, the people were exasperated by the arrests of their leaders, by the police proclamation of a peaceful meeting, and by the repeated interference with the proposed routes of strikers' processions.

The events of the Saturday night, which are admitted to have been the worst examples of police brutality, I did not see personally. But from what took place on Sunday, August 31st, in broad daylight, in the city's chief thoroughfare, before numbers of impartial and unimpeachable witnesses, it is possible to form some idea of how the police, in their then frame of mind, were likely to

Francis Sheehy Skeffington MA

behave at nighttime, in the slums and byways, and without any other witnesses than their working-class victims.

It is alleged by the police apologists that the publicly announced transfer of the place of meeting from O'Connell Street to Croydon Park was a mere blind, to draw the police away from O'Connell Street. This I know to be untrue. On Saturday night, Mr Larkin had evaded arrest; the Strike Committee did not know where he was, nor had they any communication from him. The responsibility being thus entirely cast upon their shoulders, they decided, after much discussion, that it would not be right to expose an unarmed crowd to the tender mercies of the police in the furious temper in which they had shown themselves all Saturday evening. They therefore changed the place of meeting to Croydon Park, and announced the change in Sunday morning's papers. Larkin heard of this late on Saturday night, and then sent a message to the Strike Committee protesting against their decision and declaring that, as promised he would be in O'Connell Street "alive or dead". The Strike Committee adhered to their plan, and did not communicate the fact or purport of Mr Larkin's message to their followers. Mr Larkin also sent a letter to the *Sunday Freeman* repudiating the action of the Strike Committee and repeating his intention of being on O'Connell Street that day. The *Sunday Freeman* did not publish the letter, and the only result of his sending it was to put the police on the alert. I can state positively that the great mass of the strikers had no knowledge whatever that Mr Larkin was to appear in O'Connell Street; they thought he would either remain in hiding or appear in Croydon Park. Only a handful of people, perhaps a dozen, knew that Mr Larkin was to appear in O'Connell Street. I myself learned it accidentally about half an hour before he actually appeared there.

There is not, then, an atom of foundation for the suggestion of the police that a riot was deliberately planned to take place in O'Connell Street, or that any disturbances whatever were to be anticipated unless drastic measures had been taken. With very few exceptions, the crowd in O'Connell Street at one o'clock on that Sunday was made up of idle pedestrians and curious sightseers. The total number of people in the street at the time of Mr Larkin's dramatic appearance on the balcony of Mr Murphy's hotel was, I estimate, between 100 and 200. The police estimate it about 300. On the other hand, the detailed evidence of the police witnesses before the recent Inquiry shows that there were 310 policemen in the street, even after some had been detached to follow the main body of strikers to Croydon Park. Therefore, on the admission of the police themselves, they outnumbered the people in the street.

When Mr Larkin was recognised on the balcony of the Imperial Hotel, a rush was made to get near enough to hear him. Cheering rendered his few words almost inaudible, and almost before the hotel crowd had gathered he had disappeared. When the police entered the hotel to arrest him, the crowd, now silent, remained in the middle of the street. At this moment one stone was thrown. It broke one of the plate-glass windows in Mr Murphy's shop, under the hotel balcony. There was then a pause of several minutes before the police left the hotel with Mr Larkin firmly held by two of them, in their midst. During this interval there was no attempt at a repetition of the stone throwing, which remained a purely sporadic and exceptional incident.

It is equally false to assert, as the police do, that there was any attempt of, or notion of, a rescue. When Mr Larkin was seen again the cheering recommenced; the nervous policemen took him away at a run; the crowd, or a section of it, ran alongside, continuing the cheering. Beyond this demonstration, I can state positively that no rescue was planned, or even thought of, by Mr Larkin himself or anyone else.

I was standing at the edge of the footpath opposite the door of the Imperial Hotel, when Larkin and the police came out. I joined in the cheering and started to run, with the others, alongside of Larkin and his escort. Suddenly I found myself in the midst of another body of police who had come up from behind. Like Larkin's escort, they had their batons drawn, and were batoning the crowd. They did not strike me. An officer put his hand on my chest to stop me, and then two constables seized me. The officer hastily said: "Don't touch him, but make him go back." I said: "I'll go on the way I'm going," and struggled. After a few seconds, finding themselves behind the rest of the charging policemen, the two who held me let me go, and ran on. I then continued to walk in the same direction. This brief struggle synchronised exactly with the batoning of the people all across the street and into Prince's Street. When I now looked round, the street resembled a battlefield. I saw about a dozen people lying on the ground. The nearest to me was an elderly man, whose head was bleeding freely, half-conscious. My wife and some others were helping him to his feet. He was led away, groaning, down a by-street.

I then saw Countess Markievicz with blood on her face and dress. She told me that she was rushed in to shake hands with Mr Larkin, and had been struck a severe blow on the nose by a policemen's fist.

A group of young girls, in a semi-hysterical condition, were lamenting the loss of a small child, who had disappeared in the course of the charge. While my wife and I were speaking to them, a burly constable came running across the street at our group — in which I was the only man — with his baton drawn and uplifted. The girls, some of them mere children, screamed and fled down a by-street. I called out the policeman's number, and told him I was watching him. He then stopped, apparently recognising me, and said apologetically, "I didn't do anything". I replied, "No because I called out your number in time."

The street was by this time cleared of all but police. My wife and I made our way to Store Street Police Station, where we expected to find Mr Larkin — as a matter of fact he had been taken to another station, but we did not know this. At Store Street occurred an incident, trivial in itself, which nevertheless throws a vivid light on the utter breakdown of police discipline and their shameless partisanship. As my wife and I entered the police station, a large number of policemen — forty or fifty — were lounging about the yard, sitting on a bench or standing. As we walked past them up the yard, they booed us loudly. We took no notice, went into the station house, and found on inquiry that Mr Larkin was not there. On coming out, we were again booed by the same body of police. I went back, and asked the station sergeant if it was proper for police in uniform, who were supposed to be impartial as between all classes of citizens, to boo a civilian. The Station sergeant replied that he had not heard it, — although his window opened directly on the courtyard. I pointed out that he must have heard it. He then asked me what grounds I had for thinking the groans were directed at me. I replied that I heard my name mentioned; in any case there was no other civilian there except myself and my wife. He then said he hadn't time to talk about it. I came out again, and the same crowd of police booed me a third time. This time the Station Sergeant looked out of the window, and said, "If that's intended for Mr Skeffington, stop it at once." Whereupon they booed me twice more, even more loudly, as we passed out — in direct defiance of their officer's order.

Making all allowances for the fact that I had supported Mr Larkin in the press, and that I had previously given trouble to the police in connection with the Suffragette agitation, I hold that this incident in itself shows that the police were that day in a frame of mind in which the lives and property of the citizens were not safe with them. It also shows how powerless their officers were to restrain their excited passions, even had they wished to do so. While I was not near enough to this body of police to detect unmistakable signs of drink on them, their whole behaviour and attitude were most easily explicable on the assumption that they had taken a considerable quantity of drink.

Of the incidents which were investigated by the current Commission of Inquiry, these were all that I personally witnessed. But the scope of the Commission was most improperly restricted to the months of August and September. The misbehaviour of the police continued long after that, and continues still — though exercised a little more judiciously when they think the eye of the press or public is on them. I conclude with a couple of incidents of later date.

On November 8th, or rather early on the morning of November 9th about one a.m., I was walking home along the Rathmines Road, with my wife and three friends, two ladies and a gentleman. A constable, on duty on Rathmines Road near Portobello Bridge, crossed the road towards us, planted himself in front of us, and peered into our faces. He lurched heavily from side to side, and smelt strongly of drink. We asked what he wanted, and told him to stand aside. He continued to obstruct us, and muttered insulting remarks. We asked if he intended to arrest us. He said, "for very little he would, but he knew us all, and could get us any time." Ultimately we got past, leaving him lurching and muttering on the footway. Imagine any solitary passenger, especially a woman, being at the mercy of a charge brought against her by a man in this condition! He was a very big man, and palpably drunk. I have his number.

On November 28th, my wife was arrested by a sergeant on a false charge of assault — the sergeant had assaulted her while she was peacefully distributing leaflets, and had then brought the false charge to cover his own action. The police magistrate

ignored the evidence brought forward to this effect, and she
went to prison. The next day, the Irish Womens' Franchise
League organised a meeting of protest to be held in Royce Road,
a cul-de-sac near Mountjoy Prison. A police inspector told me
early in the day that the meeting would not be permitted,
because it was an obstruction and was also "too near the prison".
When the promoters of the meeting arrived, the entrance to the
cul-de-sac was blocked by a line of police. The result was, that
whereas no obstruction would have been caused had the meeting
been permitted in Royce Road itself, the meeting now surged all
over the main road, and completely blocked the traffic for half-
an-hour or so. Along with others, I repeatedly attempted to get
through the police cordon, and was repeatedly pushed back. I
asserted that I had a right to walk down the road; if I was doing
anything illegal, let them arrest me; if not, they had no right to
touch me. To all this there was no answer except continuous
obstruction and pushing back. One constable knocked me down.

Late that evening as I was walking alone along Westland Row,
a body of police in marching order passed close to me on the
footpath. One of these deliberately lurched out of the ranks to
hustle me with his shoulder as he passed. I have his number, and
also the testimony of a passerby, who saw the act, and came up to
me, of his own motion, to give his name as a witness of this
undisciplined act.

Copy of statement of Mr Lennox Robinson, 73 Lr Baggot St., Manager of the Abbey Theatre

On the Saturday Night, August 30th last, I was going down to the
Theatre via Brunswick Street and Tara Street, towards Butt
Bridge. Everything was quite ordinary in Tara Street. Just as I
approached the bridge I saw two men leaning against the quay
wall. They were standing apparently doing nothing. Two
policemen crossed the bridge and without any parley or words
they caught hold of one and threw him into the street and the
other policeman struck the other man with his baton. There was
no disturbance and I crossed the street to the bridge. I met eight
or ten policemen coming over the bridge; they charged down
Burgh Quay towards the Tivoli Theatre. It was apparently in this
charge that one of the men was killed, but I know nothing of that
of course. I heard the crash of glass. I don't know the names of
the two men who were standing at the Bridge, I did not get the

numbers of the Police, and I do not know if they were D.M.P. men. I crossed the Bridge and found a man lying on the ground. A knot of people around him were saying that he was killed. A cab was brought round and he was brought away I think. I went on to the Theatre. The time was about 10 minutes past eight — I got to the Theatre about 10 minutes past 8 o'c.

Lennox Robinson

Statement of Countess Markievicz

We had driven down with a few friends to see if the proclaimed meeting would be held. There were no unusual crowds, our car trotted right down O'Connell Street and pulled up at Prince's Street opposite the Imperial Hotel. We noticed a great number of Police everywhere. Larkin was just finishing his speech and went into the hotel a few seconds after our arrival. A few people gathered — they were all laughing and very much amused at Larkin's appearance. A friend recognised me and called on me for a speech. I did not want to create a disturbance, so I jumped down off the car and walked across the street. As I reached the other side Larkin came out of the hotel between two police-men and surrounded by an escort of about 30 police. I ran across in front of Jim and shook his hand saying, goodbye, good luck. As I turned to pass down O'Connell Street, the Inspector on Larkin's right hit me on the nose and mouth with his clenched fist. I reeled against another policeman who pulled me about tearing all the buttons off my blouse, and tearing it all out around my waist. He then threw me back into the middle of the street, where all the police had begun to run, several of them kicking and hitting at me as they passed. I saw a woman trying to get out of the way. She was struck from behind on the head by a Policeman with his baton. As she fell her hat slipped over her face and I saw her hair was grey. She

Countess Markievicz

had a little book which fell out of her left hand as she fell. I saw a barefooted boy with papers hunted and hit about the shoulders as he ran away. I shall never forget the look on his face as he turned when he was struck. I could not get out of the crowd of police, and at last he hit me a back hand blow across the left side of my face with his baton. I fell back against the corner of Hoyte's shop, when another policeman started to seize me by the throat, but I was pulled out of the crowd by some men who took me down Sackville Place and into a house to stop the blood flowing from my nose and mouth, and to try and tidy my blouse. I noticed that the policeman who struck me, smelt very strongly of stout, and that they all seemed very excited. They appeared to be arranged in a hollow square and to be gradually driving the people into the street, and then closing in on them and batoning them. I tried to go up, down and across O'Connell Street, but each time I was put back by them into the crowd of charging police. The people were all good-tempered and there would have been no row. They were also outnumbered by the Police round about where I was.

I think I have told you everything.

Constance de Markievicz

Copy of Report to Lord Mayor of Dublin, from William Lowry, Esq. I.L.B. Barrister at Law.

Ballyliffin Hotel,
Clonmany
Co. Donegal

My Lord Mayor,

I notice from the Press that your Lordship is most properly pressing for an inquiry into the conduct of the police in Dublin, on the 31st August. There was an incident on that day on which the Press is unanimously dumb, but which I conceive is worthy of your Lordship's strictest investigation.

About 5.15 p.m. on Sunday afternoon Amiens Street Station was invaded by a large force of police, and persons waiting for the departure of trains were batoned indiscriminately in the most atrocious, brutal and cowardly fashion. One person had to be removed in the ambulance. I arrived at 5.25 by train from Howth,

in company with two friends, one of them Mr J.L. Lynd of the
Crown and Hanafar Office. The injured man was just being
removed. A state of terror reigned in the station at the time. The
porters and other officials were quite demoralised with terror. A
friend was to meet us — Mr J. Harold Lyth, Mountpelier, Malone
Road, Belfast. We made inquiries from him and ascertained that
he had witnessed the outrageous conduct of the police. One
man, an intending passenger, actually standing with his ticket in
his hand was struck down by two policemen, and then beaten and
kicked in the most savage fashion while lying on the ground. Mr
Lyth was in close proximity to this man and only escaped like
treatment by taking refuge in the left luggage office. Mr Lynd
and I questioned porters and bystanders, and their evidence
agreed with Mr Lyth's account, and was to the effect that:

(1) No attack had been made on the police from the Station
    premises.

(2) The police invaded the Station in considerable force.

(3) The police attacked people in the Station indiscriminately.

(4) Several persons were injured.

(5) A superior policeman came into the Station after his
    underlings had withdrawn, walked round, refused to
    listen to complaints, and then took himself off.

If your Lordship cares to communicate with Mr Lyth he will
furnish your Lordship directly with particulars. I am afraid no
one had the presence of mind to take the numbers of any of the
truculent crew. Mr Lynd and I made particular inquiry on this
head.

If your Lordship considers that either Mr Lynd or myself can
be of any service in the investigation which your Lordship
contemplates both of us will gladly do anything in our power. The
Crown and Hanafar Office will always find Mr Lynd. My address
after the 9th of this month will be 18 Rea's Buildings, Royal
Avenue, Belfast.

I may further state that Mr Lynd and I were driving to Amiens
Street Station at 1.30 p.m. exactly, and saw the baton charges
delivered about that time. I must say both of us were astounded.
I could see no conduct on the part of persons in the street to
justify such conduct on the part of the police. The vehicle in
which we were driving was quickly surrounded by fugitives from

the brutality of the police. So far as I could see not one person was of the type one would expect to see taking part in any riotous or other unlawful act. On the contrary, the fleeing people were of the respectable, well dressed, decent appearance to be seen any Sunday in Sackville Street, at this hour.

I expect, however, that your Lordship has plenty of evidence re. the Sackville Street incidents. I hope that your Lordship may be entirely successful in your Lordship's public-spirited efforts to bring these uniformed criminals to justice.

I am, My Lord Mayor,

Yours faithfully,

William Lowry, ILB, B.L

Copy of Statement of Joseph M. Vaughan, 1, Prospect Terrace, Kilmainham

I am a Tailor and Outfitter's commercial traveller. On the 31st August I was in O'Connell Street, walking, between 1 and 2 o'clock, from O'Connell Bridge towards the Pillar on the right-hand side going up. I saw a lot of police coming out of the Imperial Hotel, their batons drawn. Immediately they attacked the people. They had Mr Larkin with them but I did not know that at the time. I saw a young man respectably dressed (I don't know his name) go up the footpath. He was walking briskly, as if on business. He was not shouting or making any disturbance as the police were there. He attempted to get past. One of the police made as if to strike him. He had his baton in hand and struck out. The gentleman passing ducked and stepped back. I ran back also. I stopped before coming to Sackville Place. I looked back. The people were running in all directions. I saw the baton charge and people being knocked down in all directions. I got to Sackville Place and ran down about 10 yards. The police came along and one of them rushed at me. I got away and stopped again after a few yards. I saw a lady rushing over to shake hands with Larkin. She was immediately flung up against a wall. She was Countess Markievicz. I saw a policeman holding her by the throat. I could not then see what happened for a couple of minutes with the crowd, and I ran down towards Marlborough Street. When next I saw the Countess her mouth and nose were pouring blood. Her blouse was all torn. I knocked at a private house and told them, and asked for water, etc. The Countess came in and got fitted up. In the meantime an old man came down Sackville Place, I should say he was between 60 and 70. He was bleeding (from a blow of a baton I presume). He was then in a state of collapse. I went to Egan's pub for water and for whiskey for him but could not get it. I got his head bathed in a shop in Marlborough Street, near Brook Thomas' Place. I went part of the way home with him. He lived in St Lawrence Place.

There were some friends with me. These were with the Countess half way down Sackville Place. I am not a member of the Transport Union. I went as far as Amiens Street with the old man. Pat Sheridan brought him into a public house in Talbot Street (I think McCormack's) and gave him some whiskey. My three friends and I scattered when the charge commenced and the Countess was being assaulted. I saw also a man on the ground in the centre of O'Connell Street, opposite Sackville Place. He was trying to get up. Some police were rushing across and one of them struck him about the head with his baton. The man fell down again. I was too far away to see if he was bleeding and my attention was then taken up with the Countess. I heard no order to charge.

Joseph M. Vaughan,
18th December, 1913.

Copy of Statement of Henry Nicholls, Esq., B.A. B.A.I., T.C.D.,
1 Church Avenue, Rathmines

On the evening of August 29th (Friday) I went to Beresford Place about 3.30 to listen to the speeches. The crowd was very peaceable and remained quiet under the provocation given by the police forcing a way through them to let a motor car pass. When the speaking was over I was making my way home along Eden Quay when suddenly, without any provocation, about twenty police charged the crowd, of which I was one. The majority fled. I walked on and was knocked staggering by a blow between the eyes by a constable. When turning to notice his number I was struck by another constable in the mouth, my pipe being smashed. I got the numbers of both constables (33 B and 188 B) and immediately went to College Street Station to lay a charge against the constables. Two people who witnessed the assault (Mr and Miss Byrne) came with me. At College Street I was referred to Store Street when I handed in a written statement as did Mr and Miss Byrne. Next day I saw a solicitor and on Monday Mr Smith (29 Lower Gardiner Street) advised me to ask for a summons at the Police Court Office. This was refused me and Mr Smith said he would apply to the magistrate the next day. However the next morning Inspector McCaig called on me and asked me not to summon the constables, and offered me an apology. I asked him to put his apology in writing and on receiving it agreed not to proceed with the summons.

This apology and the remark of the Inspector to me, "we don't like the police to get at loggerheads with respectable people" show very clearly how they run from a summons when there is a good case against them and when the prosecutor is not a working man.

Henry Nicholls

Copy of the apology

On behalf of the constables who assaulted Mr Nicholls I apologise to him on their behalf for having done so and regret very much that such should have occurred.

Alex. McCaig, Inspector. 1/9/1913

Copy of Statement of May Byrne, 306 Iveagh Buildings, New Bride Street, Dublin, January 4th '14.

On Friday night, the 29th August last, in company with my brother I was coming from a meeting which was held at Beresford Place and when near O'Connell Bridge a body of police charged the people who were coming from the meeting. I saw one policeman strike Mr Nicholls in the face and when he turned to look after the man who struck him another policeman struck him a blow and knocked him down and about six or seven others were knocked down at the same time.

May Byrne

Copy of Statement of Mr Patrick Carton, 54 Marlborough Street, Dublin. 20 years of age.

As far as I remember on the night of the occurrence when the first baton charge took place I was at Liberty Hall and I noticed about 20 police on duty outside Tucks Entrance. There were about 300 people round Liberty Hall. I noticed a number of children singing national songs. The police advanced and drew their batons and commenced batoning the people, owing to the children singing national songs. I was on the steps and I heard a voice stating "clear the steps of Liberty Hall". I then made my way out to Eden Quay, but got a blow on the way which my cap saved me from. I saw a man lying on the ground after being batoned, whose name subsequently turned out to be James Nolan, who died owing to the effects of this baton charge. I saw a policeman going in front of Nolan and looking at him after, as I thought striking him. I took the constable's no. which was 224 C. After the constables had retreated I rendered all the assistance possible to the man and as a matter of fact went with him to the hospital. I called the attention of Inspector Campbell to the state of the man on the ground and he ordered the constable to disperse the men about. Inspector Campbell sent 52O. in a cab to the hospital with the man. I insisted on going also, and after a lot of argument I managed to step into the cab and accompanied them to the hospital. The man never spoke after he went into the hospital and on looking at him his eyes and head were all swollen and battered.

What took me to Liberty Hall was to pay my weekly subscription which I did before the charge.

I have no animus against the Police and never had any charge of any kind made against me by the police, and I merely make the statement purely for the benefit and protection of the public.

Patrick Carton

Dated this 18th December, 1913.

Copy of Statement of Mrs M Murphy, 91 Nth King Street,
Wife of Nicholas Murphy, Labourer.

On the 31st August last (Sunday evening) about ten or twelve policemen came up the street and burst in the hall door of my house, and then ran up the stairs and burst into my room which was the front drawing room, and the sergeant directed the men not to strike the woman, meaning a neighbouring woman who was with me in the room, but the policemen commenced to smash the ornaments and jugs and also took a chair and threw a dummy dog at my feet. They then left and went upstairs to the room of my friend who was with me when they arrived.

Margaret Murphy

Dated 19th December, 1913.

Reports of Police Officers (August 1913)

Statement of Superintendent Lawrence W. Murphy, D.M.P.

I was in charge of a body of Police on west side of Lower Sackville St on Sunday 31st August, 1913.

From information received shortly after 1 p.m. I entered the Imperial Hotel, and inquired for the manager. There was a short delay owing to the lift being engaged. While standing in inner hall I saw some commotion in street, a number of people running towards Hotel, looking up towards the balcony. I then heard a man's voice speaking to the crowd, and I knew it to be that of James Larkin.

Without waiting for the lift I rushed upstairs, and looked in through the smoking room and rooms of the suite on a level with the balcony. I did not see Larkin, but a gentleman indicated to me to search the rooms on the other side of the corridor.

I entered a couple of rooms, and then met Larkin coming out. He was apparently endeavouring to make his escape from back of hotel. I caught him by the arm and detained him. He made no resistance whatever, but made a remark that it was all right, or words to that effect. He was dressed in a long black dress coat, dark striped trousers, and wore glasses. He also had on a false beard. I knew him at once, having been well acquainted with his appearance.

When coming to end of corridor, Supt. Kiernan and a party of police rushed upstairs, and accompanied us to College St Police Station. I remained in charge of Larkin there until Sergeant Fagan, Detective Department and other officers arrived, when I handed Larkin over to them.

Fergus Quinn Superintendent — Dublin Metropolitan Police

That on the 29th day of August 1913 a Proclamation given under the hand of E.G. Swifte Esq, Chief Divisional Magistrate of the Dublin Metropolitan Police District was duly published wherein it was recited that information had been duly sworn representing that a number of people would meet or assemble at Sackville St. or its neighbourhood in the county of the city of Dublin on the 31st day of August 1913 and that the object of such meeting was seditious and that the said meeting would cause terror and harm to and dissension between his majesty's subjects and would be an unlawful assembly. The said Proclamation duly prohibited such meeting and strictly cautioned and forewarned all persons whomsoever that they should abstain from taking part in or encouraging or inciting to the same and duly gave notice that if in defiance thereof any such meeting or assemblage at Sackville Street or its neighbourhood should be attempted or take place the same would be prevented and all persons attempting to take part in or encouraging the same or inciting threats would be proceeded against according to law. I duly served the said Proclamation personally upon James Larkin General Secretary of the Irish Transport and General Workers' Union at 7.15 p.m. on yesterday evening the 29th day of August 1913. That I was present at a meeting at Beresford Place in the city of Dublin last night between 9 and 10.20 p.m. The said meeting was composed of about 8,000 or 9,000 persons and was addressed by James Connolly, Ex-councillor McKeon, Belfast, William P. Partridge, and the said James Larkin. The said James Connolly in his speech said that they had received notice from His Majesty the King which declared that they were prohibited from holding a meeting in Sackville St. They never intended to hold a meeting in Sackville Street. He did not know where Sackville St. was. They did not recognise the Proclamation. They intended to go to O'Connell Street on Sunday. Let no one tempt them to break the law. They should walk to O'Connell Street on Sunday and see who was going to hold a meeting and who was going to prohibit it. He said William P. Partridge also spoke and in the course of his speech said that in the words of Old Kruger "they would stagger humanity" and he called upon those present to strengthen their ranks and stand shoulder to shoulder and be determined to carry over the Tramway men to victory.

After Ex-councillor McKeon had spoken the said James Larkin next addressed the meeting. In the course of his speech he said that they were to hold their meeting when and where they liked unless it was proclaimed and then they could hold it if they were determined. He said he would ask the Lord Mayor to issue a counter-proclamation. Before he went any further and with their permission he would burn the Proclamation of the King. He then produced and burned a document purporting to be a copy of the said Proclamation and went on to say that he cared as much for the King as for Swifte the Magistrate. He never said "God Save the King" but in derision. They had a perfect right to meet in O'Connell Street but they wanted no men there but men who would stand. The Police had said that they would take his life: he was a rebel and the son of a rebel: he recognised no law. If the Employers were going to use the weapons of starvation and there was no bread there was bread in the shops or clothing in the windows. The man who was hungry and bread within his reach was an idiot. I verily believe that the said James Connolly, William P. Partridge and James Larkin have by their aforesaid language incited others to a violation of the law and of right: that there is reasonable ground to apprehend that they are likely to persist in the holding of the said meeting which has been duly prohibited as aforesaid and that there is actual danger of the peace being broken and of acts of illegality and crime being committed by reason of the speeches and incitements of the said James Connolly, William P. Partridge and James Larkin. I therefore pray that a warrant to forthwith issue to bring the said James Connolly, William P. Partridge and James Larkin before one of the Divisional Justices of the said District to show cause why they and each of them should not be ordered to find sureties to keep the Peace and be of good behaviour.

DETECTIVE OFFICE, 2ND AUGUST, 1913

Arrest of James Larkin in Imperial Hotel

About 1.10 p.m. on 31st August. I was on duty near Rotunda when I heard a good deal of noise between Nelson's Pillar and O'Connell Bridge. I went quickly to the Pillar and on being informed that Larkin was after being arrested in the Imperial Hotel I called there to make inquiries. I was informed by an office assistant that at about 1.10 p.m. the same day Mr and Miss Donnelly arrived there in a taxi-cab their rooms being engaged earlier by telephone. I then left. Later acting on instructions I returned to the Imperial Hotel went upstairs and interviewed Miss Donnelly but she would give no account of herself beyond saying that she was an amateur theatrical and that she usually lived at 21 Smith Street, Liverpool. Soon after this interview Miss Donnelly left in a cab. Constable Myles Flanagan and myself followed her on a hackney car to 144 Leinster Road, Rathmines where she entered. This is the residence of Mrs O'Regan a well-known suffragette. She again left in a few minutes and proceeded to 49B Leinster Road the residence of Count D. Markievicz where we left her. While I was in the hotel Miss Helen Maloney and Miss Gifford of Palmerston Road who are also suffragettes called to see Miss Donnelly but the manager would not allow them see her. Mr and Mrs Sheehy Skeffington were in Sackville Street at the same time. When Larkin was arrested he was bare-headed and he was taken to College Street Station leaving his tall silk hat behind. I examined the hat very carefully and found stamped on the lining the initials "C.D.M." a fact which goes to show that it belonged to Count D. Markievicz. It was subsequently sent for by the Police at College Street Station.

M. Ahern, Sergeant 14 G. Rathmines.

I then took her to her room and saw her luggage, a large trunk. I also went to Larkin's room leaving a watch on the girl's room in the meantime. In his room there was a portmanteau, old and only secured by straps. I examined contents which consisted of various articles of clothing belonging to boys, a man's trousers and some articles of ladies wear. There was also a small leather handbag locked, and a large size man's overcoat grey tweed and like one which I saw Count Markievicz wear some time ago.

I again phoned to the Detective Office stating I would detain this girl and luggage until the arrival of some other officer, and when doing so Countess Markievicz rushed in being very excited and asked to get to the phone. She rang up 498 Rathmines and asked "did the Count get home yet. I got separated, it was a success, it came off beautifully, going back now."

The girl Donnelly came from her room after the Countess left and wanted to get away. I told her what I was, and that I would not let her away until I made further inquiries. She then went to the phone and called up same number at Rathmines and said where she was and that she could not get away and please do come. Miss Moloney (Sinn Feiner) and a girl who I believe is Miss O'Regan (Suffragette) called to hotel and wanted to see Miss Donnelly but left without seeing her.

Afterwards she took a cab to 144 Leinster Road, residence of Mrs O'Regan, where she left her trunk, and then walked to 49B Leinster Road residence of the Countess Markievicz where she was shadowed by Const. Flanagan and myself.

Patrick J. Myles

Const. 11F.

30.8.1913

Arrest of James Connolly

I arrested the above named at Liberty Hall, Beresford Place between 3 and 4 p.m above date.

I told him who I was, I read the warrant for him and cautioned him. He made no statement.

M. Ahern

Sergt. 14G.

30.8.1913

Arrest of Wm. Partridge

Between 3 and 4 p.m. on this date I met the prisoner in Liberty Hall and said I wanted him and asked him to come to the Bridewell which he did and there I read him the warrant and cautioned him. He made no statement.

R. Forrest

D.O. 36G.

Public Opinion

Extract from The Irish Times 3rd September 1913.

DUBLIN'S FIGHT FOR FREEDOM

The employers of the city of Dublin have at last made up their minds to free themselves from an intolerable tyranny. The strike organisers are at bay. The struggle may be sharp, but we do not think that it will be a long one, and the result will more than justify whatever sacrifice of money or peace the city may have to pay for it. Within the last few days Messrs. Jacob and other large firms have refused to deal with members of the Irish Transport Workers' Union. Yesterday the Dublin Coal Merchants' Association came to a similar decision. They give reasons for it which must satisfy every fair-minded man. Like other traders, the coal merchants find that they must either resist the "unbearable interference" of the Union or go out of business altogether. Today the federated employers of Dublin will make up their minds on the same point. There is little doubt that they will decide to dispense with every servant who refuses to do the work for which he is paid. All this means that, if the members of the Transport Union decide to fight, thousands of them will be thrown out of employment during the next few days. It is a very serious prospect for the city, but the employers of labour have no alternative. In a letter which we print today Mr E.A. Aston pleads for patience. He tells us that batons cannot suppress permanently an industrial unrest which is deeply rooted in the misery of the slums. We have much sympathy with Mr Aston's attitude. We recognise the extreme gravity of the present crisis. We agree with Mr William Murphy that many of our employers might well examine their consciences in regard to their treatment of labour. If we wanted an illustration of the conditions of life in the slums of Dublin we have it today in the appalling story of the collapse of two rotten tenement houses in Church Street, with the loss of least five innocent lives. The housing problem, which is a radical cause of labour discontent, clamours for early and drastic solution. But nothing can be done until the tyranny which has aggravated every evil of our social and industrial life is finally destroyed. When this is done the ground will be cleared for reform. But the immediate danger brooks no delay.

Yesterday the Trades Union Congress at Manchester appointed a deputation to visit Dublin. It will come here under the most unfavourable auspices. It has been appointed, not to make an impartial inquiry, but to find evidence in support of a foregone conclusion. The deputation was instructed "to address meetings in favour of free speech, the right of organisation and free meeting, and to inquire into the allegations of police brutality". What are the facts? There is no need to champion free speech in Dublin, for that right of all law-abiding citizens has never been threatened. After Larkin's release on bail he was permitted to address a meeting in which he incited his audience to acts of violence and pillage. Does the Trades Union Congress approve of this sort of free speech? The authorities not only permitted, but protected, a large meeting of the Transport Workers' Union which was held near Dublin on Sunday. The Sackville Street meeting was proclaimed only because such a meeting held in the central thoroughfare of the city would have been a direct danger to the public peace. It is now almost certain that the charges of police brutality will be made the subject of a public inquiry. The demand is supported by a letter which the four members for the city have addressed to the Lord Lieutenant, and, for reasons which we stated yesterday, we do not resist it. In this matter, therefore, there is no occasion for the interference of the Trades Union Congress. The assumption of the Congress that the present troubles are the result of "an organised attempt to smash trade unionism" is utterly baseless. There is not one member of the Transport Workers' Union who will not be secure in his job if he consents to exchange the "red hand" for the badge of some society which confines its attention to the interests of its own members. The employers of Dublin are on strike not against trade unionism, but against the worst form of Continental Syndicalism. They are in revolt against a system which dislocates the whole industry of the city and county whenever some small dispute arises in a single trade. If the Trades Union Congress really accepts this definition of trade unionism, the whole Kingdom is threatened with industrial anarchy. The conduct and conclusions of the deputation from Manchester will have an importance which will extend far beyond the shores of Ireland.

We suggest that the deputation should be given no excuse for persisting in the extraordinary misapprehensions which prevailed at Manchester. It consists of six members. At least two of these are men with reputations for intelligence and common sense. Mr Brace, M.P., is Vice-Chairman of the Parliamentary Labour Party, and was a member of the Royal Commission on Coal Supplies. Mr John Ward, M.P., is a respected member of the Independent Labour Party, and a Justice of the Peace for the County of London. We know little about the other members of the deputation but they can hardly refuse to support any action which may be taken by the two members of Parliament. We believe that the employers of Dublin will make a mistake if they do not give the deputation full opportunities for discovering the whole truth about the present crisis. By giving the deputation the cold shoulder our employers will merely drive it into the arms of the men who deceived the Congress at Manchester. Messrs. Brace and Ward cannot refuse to listen to the employers' side of the case. The whole story of Larkinism in Dublin should be put clearly before them. They should be told, with full proof at every point, how the syndicalism of the Transport Workers' Union is ruining the trade of Dublin, stimulating class hatred, and aggravating poverty. If they are open to conviction at all, they will soon be convinced that the revolt against Larkinism does not involve a particle of hostility to honest trade unionism. If the employers take this course, they will have done, at any rate, everything which it was possible for them to do. We are not without hope that they may be able to convince the deputation of the merits of their case, and so to deprive the Transport Workers' Union of all sympathy amongst the decent trade unionists of Great Britain. If the deputation shuts its ears to facts, and accepts syndicalism as a legitimate weapon in the hands of labour, the employers of Dublin will have no responsibility for the results of that insane judgement. The firm and unanimous attitude which they have now adopted is bound to end in victory. We only suggest that, without relaxing their firmness for an instant, they should neglect no opportunity for curtailing the expense and misery of the conflict.

The Irish Worker Saturday, Sept. 13th, 1913
Open Letter to Jim Larkin from "the Irish worker".

Was Murphy Larkin?

Dear Jim,

Your performance at the Imperial Hotel on Sunday last was magnificent and not likely to be soon forgotten; but your impersonation of William Martin Murphy as president of the meeting of the Chamber of Commerce, on the following day will surely live in history.

Your denunciation of Larkin and Larkinism was fine; it could not have been better done by Murphy himself. It was well you began in that way, otherwise you never could have got home the fine thrusts you made afterwards without arousing suspicion as to your identity.

Even as it was, when you told the meeting that, "the employers of Dublin had bred Larkinism by the neglect of their men" many of those present rubbed their eyes and wonderingly asked themselves "where were they?" and I feared for a moment they would see through your disguise.

However, they looked more at ease when you assured them that employers had nothing to fear from Trade Unionism — the good old-fashioned kind — which enabled them "in 99 cases out of 100" to starve the workers into submission, and how difficult it was for Larkin to get the workers to understand this. How you must have invariably chuckled on hearing that august assembly applaud what was really the case for the Transport and General Workers' Union and the newer Trade Unionism.

Surely no worker after the testimony of this highly enlightened body can have any further doubt about the efficacy of the newer Trade Unionism and the futility of the old.

If the employers who attended that meeting have any sense of humour left they will give up talking about their superior intelligence, when they learn how badly they have been had.

But who could have believed, however, that they could not realise that they were being duped, even when, as "a last parting shot" you told them to "go and examine their conscience as to how they were treating their workers".

They were too dense. I rather think their much vaunted intelligence must be a negligible quantity, as those who attended that meeting don't know yet what to think of your speech.

One of the members was overheard remarking to another at the conclusion of the meeting: "Was Murphy really in earnest, or was he Larkin?"

Yours admiringly,

Red Hand

The Irish Worker

Sat, 6th September 1913

Mr James Larkin on the way to be tried

Message from Jim Larkin

Men— be MEN! The fight goes well — we are winning, and shall smash Murphy and his Federation of tyrants to smithereens if you keep straight on. I am in good health and spirits in this "home from home". My sympathy goes out to the bereaved relatives of our comrades, Nolan and Byrne, and of those who lost their lives in the deplorable disaster in Church Street. The Dublin Corporation is criminally responsible for the deaths of the Church Street victims — sacrificed on the altar of Capitalism and Landlordism!

Men and Women of Dublin! PAY NO RENT until the Lock-Out is withdrawn and the victimised tramwaymen are re-instated.

Jim

The Irish Worker Sat. Sept. 6th, 1913

Irish Transport and General Workers' Union
General Lock-Out

A MONSTER
Demonstration
TO CLAIM THE RIGHT
OF FREE SPEECH

WILL BE HELD ON

SUNDAY, SEPTEMBER 7TH, 1913

UNDER THE AUSPICES OF

The British Trades Congress, the Irish Trades Congress and the
Dublin Trades Council and Labour Party

IN O'CONNELL STREET

Mr Thos. McPartlin, President of the Trades Council, will preside.

SPEAKERS

Messrs J. Ward, M.P; W. Brace, M.P.; J.A. Seddon, ex-M.P., (National Union of
Shop Assistants); J. Hill, (Boilermakers' Society); Harry Gosling, (President
National Transport Federation); Councillor Jack Jones, (Gas Workers'
Union), representing British Trades Congress; and Messrs. Arthur Henderson,
MP.; G.N. Barnes, M.P.; and G.H. Roberts, M.P. (representing the Labour
Party); Mr Rose, E.C., and Mr Freeland (Organiser Amalgamated Society of
Engineers); and representatives of the Irish Labour Movement.

CHAIR AT 1 P.M.

WORKERS OF DUBLIN!

ATTEND IN YOUR THOUSANDS AND ASSERT YOUR RIGHT TO FREE SPEECH

Transport Workers' Strike, Dublin, 7th Sept. 1913

The following memorial to Herbert Asquith, Prime Minister of Britain, were sent by the undersigned members of the British Parliamentary Labour Party.

Memorial to the Rt Hon. H.H. Asquith, MP.

We, the undermentioned Members of Parliament belonging to the Labour Party beg to submit to the Prime Minister that the prosecution of Mr James Larkin for seditious speeches and his continued imprisonment since his conviction are grave scandals in view of the fact that highly-placed people are allowed to make speeches with impunity which appear to the average person to be far more dangerously seditious: and that this gives reason for the widespread allegations that there is in this matter one law for the rich and powerful and quite another for the working classes.

We beg to point out that there is a very general belief that substantial injustice has been done to a man who has been leading a great struggle for improving the conditions of the workers of Dublin and whose efforts in their larger aspects are regarded by the general public with sympathetic approval.

We therefore venture to express the hope that the Government will no longer delay to recommend the exercise of the Prerogative and thus to terminate the imprisonment of Mr Larkin.

Wt. Abraham	W. Adamson
George N. Barnes	C.W. Bowerman
J.R. Clynes	Charles Duncan
A.H. Gill	F.W. Goldstone
J.G. Hancock	J. Keir Hardie
Arthur Henderson	John Hodge.
Walter Hudson	James Parker
Joseph Pointer	Thomas Richards
T. Richardson	G.H. Roberts
Albert Smith	Albert Stanley
Will Thorne	Stephen Walsh
George J. Wardle	Alex Wilkie
William Brace	Fred Hall (Normanton)
W.E. Harvey	W. Johnson
Philip Snowden	J.E. Sutton
J.H. Thomas	John Wadsworth
John Williams	Ramsay MacDonald

IRISH TRANSPORT GENERAL WORKERS' UNION

James Larkin
General Secretary
Head Office: Liberty hall
Beresford Place
Dublin, 29th July 1914

Dear Mrs Quinn,

I regret that I was not in when you called yesterday. Let me express my sincere condolence for your loss. I was talking to Pat the night before I went to London, I did not think I would be told he would be called away so suddenly. I want you to depend upon us in anything that you may want doing, you can depend upon us nothing will be left undone to help you in every way. I would ask that the Citizen Army should get your permission to convey the body to its rightful place. As you are no doubt aware that Pat was whole souled in his enthusiastic support for the army.

Food Kitchen, Liberty Hall

Jim Larkin gave instructions that the women and children were to be fed first.

Kindly notify me at once and I will have the men there in full uniform. The friend who brings you this note, Mr Roland Kenny, countryman of our own represents Reynold's newspaper and I would be very pleased if you would give him full information as to the happening and also to the connection that your lamented husband had with our Union and the victimisation of him because of his loyalty to trade Unionism.

I am,

Yours most sympathetically,

Jim Larkin

This copy letter was given to me by Jer O'Leary, my "stage" grandfather. As can be seen Big Jim thought of the personal tragedies of others even in times of great stress.

The Lock-Out lasted for many more months, which would not have been possible without those locked out receiving the wholehearted support of their spouses and families, at a time of great hardship. The food kitchen in Liberty Hall in 1913 played an important part in assisting the morale of those who were locked out. Many people from around the country supported the effort to try to ensure that people who were seeking some crumb of human dignity, did not starve. Delia, Jim's sister, who had been a nursing sister in Liverpool, gave up her job to help with Jim's Union activities and helped at the kitchens in 1913. Many others also helped out, the Sheehy-Skeffingtons, Countess Markievicz, Helena Maloney, and others.

My grandfather believed that it would be important to secure sympathetic strike action in England. This was frowned on by a number of the Labour leaders and administrators in England.

Jim organised his "Fiery Cross" Campaign and held meetings in London, Manchester, Liverpool and other venues. At these meetings he was critical of the bureaucrats of the movement, but won the hearts of the working people throughout Britain. people were rushing to send money for the relief of those involved in the Lock-Out in Dublin but he believed that having food delivered by ship would be of great spiritual value as well as lifting the morale of the men and women of Dublin. The sight of the "SS Hare" steaming up the Liffey must have been an inspiration. The stresses on families of workers involved in the dispute were enormous and many people in Britain offered accommodation for a few weeks to children of those affected by the Lock-Out.

The position taken by the hierarchy of the Church was that the children were being taken to a pagan country where their faith would be under attack. Once again the police took action against people who wished to send their own children to England for a week or two, by condoning and in fact, supporting the kidnap of children from their own parents or those in charge of them. The State did nothing to alter this position.

Sunhall, Liverpool, Public Meeting, Dec. 1st 1913
Jim Larkin, James Connolly, "Big" Bill Hayward and their Liverpool colleagues

The following copy letter was addressed to Dr Walshe, Archbishop of Dublin by Ben Tillet, a prominent trade unionist from England.

The Secretary
The Labour Party.
4 November 1913

To the Most Reverend The Archbishop of Dublin,

My Dear and Reverend Sir,

The Executive of the Book Wharf, Riverside and General Workers' Union have instructed me to make protest against the unjustifiable attack and aspersions upon British workmen.

As a matter of fact, a large proportion of the members of our organisation have the honour to be Irish in race and Catholic in religion. The Inspiration of help came from the Irish sympathisers resident in this country, and the only desire was one of interest and love for the starving children of Dublin. It is understood that the poor of Dublin are worse off than the children of London, if that is the case, then God help these helpless little ones.

We in London would have been glad if during our dispute last year we could have been gladdened with the offer of help from Dublin Workers and the Priests. That the element of religious bias should now be introduced appears on the surface to be a travesty of the true Catholic religion, which is assuredly a world religion and not as is being claimed by the Hibernian Society and the Priests, an Irish religion. Besides being the greatest world religion, it is the best organised International religion; its priests are in every centre of the civilised world. With such a vast and comprehensive religious machinery, and a perfect distribution of religious institutions, surely it was possible for any of the priests to take charge of the religious training of the children, no matter in what centre the children would be housed.

The men and women whose great and humane interest prompted them to offer their homes can claim as good and as true an interest in the spiritual and moral welfare of the children, as a professional theologist, and with that interest would have willingly co-operated with the priests. The fact that the majority of those coming forward with offers of help to the parents and children of Dublin, are both Irish and

Catholic, should have saved them from the insult offered them by the calumny of those who abuse both Irish nationality and the Catholic religion. Thousands of our members, both Irish men and women have sacrificed, even out of their scanty incomes, money in support of the children and the families of Dublin. The Priests appear to have taken the attitude of the disciples who drove back the children from the Nazarene. You will remember the immortal command of "Suffer the little children to come unto Me": in fact that beautiful spirit of poor, helping the poor, gave of their best to the children.

Our membership resent as brutal and unchristian the attacks made upon the British workers and the Irish resident in this country, and trust that you will use your great office for the purpose not merely of relief, but for the overthrow of the system of robbery by which the children and parents are robbed of the ordinary decencies of life. You must know that poverty is the bad mother of vice and disease. Do not forget your sacred duty is to overthrow the weight of your office, and courage and convictions, on the side of those demanding in the name of God and Humanity, that the causes of destitution and death should be removed. We are proud that the poor mothers of this country could stretch out mother-arms to the starvelings of Dublin and we are proud of the Christlike love, which prompted our people to help yours.

With respectful regret at your bias.

I remain,

Yours sincerely

Ben Tillet

General Secretary

Ben Tillet's letter to the Archbishop of Dublin regarding the invitation to strikers children going to England gives a clear and eloquent picture of the circumstances.

Jim Larkin's comment about the formal stance of the Church was very brief and to the point.

He said: "It's a poor religion that cannot afford a couple of week's holidays."

Irish Worker 20th Dec. 1913, by Jim Larkin

CHRISTMAS 1913

While we are writing this the one question agitating all Dublin is whether this Christmas will see a relighting of the Fiery Cross or the ringing of Christmas bells of peace and rejoicing. Possibly no more grim commentary upon the so-called civilisation of today could be instanced than that fact. Here we have a great city held up by a war between two classes, and in that war the contending classes are represented, on the one hand, by those who control the wealth, the capital, the armed forces and all the means of coercion; whilst, on he other hand, all that is represented is toiling men and women, with no assets except their brains and hands, and no powers except the power to suffer for a principle they esteem more valuable than life itself.

But to the side of this latter class has been drawn gradually as if by a magnet all the intellect, the soul and the spirit of the nation, all those who have learned to esteem the higher things of life, to value the spirit more than the matter.

Publicists of all kinds, philanthropists, literary men, lovers of their kind, poets, brilliant writers, artists, have all been conquered by he valiant heroism of the Dublin workers, have all been drawn within the ranks of the friends of the fighters of labour — all have succumbed to the magic charm of the inobtrusive men and women whose constancy amidst sufferings has made this fight possible. Whoever signs the document of settlement (if any is ever signed), whosoever is acclaimed as the great one of the treaty of peace (if there ever is a treaty of peace), the real heroes and conquerors are to be found in the slums, and in the prisons, where men, women and girls have agonised and are agonising in order that their class may not lose one step it has gained in its upward toil to freedom.

These thoughts come crowding upon us as we write. We think also that, despite all the adhesion of all the brilliant ones and all those in the highest odour of sanctity to the cause of the workers, the settlement is still in the hands of those who control the economic power. Poets artists, authors, humanitarians, and archbishops may plead and beg for the ringing of the bells of Christmas for ever. The final word still rests with those who control the money bags; and thus we learn, hard facts teaching us, that in this gross travesty of civilisation under which we live today neither soul or brain is the equal of gold.

"The clinking of the silver dimes life's melody has massed, And nature's immemorial chimes are jangled, harsh and jarred." And so Dublin lies in the grip of the power of the purse; and on this fateful Friday the issue still hangs trembling. A few hours may determine whether the verdict will go forth for the joyous ringing of the Bells of Peace or for the militant call to all lovers of their kind to grasp and pass from hand to hand again the dread but inspiring Fiery Cross.

British TUC and Labour Party View of 1913

In the course of my research in England I visited the Labour History Museum in Manchester. I had been in contact with them in advance and the Director, Mr Nicholas Mansfield, and the archivist Stephen Bird, had been most diligent on my behalf. They had located the appropriate files referring to the Labour Party in Britain in 1913.

The information contained therein is currently not readily accessible in books written in Ireland about that period. These documents, while I might not agree totally with their content and conclusions, nonetheless demonstrate much of the thinking of the TUC Executive and Labour Party members of that time.

I believe that to give a precis of the documents would be insufficient, therefore I have reproduced one of them in full with grateful thanks to the Museum of Labour History, Manchester. Copies of two other detailed reports I have passed on to the Labour History Society on behalf of their British colleagues.

Trades Union Congress Parliamentary Committee,

General Buildings Aldwych, London W.C.

Report of the Deputation appointed by the Manchester Congress to deal with the Trade Union Crisis in Dublin.

The following resolution of Congress was the instruction to the delegation:

"That three members appointed by the Parliamentary Committee and three appointed by the Congress be sent to Dublin to address meetings in favour of free speech, the right of organisation, and free meeting, and to inquire into the allegations of police brutality. The deputation shall report to the Parliamentary Committee, who shall take such action as may seem to them desirable."

In accordance with this resolution Congress appointed Messrs. W. Brace, M.P., John Ward, M.P., and J. Jones, while the Parliamentary Committee appointed Messrs Harry Gosling, J.A. Seddon, and John Hill.

The deputation proceeded to Dublin, and immediately on arrival met a number of Trade Union representatives, including some of the Executive of Dublin Trades Council, at Liberty Hall, the headquarters of the Irish Transport Workers' Union.

On the following morning, September 4th, the deputation interviewed the Lord Mayor of Dublin at the Mansion House. The Lord Mayor very willingly gave evidence on the position of affairs, which considerably assisted the deputation. We also interviewed several of the employers concerned, including Mr Murphy, who, whilst finding fault with the later developments of the methods of the union, admitted that great service had been rendered to large sections of the very poorest of the workers in Ireland by the Irish Workers' Union.

From the evidence obtained we are satisfied that the Irish Transport Workers' Union had been doing good work – that it had considerably raised the wages of the various sections of industry which it had organised. The union had brought hope to thousands of the lower-paid workers of Ireland.

The Irish Transport Workers' Union and its General Secretary, Mr J. Larkin, had adopted a very aggressive policy, attacking employers individually, extending the use of the sympathetic strike, the refusal to handle what is termed "tainted goods", thereby involving sections of the community previously untouched by these disputes. This policy is being met by the employers with an equally aggressive policy of a sympathetic Lock-Out.

Mr William Martin Murphy, the chairman of the Dublin Tramway Company, determined to oppose Mr Larkin in his efforts. He also determined to oppose him and the Union in all other sections of industry where the Union had members, and to this end he created the Employers' Federation, who have now issued a form for all their employees to sign, of which the following is a sample:

FORM OF AGREEMENT

I promise that, while I am in the employment of _____ _____, I will not belong to or support the Irish Transport and General Workers' Union or any other Trade Union affiliated with it.

(Signed) ....

Factory No. .... Department ....

Date ....

Mr Murphy, who is the proprietor of three Irish newspapers — the *Daily Independent*, the *Evening Herald* and the *Sunday Independent* — was also able to apply the powers of the Press against Mr Larkin and the union. In one of these newspapers Mr Larkin was called "a mean thief".

The Irish Transport Workers' Union runs a newspaper called the *Irish Worker*, and in his paper Mr Larkin replied to Mr Murphy with more vehemence than courtesy, and at the time of our arrival in Dublin the dispute had degenerated into a personal quarrel between Mr Murphy and Mr Larkin, and this was going on with thousands of workmen out of employment, the city of Dublin under a semi-military regime, and the whole population suffering serious inconvenience and loss.

Regarding the police attack of Saturday, 30th August, on members of the ITGWU at Liberty Hall (continued subsequently to Eden Quay, where two of them were batoned to death) and the break-up of the meeting in O'Connell Street on Sunday, 31st August, we found no justification for the action of the police, which resulted in serious injuries to hundreds of citizens.

The police have claimed justification for their conduct because of a speech made by Mr Larkin on August 28th, in which he is alleged to have advised all workers to attend the Sunday meeting in O'Connell Street, but advised all women and children to stay away, as he said "this will be a job for men". Other statements of an inciting nature were attributed to Mr Larkin, but he and his colleagues and other Trade Unionists whom we interviewed deny any allegation of incitement, and state that the meeting would have been peaceful and orderly but for the action of the police.

Regarding the chief mission of the deputation to hold a Free Speech and Trade Union meeting in O'Connell Street, we learned from the Lord Mayor that he had no powers to permit or prohibit such a meeting.

The police force, both the Dublin Metropolitan Police (who are armed with batons) and the Royal Irish Constabulary (who are more of a military force, being taught to shoot and use the sword) are all controlled from Dublin Castle, and are immediately under the Chief Commissioner (Colonel Sir John Ross).

Neither the Lord Mayor nor the Corporation were consulted with regard to the bringing of extra police into the city, nor were they consulted with regard to the prohibition of the meeting on Sunday, 31st August.

In pursuit of our determination to hold a meeting on Sunday, 7th September, we sought an interview with the Lord-Lieutenant (Earl of Aberdeen), the Under-Secretary (Sir J.Dougherty), whom we met at the Castle on Thursday, 4th September, with other Castle officials being in attendance. Having explained our intention, the Lord-Lieutenant and the Under-Secretary did all in their power to dissuade us from our purpose, advising us that there was sure to be considerable destruction of property and bloodshed, and that we were taking our own lives in our hands.

No amount of persuasion from the Lord-Lieutenant, the Under-Secretary, or other authorities in Dublin, however, could dissuade us, and we firmly reiterated our determination to carry out the mandate of Congress.

We found the Lord-Lieutenant most courteous, and he sought several subsequent interviews with us with a view to persuade us to hold our meeting at some other part of the city, and it was not until the afternoon of Saturday, September 6th, that we persuaded the Castle officials not to actively prevent our meeting being held. Since our first visit the Lord-Lieutenant had been in communication with the Attorney-General for Ireland, the Chief Secretary (Mr Birrell), and Sir James Dougherty, and they finally intimated to us that although they could not sanction our meeting they would take no steps to prevent the meeting being held. On our strong representation that the presence of the police was the cause of the previous trouble, and that we could not be responsible for order unless they were removed, and that we would appoint 300 marshals from our own ranks, the authorities withdrew practically all the police from O'Connell Street on the Sunday. We also succeeded in securing the suspension of all vehicular traffic during the time the meeting was in progress.

At the meeting the vast multitude of Trade Unionists and citizens were addressed from three platforms by your delegates (Messrs. W. Brace, M.P., J. A. Seddon, H. Gosling, John Hill, John Ward, M.P., and J. Jones), the Labour Party representatives (Messrs. A. Henderson, M.P., G.N. Barnes, M.P. and G.H. Roberts, M.P.), and representative Irish Trade Unionists

73

appointed by the Dublin Trades Council, and the following resolution, which was submitted simultaneously from all three platforms, was carried with great fervour and enthusiasm:

That this mass meeting of Trade Unionists and citizens hereby assert the hard-won rights of free speech and Trade Union combination, including picketing and the right of every worker to select his or her own Trade Union without the interference of any employer, recognising that collective bargaining is the only means whereby improved conditions can be secured; further, we demand an immediate and independent public inquiry into the conduct of the police on Saturday and Sunday, August 30th and 31st last, which resulted in the arbitrary imprisonment of Trade Union leaders, and in the serious wounding of hundreds of peaceful citizens and the death of two of our comrades.

The meeting was a perfect success, having not a single incident of the slightest disorder, and after the passing of the resolution the great crowd quietly dispersed.

This great orderly demonstration, in the absence of all police, on the spot of the previous Sunday's meeting, is indisputable proof of the peaceful intentions of Dublin Trade Unionists and the unwarranted brutalities of the police on August 31st.

While in Dublin your deputation applied themselves to the immediate and pressing necessity of bringing about the usual Trade Union procedure in attempting to settle existing disputes by friendly conference between the employers and representatives of the men concerned. In this effort we had the consent and co-operation of the Trades Council and the representatives of the Irish Transport Workers' Union.

We visited Mr Larkin in Mountjoy Prison, who expressed every confidence in his fellow officials who were acting in his absence, and advised us that whatever they would do he would confirm. Thereupon, we met the representatives of the employers concerned in the Shelbourne Hotel and 12 noon on Friday, September 5th, and, after a long conference, in which we vindicated the right of every workman to choose and join his Trade Union, the right of collective bargaining, the right to picket, etc. we succeeded in arranging a conference between the employers and representatives of the men for Monday, September 8th.

This conference consisted of eleven representatives employers and eight representatives of Dublin Trades Council, representing practically all the larger trades of Dublin, and including the Transport Workers. Four of our deputation attended. The conference lasted about seven hours. The whole position was reviewed, and so hopeful was the outlook that an adjourned conference was arranged on the motion of the employers present. The time and place of this conference was fixed. To our great surprise and disappointment we received at a very late hour notification from the employers of their intention not to attend the conference as arranged. But, recognising our obligation to the Dublin Trades Council, we proceeded again to Dublin on Saturday, 13th September. On our arrival we met the Trades Council and discussed with them the new situation, and with their consent we made further attempts to persuade the employers to adhere to their arrangement to meet us on the Monday. These efforts were continued till a late hour on Monday night, when a final refusal to again meet us was given by the employers.

From information obtained since negotiations broke down, we are thoroughly convinced that the Dublin Employers' Federation Limited are not prepared to make any kind of agreement with responsible Trade Union representatives, and are determined to crush out Trade Unionism in Dublin.

The result of our mission may be briefly summarised as follows:

FREE SPEECH

The task of asserting the right of free speech and free meetings in O'Connell Street, which is the principal thoroughfare of the capital of Ireland, seemed almost impossible. The Irish Attorney-General, in the presence of the Lord-Lieutenant, the Under-Secretary, and the Chief Commissioner of Police, read to us extracts of Irish law, and advised us that we had no right to hold a public meeting in O'Connell Street, which was primarily a place of public thoroughfare. He warned us of our legal risks in attempting to hold such a meeting. The Under-Secretary reminded us of the valuable property in the vicinity which was owned by parties to the existing dispute, and which it was his duty to protect. He also spoke of the state of feeling existing, which was sure to be intensified by public meetings, and the inevitability of further serious conflict with the people and the police. The Lord-Lieutenant in supporting his officials did all he could by pointing out our own personal danger and responsibility to dissuade us from holding our meeting in O'Connell Street.

We have already cited the steps we took to ensure order, which enabled us successfully to carry out to the full the mandate of Congress.

TRADE UNION COMBINATION

This right is seriously menaced in Dublin by the Castle authorities, who, in our opinion, are using military authority and armed force to assist the employers in coercing Trade Unionists into abject subjection to the illegal and unfair conditions laid down by the Employers' Federation. We have ample evidence to prove that the legal right to picket is ignored by the authorities, and, when attempted, made by the police a sure means of arrest, in all cases followed by imprisonment. This aspect of the question must have careful attention when the public inquiry into the conduct of the police takes place, as there is evidence of Castle officials and relatives being financially interested in some of the firms in dispute.

ALLEGED POLICE BRUTALITIES

On this question we have tried to keep an open mind, but the persistent delay of the Dublin Castle authorities in opening the inquiry is justification for our gravest suspicions that the allegations of unprovoked brutalities, both in the streets and in private residences, committed by the police are only too true. Your deputation, backed by the unanimous resolution of the citizens of Dublin, have voiced the demand of Congress for a public, immediate, and impartial inquiry, and it will be the duty of the Parliamentary Committee to watch the composition and character of the tribunal, and also the proceedings of that tribunal, in the interests of Trade Unionism.

Harry Gosling   John Ward
J.A. Seddon   John Hill
J. Jones   W. Brace

Two Continents Apart

Jim Larkin, outside
Croydon Park, 1914

Peter Larkin

James Larkin

One hundred million men and women go
inevitably about their affairs,
In the somnolent way
Of men before a great drunkenness.
They do not see you go by their windows, Jim Larkin,
With your eyes bloody as the sunset,
And your shadow gaunt upon the sky...
You, and the like of you, that life
Is crushing for their frantic wines.

— Lola Ridge, *The New York Nation,* May 2nd 1923

Big Jim in America

A new chapter in Big Jim's life began on October 14th 1914. On that day he left for America. It is my opinion that his workload for the previous ten years — in Liverpool, the docks of Britain, Belfast and finally in Dublin with the Lock-Out — had drained his immense energy to the limit. He needed time to recharge his batteries, expand his experience and find fresh inspiration.

On his way to America he first visited Liverpool to see the remainder of his family who still lived in that city. The night before he sailed he spent with a former workmate Fred Bowers, with whom he had worked on the construction of the Liverpool Anglican Cathedral. Together, prior to the setting of the foundation stone, they had done what was common for many masons and put a time capsule of socialist tracts and publications underneath the stone. I do not regard this as inappropriate as the basic tenets of pure socialism are quite akin to those of Christianity. He and Fred stayed up most of the night talking about the past, as well as their hopes for the future. Jim left for America the next day.

He arrived in America in November of 1914. He rapidly became involved in the political movements of the time speaking at public meetings, working for the Industrial Workers of the World. This general union was called colloquially the "Wobblies". It is interesting to note that his brother Peter started work for the same union early in 1915 in Australia. Apart from working for the members of the same union Jim and Peter were both subjected to constant harassment by the authorities. In both their cases this led to unfounded charges of criminal syndicalism and they were jailed unjustly. The spurious charges they faced were merely a cover for the authorities' opposition to their expressions of concern for people who were living in great need. They caused the ruling classes to feel uncomfortable and this was regarded as a grievous offence by people who were living in luxury and were extremely sensitive to criticism aimed at them from any quarter.

Bertrand Wolfe, in his book *Strange Communists I Have Known*, gives an example of the type of attitude that existed amongst the general public who did not know what to make of Big Jim. He refers to Jim speaking at a meeting in San Francisco where he reported that Jim was heckled by a member of the audience whose one form of amusement appeared to be attending public meetings. In an attempt to provoke controversy he said to Jim, "What is your view of birth control?" Jim thought this might be a personal attack on him and his country so he replied, "It is a pity your mother did not use it".

In 1917 Jim also gave an oration at the funeral of Joe Hill, an organiser for the IWW who had been shot by goons hired by employers. In fact, on one occasion while Jim was attempting to organise a factory in the South he escaped lynching by a hair's breadth. I was told that the Mayor of the town from which he was chased was called Daniel O'Connell!

One of the cities he visited was Chicago. The President of the Chicago Federation of Labour was a gentleman called John Fitzpatrick whose birthplace was Athlone. The poster about a meeting on March 12th 1916 which was chaired by John Fitzpatrick and featured Jim Larkin and Con O'Lehane. This poster was kindly given to me by Mrs Eileen White who was related to John Fitzpatrick.

When going to America Larkin was given a note of introduction to John Devoy by Tom Clarke, who was then one of the leaders of the Irish Republican Brotherhood in Ireland, while Devoy virtually controlled the Clan-na-Gael in America.

In America Larkin tried to make it appear that the note of introduction from Clarke constituted credentials which entitled him to be present at all meetings of the Clan-na-Gael at which important action was decided upon, but he was informed that the introduction was not capable of such interpretation and was refused admission.

The Clan-na-Gael paid for his expenses in America for some time and also the expenses of his wife and children when they returned to Ireland. Larkin, however, soon got mixed up with Socialists and made an attack on the Clan-na-Gael which ceased to make him an allowance, but not before he had obtained a grant of 2,000 dollars to cover his expenses to attend a Socialist Conference in Stockholm or Russia. It is not clear if he ever attended the Conference and he has been accused of pocketing the money without going.

It is significant that the very many people in America who supported Jim's efforts on behalf of workers were almost exactly the same groupings as those who supported his work in Ireland and England. Likewise with those who opposed him.

His first formal clash with the authorities resulted in him spending some time in Comstock Jail. Amongst those who visited him was Countess Markievicz. A copy of her letter to Bob de Coeur of the Citizen Army, about her visit to Jim in jail, is included here courtesy of the Office of Public Works, Kilmainham Jail.

Copy of letter (undated) written by Countess Constance Markievicz from New York to Bob de Coeur (Citizen Army)

My dear Bob,

I am writing to you for the benefit of the Council as I actually remember your address. We had a fair crossing, and got a great reception on landing.

The first thing I did was to make arrangements to go and see Jim L. We fixed it up for Weds. 12th. Mrs Jack Carney came to see me and told me how to go ahead. She often goes to him. I started off Weds. evening travelling all night, changed at Albany in the early morning and ran through Saratoga, where the English were beaten, and arrived at Comstock at about 9.30 Thursday morn. The Prison is a huge red building in the middle of a farm. No wall round it, no horrible big gate, just a door and a Porter's lodge where a most

81

obliging official at once went off to look for J.L. He then brought me into a snug room and left me on a comfortable seat to wait. There was quite a crowd of men and women talking together and smoking in the room. Then the door opened and in came our friend. His face has not changed a bit, perhaps its a little less careworn and thin, he has the same old fire in his eyes but his hair is almost white. He gave me a hearty greeting and introduced me to the head officer and arranged with him to show me round the Jail later. Then we started talking and he posted me up a lot about things in America. He seems to be well up in everything that is going on at home, except about the late Commandant. He understands the political situation absolutely — I could see it fretted him dreadfully to be shut up just now when he could do so much, but he was awfully brave and made the best of everything. He told me that the food is excellent and heaps of it, beds comfortable wire mattresses, and work is done in quite an easy pleasant way with no rude officers shouting at you and trying to speed you up and there is no spying on you. You have heaps of visitors who can bring you all sorts of things and talk with you without restraint. You can talk among yourselves and smoke. In fact, he said, that physically he had nothing to complain of. He made the best of everything in a splendid way — the only thing, he said, was the confinement, and I could see how he suffered from his enforced idleness, when he can see so much to be done.

At midday J.L. had to go and report himself. When he came back he introduced me to two of his fellow prisoners who also had visitors and asked one of them to get me some coffee. He not only got me some delicious coffee but asked me to share their dinner, and we all sat down and I got some nice chicken sandwiches and cake. Think of it in a Jail! After dinner we went on talking and I told him all about the Army and gave him greetings from the Council and all his many friends. He told me that he was against the organising of a strike in Dublin for his release, because it would not help, and believes his release was blocked by England possibly at the instigation of the Free Staters.

He is on very friendly terms with our crowd and it was his work for the Republic that got him locked up. He blames Devoy and Cohalan, and says that they could get him out tomorrow if they wanted to. I had to leave at 20 to 4 to catch the train. Before leaving the Prison the Chief Official came back and he and J.L. took me round the place. Its all more unlike a prison that you could imagine. In one room a band was practising, all prisoners, it was a huge room and all round it were baths! In another room they were printing, then I saw the tailoring, shoemaking, mat making. Then we saw the kitchen, bakehouse and store rooms. Everywhere the men were talking and behaving just like you do in real life. Then we saw the cells. They are in the middle of the passage, with no door or window, but a gate which faces a huge window. Everyone has lots of pictures and ornaments.

The real tragedy for a man like Jim is the confinement, and the isolation. There he is, a man of great brain and tireless energy, shut up with a crowd of Blacks, Chinese and criminals of every race, located at the back of beyond, and hearing daily of the dire stress of the country to which he belongs. He told me — without my asking — that he had to wire to stop that strike for his release that there was so much fuss about. He says it couldn't have helped. He blames Judge Cohalan for his imprisonment. But indeed he talked very little about himself, he just made the best of everything, and tried to tell me things that would be useful.

Now I must end this or I will not get my letters off by this mail.

So goodbye and good luck to you all. Mise do chara i gcuis na hÉireann,

Constance de Markievicz.

Please write to me

8 East 41 St. (c/o Austin Stack, Irish Delegation)

New York City.

My grandfather renewed his friendship with Jack Carney and his wife Mina in America. Jack Carney was editing a newspaper in Duluth. There is also included here a copy letter from Jack Carney, again courtesy of Eileen White.

52, Merrion Square
Dublin Jan 24th, 1934

My Dear John Fitzpatrick,

There is no need for me to tell YOU how happy I was to receive your letter. A letter from John Fitzpatrick is an event of such rare occurrence that when it does arrive even the leprechauns take on a merry twinkle in their eyes. It is now 12.30, past midnight, just after leaving Jim. We have come home from the Union headquarters where we spend all of our time in work or play. Our Union activities are many but the work is child's play when your heart and soul is in it. I am on the Dublin School Board. I also manage a factory run by members of the Union. It employs around twenty men. The firm who own it went broke, so Jim took it over on lease. They make spades and shovels. We keep going and a slight loss is made up by the Union. And when I see the smith swinging on the anvil I always think of big hearted John Fitzpatrick. We are not competing with the U.S. Steel Trust but 20 families are eating and living and a small contribution like that helps a lot. It has given me a wonderful experience. Arising out of the factory management I attended the convention of the employers of the Free State. Some four hundred had gathered together in the Metropole ballroom. There was no discordant note, all was merry and bright until they moved a resolution calling attention with "disfavour the expenditure of considerable sums of money on the unemployed..." I went to the microphone. I only had five minutes, but I was cool and collected, though my whole being was consumed with a seething rage, mingled with a contempt to all of these well fed gentlemen who talk so glibly of spending money on their trips to Europe and ask for reductions in income tax and want to cut down the unemployed relief. I told them that I supported the policy of building up Irish industries but now I could see that after having driven the English invader out we would have to drive out a worse invader — the invader of the homes of the poor and unfortunate unemployed. There were few cheers. Many of the employers knew me. Ten voted with me for the rejection of the resolution. But the sullen silence of the convention seemed menacing and one big employer got up and said it ought not to go forward they were against the poor, etc. I walked out with all eyes turned on me, but I left them thinking and that is the trouble. You build up one set of exploiters after driving another set out. The petty employer is the worst tyrant. You can argue with the big employer but the petty employer is beyond all reason. On foreign policy I support the present Government. On domestic questions I differ. Only the trade union can understand the worker. No body else tries to or could if they tried. President De Valera means well and he is honest. Do not believe the yarns about O'Duffy. He has just been challenged to fight an election but refused to accept the challenge. His record is a terrible one. There are 77 executions he superintended — executions of his own people. These dead rise up in their graves to confront him at every turn of the road. The blue shirts dare not parade in any large town without police protection. It is the press that makes O'Duffy and it is that press that was never friendly to Ireland. The Labour Movement is now passing through another phase, namely, the driving out of British Unions. Eventually they will go, but I am afraid they will have to be driven out by fighting them. If they were so loyal to Ireland as they say they are they would get out. They secured a foothold here in 1917 just after the Easter Rebellion. They came when our people were torn in anguish at the loss of their leaders. Their time is short. Jim is not so active at present. I think he made a mistake in 1923, but he has kept the past. Without him wages and hours would have been terrible. It is no soft job working with him, but one likes it because the man is hopelessly and may I say wonderfully honest. He does understand his people and though at times he would drive you to drink with his generous hand and heart you are glad he is what he is because of what he is. He is not without his faults but I prefer his faults to the virtues of some of the leaders here.

Building trades here had a terrible setback in 1930, but are slowly getting back into form. There is much activity here. The brick factories cannot supply enough bricks. The Government is putting through an extensive housing scheme, though the rents are not as economic as they might be. Those who need them the most cannot afford the rents. If anybody in the building trade would send me some technical stuff on house building in America I would be more than obliged to them.

Railways for a long time here had their work done in England. after a fight of six years Jim Larkin got them to remodel their shops in Dublin. They are now spending 500,000 dollars on new shops and so all work will be done in Ireland. There is on a foot a scheme to co-ordinate the bus and railway traffic. Every part of Ireland is now reached by either bus or train. Here the buses are dearer than the trains. Huge motor transport cars carry pigs and sheep, also cows, into Dublin. The Economic War makes food cheap. Best steak as low as 14 cents per pound. In Roscommon you can get pound of steak, stone of potatoes and six head of cabbage for 35 cents. All stuff arriving in packets is taxed 1d per shilling so all the firms send their stuff here in bulk and have it packed here. There are 5000 girls employed in the sweep offices. It is the largest industry in Ireland outside of Guinness's. The price of turkeys at Xmas was 10 cents per pound. In England turkeys sold for 52 to 60 cents per pound because there was a shortage due to the economic war and boycott of Irish birds.

I could write sheet after sheet, John, but even I must sleep for I rise at seven-thirty. I am sorry about Jim Brennan. A great scout. I have forgotten his address and if you know it send it on. Ed Nockelu, the shrewdest guy in the American Labour Movement. It is impossible to think of you without him or him without you. Amos and Andy! I will send your note on the radio to the press so that the people can read it. And now to the end. DUBLIN! Soon it will be spring. Spring in Dublin. Nowhere do men feel the wonder and exhilaration of spring as here in this great city, and in no city is the glory of Spring so amazing and stimulating as here in Dublin. I love this city. I could do better in London or Paris, but Dublin on bare living is so much better. The very memories of Dublin are sufficient in themselves to carry one on through to the heights. Here in this square walked Oscar Wilde, Emmett, Tone and others. The world still speaks of them. Here was born great hopes and here trod aristocrats whom the world has forgotten. Across over the square, behind yonder tower was born Castlerach, of whom Byron wrote, "So he has cut his throat at last! He? Who? The man who cut his country's long ago!"

So John I bid you goodnight and good morning. Remember me to Ed and to all the crowd. I am interested in what you write of President Roosevelt. I shall view his program with interest. I hope your optimism will be justified. Mina will be glad to hear I have heard from you. She is now a great sculptress. Someday I will send you pictures of her work. She is a great woman, above all she is Labour and thanks to John Fitzpatrick who was so impressed in the day I took her to the Federation meeting. My best to you, John and if someday you can find time for a holiday there will be a great welcome for you.

So long John

Jack Carney

The culmination of Jim's sojourn in the United States was the major trial when Jim was tried for criminal anarchy (it is well documented and took place in New York in May 1920). He was convicted and sentenced to 5–10 years indeterminate imprisonment in Sing Sing Prison.

LARKIN GOES TO PRISON FOR LOYALTY TO THE WORKING CLASS

"The conviction and sentence of Big Jim Larkin was not surprising to those who are acquainted with the brand of Justice meted out in American courts to those who have dared challenge the supremacy of the Industrial potentates. Jim faced the usurpers of law single-handed. Prosecutors and persecutors were flayed mercilessly by this silver-tongued orator from the Emerald Isle. A biased jury, a judge to whom real Americanism is a dead letter and a labour-hating district attorney played their dirtiest. These servile tools of capitalism will yet live to see their dastardly work undone. Years ago when Larkin was incarcerated by the British Imperialists the workers on the other side of the Atlantic declared a general strike."

COMRADES–

You can assist in liberating Jim Larkin from Sing Sing to-day as you did in getting him released from Mountjoy Jail in 1913, if you show the same earnestness and determination NOW as you did THEN. Ways and means will suggest themselves to you. Remember Jim Larkin has been exiled from his wife and four children for six long years because of his work for you.

THINK OF IT

Issued by the Larkin Release Committee

BERNARD CONWAY, *Chairman*
MICHAEL CONNOLLY, *Treasurer*
DELIA LARKIN, *Secretary*
SEAMUS McGOWAN, *(Capt. I.C.A.)*
HENRY DALE
STEPHEN HASTINGS *(I.C.A.)*
MICHAEL O'MAOLAIN

Look out for date of Public Meetings

Whilst in America in 1971 I ascertained that Jim had had many visitors in Sing Sing — a great many from the Labour Movement, members of AFL/C10 unions, writers and artists, specifically people such as Paul Robeson, the bass singer, Charlie Chaplin and Merle Oberon the actress. A number of people in the entertainment industry were blacklisted for performing what was, in fact, one of the corporal works of mercy in visiting someone who had been incarcerated unjustly.

In 1923 Governor Al Smith of New York pardoned Jim. It was suggested that he return to Ireland forthwith. He was released from Sing Sing prison on 17th January, 1923 and soon afterwards announced his intention of returning to Ireland with a shipload of food stuffs for the neglected and starving Nationalists of Belfast. He cabled the ITGWU in Dublin to send him £500 to enable him to secure the ship and food and at the same time appealed for a volunteer crew to man the boat. His request was refused by the Union and he was therefore deprived of the theatrical display which he loved so much of arriving in Ireland with a cargo of food for the victims of the Belfast dispute. He returned to Dublin on 30th April, 1923.

Whilst Jim was in America his brother Peter was in Australia and his sister Delia was in Ireland. Peter later went to America to help raise funds for Jim's defence.

In an interview with Patrick Nolan of *The Irish Times* in 1965, James Larkin Jnr confirmed that in 1919 Michael Collins and Joe McGrath smuggled himself and Thomas Foran, President of the ITGWU, to the USA where Big Jim had been in prison. Jim Jnr remained in America for 6 months.

The chronology of Jim's arrest and imprisonment in New York is as follows:

Nov 7th 1919 — Arrest in New York.
Nov 10th 1919 — Charged with criminal anarchy.
April 7th 1920 to April 27th 1920 — Trial.
May 3rd 1920 — Sentenced to 5-10 years.
May 22nd 1922 — Released on appeal — Refused.
Jan 17th 1923 — Pardoned by Governor Al Smith of New York.

There seemed to be general panic amongst the authorities when Jim Larkin's name was mentioned. A report in the Australian *Argus* of 30th August 1917, says:

The Prime Minister (Mr Hughes) was asked by Mr Orchard (NSW) in the House of Representatives yesterday; if he had seen the press report that the notorious Jim Larkin was on his way to Australia; if it was the intention of the Federal Ministry to allow this stormy petrel to land on these shores; or whether, in accordance with the wishes of a large section of the people of this country, the Ministry would compel him to seek some other Mount Ararat. (Laughter). Mr Hughes replied, amid cheers, that instructions had been issued that Mr Larkin was not to be allowed to land here. (Ministerial cheers). Dr Maloney — 'why don't you crucify him?

LARKIN PARDONED
LEAVES SING SING
OTHERS MAY FOLLOW

Govenor Grants Unconditional Release, Holding That Prisoner Had Suffered Sufficiently.

DOES NOT EXCUSE OFFENSE

He Expressly Repudiates Views Voiced by Larkin, but Questions Whether They Are Criminal.

LIKELY TO FREE FOUR MORE

Peter, and Australia

Peter Larkin was the third son of Jim Larkin and Mary McAnulty. He was born in Liverpool in 1880. His early life mirrored that of his elder brother Jim. He faced the same hardships with equanimity. He was shorter than Jim but stockier. He worked at the North end of Liverpool Docks and assisted Jim in organising the dockers from 1903 onwards. His profile in the Labour Movement was slightly less obvious than Jim's however they shared common views on workers' rights. At a later time they also shared common convictions for criminal syndicalism albeit on two different Continents — Jim later in the USA and Peter in Australia. During that later period they also served as members of the IWW (the Industrial Workers of the World) in those different continents.

The next formal record we have of Peter is that he continued working on the Liverpool docks. In 1914 he moved to London and worked briefly on the docks there. In early 1915 he arrived in Australia as a seaman. A description of Peter in *Sydney's Burning* by Ian Turner is as follows:

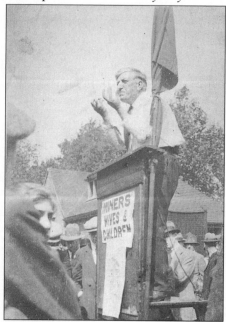

Peter speaking at a miners' meeting

Peter Larkin was heavily built with an untidy mop of hair, surrounding a moon face dominated by a great bulbous nose. Larkin looked the man to wield the Shillelagh. He already had years of experience as a labour agitator behind him. Now he worked in the waterfront and spent his spare time agitating for Home Rule for Ireland and industrial democracy. Together with a colleague in the IWW he had recent convictions arising out of propagandist activities in Australia. A trial took place of 12 members of the IWW in Sydney as the following newspaper article reports:

ALLEGED TREASON

POLICE RAID

PREMISES OF THE I.W.W.

A raid was made upon the premises of the Industrial Workers of the World in Sussex Street, on Saturday morning by a body of police, under Inspectors Walker and Campbell.

A search of the premises was made, and a quantity of materials seized, and four men were arrested, and charged with treason. The names of those arrested are, Charles Reeve, 30 years, bricklayer, a native of England;

Thomas Glynn, 35 years, journalist, a native of Ireland;

Peter Larkin, 46 years, seaman, a native of Ireland;

John Hamilton, 42 years, painter, a native of Victoria.

The arrested men were at once taken to the Central Police Court and had the charged proffered against them.

Among the material seized was literature, pictures, flags, and photographs all of which were lodged at the Central Police Station.

Part of the charge read that the accused feloniously and wickedly did compass, imagine, invent, devise, or intend to levy war against the King within his Majesty's dominions.

Sydney Morning Herald, Monday 25/9/1916.

Most of the evidence appears to have been concocted by informers. Before sentence was passed Mr Justice Pring asked if they had anything to say, Peter Larkin's response was as follows:

You ask me have I anything to say! Have I anything to say against a Star Chamber? Why, I ask you, should I bring to this country but a few months ago the wife of my bosom and the child of her womb and then perpetrate the foul crimes with which you charge me. No such thing as crime can be laid at my door or at the doors of any of my ancestors. I am not guilty, even if all the juries of the world say I am. I leave it to my own class, who knew me, and I say again if my class condemns me I am prepared to take the medicine.

The other accused made similar responses. However, seven of the accused were given 16 years hard labour. Peter and three others were given 10 years hard labour and the remaining accused were given 5 years hard labour. The manipulation of the legal process in that trial was very similar to that undergone by Jim, in America. Whilst we have proof of Jim's belated pardon by Governor Al Smith of New York, all I can deduce with certainty is that Peter did not serve out his full sentence. He was in Dublin by 1921 as he was sent for by old members of the Union to help organise a defence fund for Jim in prison in America. He was then sent out to New York as the Defence Committee's secretary-treasurer based in 53 Jane Street, New York from where he sent over the article reproduced here.

In this particular article he commented on the industrial scene in Ireland from the time of the dispute in Belfast in 1907 to the Lock-out in Dublin in 1913. This was from the view point of one who had suffered wrongful imprisonment at the hands of the authorities and who was battling for his brother who was suffering the same fate. In penning the article he was direct in the extreme.

My last comment is that the final two sentences should be disregarded — no communications or funds should be sent to 53 Jane Street, New York City!

IRISH CRISIS

&

JIM LARKIN

by Peter Larkin

In response to repeated requests for information as to the present conditions existing in Ireland I am setting down my view of the situation as it presented itself upon my return from Australia some few months ago.

Knowing from actual experience the story of the working men and working women of Dublin in 1913, in their tremendous struggle against the combined forces of the Irish employers, British employers and the British government, I was painfully struck upon my return from Australia by the entire absence of enthusiasm among the ranks of the very people I had seen fighting so nobly in 1913. The old place seemed dead and as I walked around the places where the Old Guard congregated and heard their story I sensed the reasons for the lack of enthusiasm. Irish Labour has lost faith in its present representatives. Neither Free Staters, Republicans, nor labour members of the Dáil can enlist the support of the Old Guard of Irish labour in any attempt that stands for industrial betterment or for national independence. No clear call is issued by the leaders of the Irish masses. The situation is tragic beyond words.

Wherever I went I heard the cry, "When will the big fellow (Jim Larkin) be back again in Dublin?" One section has openly

92

declared that it will not pay any more dues into the Union until Jim returns. They back up their resolve by pointing out that the fighting Union of yesterday has become a haven of rest for the careerists and opportunists. The backs of Irish labour serve the leaders as stepping stones to power. The old slogan, no longer resounds through the Union halls. The slogan that rallied the masses of Ireland to victory has been superseded by the English formula which makes of the rank and file a consciousless mass, wandering aimlessly about like so many dumb sheep, whose only function is to pay dues.

The Old Guard of Irish Labour has no love for the "Free" Staters. They describe them as "a lot of damned scoundrels who would not only sell Ireland, but the mothers who bore them, in order to bask in the smiles of the Empire". Their candidly expressed opinion of the Republicans is that they are honest and sincere determined people, but lack the clearness of vision to recognise that their cause is hopeless without the driving forces of organised labour, with a clean cut industrial purpose behind them.

To sum up, the Old Guard of Irish Labour feels that the recent struggles in Ireland have not produced the men and women that came out of the big industrial battle of 1913; men and women with the vision to see and the force to act upon the ideas necessary to bring the masses out of the bogs of chaos and treachery, which the wily English politicians, with the aid of the "Free" State generals and "wee" parliament bloodpirates of the Carson type, have led them into. There are no Pearses, Connollys, Clarkes or McDonaghs now!

It must be admitted, when we consider the knowledge that Collins, Griffiths and Mulcahy possessed and utilised, knowledge of the machinery built and used by the Republicans during the time of terror, that their acquaintance with the whole movement was of great material value in aiming a disastrous blow at the Republican movement. Where the Republicans, previous to the treaty had proven themselves to be adept at fooling the best military and secret service men of the British empire, once they had seduced those who were prepared to sell the information they acquired as Republicans, their knowledge was of the greatest intrinsic value, for the disorganisation of the Republicans. The latter were compelled to reorganise and adopt new tactics.

Had there been a clear-sighted, decisive-minded man at the head of the Republican forces, as newly organised, who instead of talking and temporising and discussing the treaty, had arranged those who signed the treaty before the representatives of the Dáil for High Treason and dealt the signers their just deserts, the "Free" State could never have existed either in name or in fact.

It is the same old story. Until the Irish masses recognise that all struggles have an economic basis, and that they must be fought and their results determined by a subject class with an ideal, their struggles will fall far short of their objective. The masses must depend upon their own power, not upon the prayers of a Moses. He never has come. He never will come.

The whole field of Irish economic freedom must be plowed over again. Conditions are deplorable. In Belfast, people live in fear and dread of assassination. The Craig gang is no respecter of persons. Anyone who is known to hold either nationalistic-labour, republic or socialistic ideas, Protestant or Catholic, is murdered or driven out of the six countries.

There are operating in the North 42,000 special constables, in three classes, and the function of each class is a component part of a well thought out and devised scheme to make Ulster today, as in the past, the stronghold of reaction and British imperialism, for while the capitalist class holds Belfast, Irish freedom, either political or economic, is impossible.

To the merest observer, therefore, the North is the key to the Irish situation. This explains England's determined resolve to hold that part of Ireland. Students of Irish affairs slowly, but surely, acknowledge this fact.

The special constables are comprised most of ex-soldiers, the scum of the British slums, in charge of cadets of the property class. They are also backed up by British soldiers in full war kit and "Free" Staters are working hand and glove with them on the border line. This being the case, it is easy to understand why those who are on the run in the north of Ireland are at a greater disadvantage than men of the Republican forces in the south, west and parts of the south-east, where the people are almost solidly Republican.

The "Free" State government, in my opinion cannot last, inasmuch as Ireland cannot stand the financial strain. It is common knowledge that the "Free" State government and army are being backed up with British war material and finance.

The treatment of prisoners in "Free" State jails, is worse than ever it was under the jurisdiction of the English garrison. Prisoners have been brutally murdered in their cells for refusing to "squeal" on their comrades. Men have been branded with red hot irons.

The knout is being used freely, not only in the North, but wherever the Free State functions. Prison ships are becoming the order of the day. Credulous Irish men and women, visiting New York go down to glut their hatred of England by going through the old convict ship *Success* no doubt have cold shakes down their spines, looking upon it as a thing of the past.

Well, if the Irish men and women, who view this boat with holy horror will cast their thoughts toward Ireland, they will see in their mind's eye, what is only too plainly visible to the people at home — the convict ship *Agenta* in an Ulster lough, and in its penal cells, Irish rebels who long for freedom and work for it — or who did before they were captured by British agents and put on a convict ship.

The *Agenta* was built in America and purchased from the U.S. government. The American people whose money went to build it, are made innocent participants in the outrage. The Craig government operates to berth the rebels in the north in the *Agenta*, but the "Free" State government, not to be outdone by "Christian" England, has a convict ship for rebels in Dublin Bay.

The same creatures guilty of this crime against their own flesh and blood will thump their craws in the churches and chapels of Christian Ireland, and shed tears when they think of barbaric, blood-thirsty Cromwell who, in his day of making Ireland safe for the Empire, banished Irish girls and boys to the West Indies, to become slaves of the planters. The latest idea of the "Free" Staters is to out-Cromwell by deporting those who refused to swear adherence, or in other words sell their birthright, to some lone isle.

St Helena has been mentioned, I don't believe St Helena will be chosen, for having visited that isle and lived there for a time, I know that it is often visited by passengers between London and the Cape. There might be found means of communication and the outside world. I believe, according to information I gleaned, while in London, that they have in view, under British guidance, an island, taken from Germany, in the South Seas. This island is rampant with fever and possesses of Irish slaves driven by gangsters to fill the coffers of British imperialists and capitalists.

The remarkable thing about the atrocities being perpetrated upon the people of Ireland, is the silence of clerics of all churches, labour leaders in England, and the press of the entire world, I have in my possession a compilation of facts, arranged by an Australian exclusively from sworn and verified affidavits obtained while touring the North recently. Lack of finance, up to the present has stopped me from publishing it. It has the greatest news value and is sensational in the extreme. I would like to know where are the Irish working classes I have heard of so often in this country, what are they doing, and why have they nothing to say in answer to the despairing cry coming from the finest section of Irish organised labour in its hour of extreme agony. This section has proven itself in its past struggles. Irish labour was on its knees previous to 1907, when Jim went to Belfast. He showed them the light and ably and well they followed it. Catholic and Protestants united for the first time since King Billy defeated King Jamie, the Scot, in battle on the banks of the Boyne.

For 11 weeks, in 1907, the Protestants and Catholics of Belfast stood shoulder to shoulder, as Irish men and women and neighbours.

There were neither assaults made, nor insults offered during that time and the world was treated to the spectacle of a labour parade in which the peoples marched in their thousands to the strains of two score of Irish bands, one half of them from Orange societies and the other half from Catholic parishes. It is difficult to realise now that it was an Orange band which led off with Moore's fine Ulster song, *Let Erin Remember the Days of Old*, its notes caught up by Catholic and Orange bands down the line.

Picture Ulster of today, under the Craig-Law regime, where assassination, bigotry and torture are being used to break up the solidarity of labour —the common bond of the common people.

Wexford, Waterford, Cork, Sligo and other towns wherever Larkin enunciated his gospel, show that the Irish working class, if given a clean lead from out of its own ranks, will manfully respond.

The Dublin rank and file wants to know what Irish American working men are going to do about it. It is common knowledge among friends and foes that Jim Larkin is the man who can take hold of the situation in Ireland and bring the people out of chaos into peace. The Old Guard sent to Australia and bade me hope to consider this question, and it has sent me here, full of home, that I can express its plea and induce Irish men and women in America and all fair minded Americans to break the bonds and set the prisoner free.

Will the good and true suspend all differences and come in force to answer the faith expressed in Ireland? Will they send back to the poor and strong in Ireland their trusted leader and save the Irish Labour Movement and the Irish people from disaster?

If you, who read this, think it worth while to help get Jim out of prison, will you act at once? Send along your contribution. The Larkin Defence Committee here has made me secretary-treasurer and placed in my hands the full responsibility for funds given in Jim's name. All communications should be sent to me at 53 Jane Street, New York City.

Larkin and Debs

Larkin is still in Sing Sing and not an honoured guest in the White House. Will not someone prompt Warren Harding to give a banquet in the White House to America's noblest and place Debs on his right and Jim Larkin on his left? He would learn more by listening to them for an hour than he'll ever learn from his sharp-mouthed Mellon or his slobbering Duaghtery with injunctions to make the constitution ridiculous, by imprisoning the workers and freeing the robber-instincts! Debs' sweetness and Larkin's wisdom might teach even him how foolish is his 'normalcy! – Frank Harris

Irish Citizen Army by James Connolly

The Irish Citizen Army in its constitution pledges its members to fight for a Republican Freedom for Ireland.

Its members are, therefore, of the number who believe that at the call of duty they may have to lay down their lives for Ireland, and have so trained themselves that at the worst the laying down of their lives shall constitute the starting point of another glorious tradition – a tradition that will keep alive the soul of the nation.

Peter returned to Ireland in 1923. With the foundation of the Workers' Union of Ireland he became its first National Organiser in 1924. He held that position until his early death in 1931 at the age of 51. There is no doubt in my mind that Peter's premature death resulted from, in large part, the actions of the Australian judiciary and the harsh sentence that was passed on a man whose only fault was that he cared for his fellow man.

In 1930 Peter and his wife, Annie, attended the wedding of their only child, Esther, in London to George Russell, a Scotsman. In the 1950s Esther and her husband returned to Australia where their family is still living. Esther died in 1992.

In November 1947 Peter was re-united in death with his brother Jim when he was re-interred in the joint grave in Glasnevin Cemetery. Delia was subsequently buried with them. I was present at Peter's re-internment ceremony in August 1947.

Peter Larkin's funeral

Peter and Annie Larkin at the wedding of their daughter Esther to George Russell

Delia

Delia Larkin, after the formation of the Irish Women Workers' Union in 1911, became the first General Secretary of that Union. It was primarily founded because of two conflicting reasons, at that time the majority of men made it clear that they did not want women members in their Union, this compliment was returned in full by very many women prospective Union members.

In a couple of the photographs taken during the period of the Lock-Out, of significance would be the average age of the members which appear to be in their teens.

Delia Larkin and members of the Irish Women Workers' Union.

Delia, as with her brother Jim, believed that a union should care for more than the body of the member, but also for the mind and the spirit. She was directly involved in organising a choir and also running dance classes and amateur drama classes. She organised tours of England and Ireland to publicise the cause of women workers. She also was an important propagandist for the Women's Suffrage Movement.

Middle: Hugh Larkin in Army uniform

It was as a result of the amateur dramatic society that Delia ran for the Workers' Union of Ireland that my late father and mother met in Unity Hall, Marlborough Street. My grandfather had met my mother prior to our parents meeting.

I had the pleasure of meeting Aunt Delia on many occasions mainly in Wellington Road. She had married Pat Colgan, a member of the Executive Committee of the Workers' Union, late in life. Jim lived with them. I was young when I met her and I remember her clearly. She frequently wore full-length black taffeta dresses. She also wore her hair drawn back and very tidy. At my age then she struck me as being a very kind yet strict school-mistress. It was not until very recently that I learned of her early career as a nursing sister in Liverpool. I have particularly fond memories of being asked to assist in the harvest of the Victoria plums, gooseberries and raspberries that proliferated in the walled back garden of 41 Wellington Road. Much of the harvest did not reach the kitchen! I regard Aunt Delia as being a lady of great fortitude. I believe her affection for her older brother, Jim, came close to hero-worship with much justification.

OTHER FAMILY MEMBERS

Although in the course of research I have been assisted greatly by Peter's family in Australia and Hugh's great-granddaughter, Rebecca, in the USA, there is, like in almost every other family, no trace of descendants of other members of our family. Specifically I mention, again, Hugh, Patrick and Barney Larkin, brothers of Big Jim's father, who all emigrated from Killeavy in the 1840s or 50s. There is also Margaret who was Big Jim's sister, born in Liverpool in the 1880s. I would welcome any information about descendants of the above.

My effort is something like a snapshot or snapshots of the family and there are faces missing which would be marvellous to put in context.

Jim's Return and the Formation of the Workers' Union of Ireland

While Jim's arrival in Dublin in 1911 created apprehension amongst employers and also sections of the Labour Movement; his triumphal return from America was welcomed by the vast majority of the populace.

However, both the employers and the apparatchiks or functionaries of the State and its minions, as well as some of Jim's erstwhile colleagues, viewed his arrival with apprehension. His colleagues on the Executive of the ITGWU, knowing that here was likely to be disagreement with the "stormy petrel" of the Union, were right to be concerned.

My grandfather's own feelings about that situation, as he told me, were that although there were some serious personal disagreements, he saw the major problem as being the alteration of two rules of the Union. Whilst he was in jail in America I can recall clearly him telling me that these specific rule changes allowed for:

1. On the occasion of a member receiving an increase in pay, the first week's payment of the increase would form a levy from the member to the Union.

His view was that members paid their standard contribution for service from the Union and should not have to pay twice. Levies should only be raised in support of members in need.

2. The rules had been altered to allow that officials appointed by the General Executive Committee could be selected and act as full voting delegates at annual conferences of the Union or of Congress.

Jim was very pragmatic and saw this as a way in which it was possible for the Executive Committee to control significant numbers of delegates. Whilst my grandfather believed in the democratic process, he found it difficult, in the heat of battle, to arrange committee meetings on every day-to-day issue that arose.

I believe that he would have welcomed the recent formation of SIPTU. Whilst the first rule he objected to was inactive in the Transport Union for many years, the second rule was still in being until the amalgamation of the Federated Workers' Union and the Transport Union.

I have included here courtesy of the William O'Brien gift in The National Library of Ireland, one of the many documents that were issued specifically to damage my late grandfather's credibility. The one matter of significance is that these documents were issued and circulated unsigned.

THE GREAT

"I AM."

WHO MADE THE WORLD?

JIM LARKIN!!

WHO DID HE MAKE IT FOR?

JIM LARKIN!!

Shortly after his return he went to the West of Ireland for a few weeks to recuperate from the stresses of imprisonment. He stayed in Lissadell, the family home of the Gore-Booths. Countess Markievicz was a Gore-Booth and had consistently, together with her husband, supported Jim in his endeavours.

My wife, Brenda, and I had the pleasure, in he late 1980s, of visiting Lissadell ourselves. The atmosphere of the house was peaceful and we met the late Aideen Gore-Booth, a lovely lady, who remembered Big Jim. The visit was very evocative of the time with which we are now concerned.

Jim, in talking to me, had said that he had no intention of being involved in any break-up of the ITGWU. As I understand, a few branches of the Union contacted Peter and said they were not prepared to stay in that organisation whether Jim went with them or not. I understand that his sister Delia went to Lissadell with this information. Subsequently and reluctantly he decided to go ahead and form the Workers' Union of Ireland.

At this time he also came to a crossroads in his own personal life. after he returned from America, with the effects of imprisonment and hardship, it became obvious that he and Elizabeth had grown apart and could no longer live together. For the rest of his life he held her in great affection as she did him. Elizabeth's life had been one of great difficulty as she had, almost single-handedly, raised their four sons, Jim, Denis, Finton and Barney. It is appropriate to say that the four brothers held their father in very high esteem and respect and they loved their mother.

After a traumatic beginning the Workers' Union grew slowly. Peter, a founder member, acted briefly as Secretary to the provisional executive committee. He then returned to work with London dockers. He was appointed first National Organiser late in the 1920s and continued in that position until he died in 1931 at the age of 48.

The Union, from its inception in 1924, operated on the basis of an open door policy, where members were able to visit the General Officers with problems when other officials were not available. Throughout the time from 1924 to the foundation of SIPTU, officials have worked on a principle of assisting each other when an emergency arose. This helped provide on-going service for the members.

I have no doubt that my grandfather would have welcomed the re-unification of the separated members from the Irish Transport and the Workers' Union.

Peter Larkin, Jim Larkin, and colleagues on holiday in Harlech, North Wales

Although there had been much in the way of differences, including the co-operation of certain senior Transport Union officials with the government and with the police, I am totally convinced that my grandfather was big enough to recognise that his presence at certain meetings would result in disputation with others. Equally, Big Jim Larkin would not retain bitterness against former comrades. For my own part, when, finally, talks on the amalgamation of our two great Unions were coming to fruition, I was delighted to approach the campaign in a positive way, knowing well that my grandfather and other deceased members of the family would have fully supported the move.

My own experience since joining the WUI in 1970 had been positive in the sense that I had the opportunity to work quite happily with my colleagues from the Transport Union throughout the country.

Finally, in this section, I wish to refer briefly to a meeting I had in Swords with Martin King, regional officer, Dublin No 2 Region, SIPTU. He reminded me of the first time we met. In answer to a request from me he came to Parnell Square to meet the members of No. 3 Branch Committee which, with the amalgamation, was ceasing to exist, and all the members were transferring to his region in different branches. I thought that meeting was very cordial and brother King was most co-operative. However when we met again in Swords Main Street he said that that meeting was the most intimidating meeting he had attended as he was surrounded in the Executive Room in Parnell Square by the photographic presence of Big Jim Larkin, Jim Larkin Jnr, Denis Larkin and in person my humble self.

Big Jim – More Quotes

I will conclude this section with quotes from interviews I had with James Plunkett Kelly, Joe Deasy, Dr John de Courcey Ireland. Later on, through the book there are more quotes from he same contributors as well as Brendan Hayes, Matt Merrigan Senior, Donal Nevin, Tom Crean, Francis Devine, Billy Attley and others.

JAMES PLUNKETT KELLY

JPK worked for the Dublin Gas Co and joined the Union when he was 18. He later joined the WUI as a Branch Secretary with the same rates and conditions.

It came to holiday time "I asked for 2 weeks holidays from Big Jim Larkin,

'No,' he said, 'There are no holidays in this job, you just do the work; this is a vocation. Trade Unionism is a vocation rather than a "job"'.

I was afraid of my life but I stood up for myself,

'Mr Larkin, I've got kids at home and I haven't been at home at night for a long time and I am surely entitled to holidays.'

This was in Thomas Ashe Hall. 'You had better talk to the young feller,' he said.

I said I would go to see young Jim — his office door had frosted glass. I knocked, 'come in young Kelly'. The big feller himself was talking to young Jim'. There you are young Kelly, I recognised your shadow, not as there's much of it'. he said.

I got my fortnight's holidays, although I only took a week because, as Jim said, trade unionism is a vocation rather than a job".

On another occasion, we were looking out of the window on a very rainy day. A messenger boy passed by on a bicycle, he was soaked to the skin and he had a big basket on the front of his bike. Jim said, "that has to stop. Look at that child. That child is not physically capable of doing that sort of work."

His mind switched rapidly and the next thing he said to me was, "Tell us, Were you ever up in an aeroplane?"

I said no, then he said,

"It's a marvellous situation. You go up in the air, climb a certain amount, go through the clouds, the sun is shining all over the clouds, you look, and it is absolutely beautiful".

A group of us in the Gas Co. were threatened with dismissal. We organised an unofficial strike. I went to see the Big Man and told him we had stopped, and the reason and then he said, "come on, young Kelly — we'll go across."

We went round to the Gas Co. in D'Olier Street from the Thomas Ashe Hall which at the time was having new floors put in. During the course of these repairs Jim fell through the floor. At 69, he was badly hurt and I believe this is what killed him soon after. When he got to the Gas Co. he noticed the public doors were shaped rather like coffins. We met Mr Robertson, the General Manager, who said "Well, Mr Larkin, we cannot put up with this."

Jim looked at him and said, "Mr Robertson, why did you build these doors looking like coffins, they depress me".

It defused the situation. Mr Robertson looked startled but Jim sorted it out and got us all back.

When Big Jim was attending a meeting at the time that he was living in Auburn Street, in the course of the meeting he stopped, got up and said, "There's trouble at home." He left. The following day we heard that some anti-Larkinites had thrown Young Jim into the canal near Auburn Street.

Alfie Byrne was walking down Dame Street with Big Jim and Barney Conway. Alfie was approached by a woman who asked for some money. He replied "My dear woman, I just haven't got it. Jim will you lend me a shilling?"

"I haven't got it," says Jim "Barney will you?"

Barney gave the shilling to the woman. Alfie went off and Jim said to Barney,

"you fool! Why did you give her the shilling? You should have said you hadn't got it. She'll go off and say, "They had the shilling but poor Alfie didn't".

Then Jim said,

"Never mind, you'll get it all back in Heaven and hundredfold".

"Yes," said Barney, "I'll get it back a hundred pints".

In chatting to Frank Cluskey, he once told me an apocryphal story about Barney Conway. Barney was one of the stalwart members of the Union. You would go in to him and ask him about a verbal agreement that you had reached with an employer and he would reply, "A verbal agreement — it's not worth the paper its written on".

My own experience in dealing with over 500 employers over 24 years showed me that Barney Conway was right but for a very few honourable exceptions.

The Big Feller came when we were at the Hall door yarning one day, there was a man pushing a barrow cleaning the streets. He said to me,

"You see that fellow? He is going to retire in 3 or 4 weeks, he'll die in about 6 months because he has no occupation. You may look down on him but that is his job and he talks to people every day and he will be at home all day with nothing to do. He will die because he has no interests."

That shows how perceptive Big Jim was.

JOHN DE COURCEY IRELAND

There is a speech I well remember Big Jim making at one meeting:

"Well, you knew me well enough to know that if you have a genuine grievance I will fight for you to the end, but if you think that we can change the world through Trade Unionism like I think and you can do it without doing a decent day's work or working properly or keeping hours properly, you are going up the wrong path altogether and you will hear about it from me."

He is the only Trade Union leader I ever heard speak like that, and of course he got enormous applause.

I believe Big Jim was a long-term optimist but a short-term pessimist. He was the first person who warned me not to have too much faith in the Soviet Union. He personally was immensely attached to the Russian Revolution which took people out of an awful war. He said to me, "I am afraid they have lost their idealism". Big Jim Larkin never lost his own idealism.

I, myself don't believe any Labour politician can really understand what poverty is about unless they walked up and down city streets sniffing somebody else's dinner, and knowing they are not going to get one themselves.

In 1943 at the General Election big Jim asked me to take the chair at the first meeting which was at the Five Lamps. I had nothing to say other than,

"You all know the candidate and I'll now ask him to speak".

It was the most marvellous speech I ever heard. He started off by telling stories about a sea voyage, a shipwreck, he gripped everybody's imagination. Everyone was wondering what he would say next. He had the whole crowd completely mesmerised when he started to talk about the real issues.

In 1943 I remember Big Jim at a meeting saying,

"We call each other comrade, comrade means that we are closely associated in a kind of crusade and we happen to be the reflection of the picture of the Society

that's going to come, and we've got to show that we co-operate because that society is going to be one of co-operation."

JOE DEASY (PRESIDENT, IRISH LABOUR HISTORY SOCIETY)

In 1944 I first saw Big Jim at the Labour Party conference in 1944. His interventions in speaking on resolutions were very constructive.

I was elected to Dublin Corporation in 1945, at which time he was Chairman of the Housing Committee, which was a Committee of the Full Council, it was an experience to see the way he chaired the meeting. everyone got a fair say, which Jim, after each speaker had made his contribution, would sum up, whilst pointing to the next speaker.

In 1945 the Labour Group had decided to support him for the position of Lord Mayor. It would have required the votes of Fine Gael to elect him. The Fine Gael Group contacted General Mulcahy in the Dáil, they were instructed not to support Jim Larkin, but they could support any other Labour member of the Corporation.

In the 40s, I was selected to serve on a Housing committee for the Labour Party. I had to meet with Big Jim in Thomas Ashe Hall, I met him for over an hour and a half on the topic of Housing. Back in the 1920s he had said a number of bitter things about Tom Johnson. On this occasion he was full of praise for Tom Johnson, giving him credit for his work on Housing Legislation, and also his lifetime of study of the subject.

One of his attributes was that he could attack very, very venomously, and then expect you to forget it and be friendly afterwards.

An important event took place whilst I was a member of the Corporation and present. Big Jim moved that the Freedom of the City be conferred on George Bernard Shaw. His nomination was most articulate, it showed an intellectual aspect of Jim that is not widely enough acknowledged. Jim was a most widely read man. He had also met George Bernard Shaw in 1913. The vote was carried with three objectors. One of these was Alderman Butler.

I have a very happy recollection, later that day, I walked down Dame Street in the Company of Big Jim and Barney Conway. Jim was very pleased with himself and deservedly so. I'll always remember that in the debate, even though Alderman Butler had opposed the motion Jim said about Butler, he had every respect for him. "A man who has endured as much pain in his life as I have."

Later Jim was mulling over the debate, and he said of Butler, "A very decent man, but he would burn you at the stake for the good of your own soul".

Continuation of the
Larkin Tradition

The Chess Masters: Jim, Denis and Jim Jnr

Jim Jnr, Denis, Barney, Finton with their mother Elizabeth Larkin, 1915

Jim Jnr and Denis Larkin

Jim and Elizabeth Larkin had four sons; Jim Jnr, born in Liverpool; Denis, born in Rostrevor Co. Down, and Finton and Barney born in Dublin. Of the four sons, the first three received their primary education in St Enda's in Rathfarnham, which was a school run by Padraig and Willie Pearse. Their youngest brother, Barney, was not yet old enough for school.

Finton went to England, as did Barney, but they both followed different paths in life. Finton went into the retail trade and for many years, with his wife Edie and children Brian and Sheila, ran a family newsagent's in Grafton Road, Kentish Town. During his life Finton had a difficult time as it appeared he had inherited asthma from his late grandfather. Barney joined the RAF and spent some tours of duty in Rhodesia. In later years he worked for BOAC as an aircraft engineer. In the late 1950s he married Evelyn. Barney was taller than his father — he was over 6'4" in height. The Dublin term that he was "as skinny as a whippet" would be appropriate in his case. When I was small I can remember cries of "mind your head" as he came through the front door in 10 Marino Park! Like his brothers I remember him with great affection.

Some people may think it strange that the two older brothers should find their life's work in the Labour Movement, with great success. I do not find it unusual, as, if one looks at very many families whether farmers, electricians, or doctors the same thing happens. This comes about by children being reared in an atmosphere which is conducive to interest in their parents' work. In looking at the life and careers of my late uncle, Jim Larkin Jnr, and my late father and mother, Denis and Anne, I have found it extremely difficult to separate the working lives of the brothers. Both had immense talents as negotiators and communicators, and they also had a personal closeness that, when applied to their work together, produced a result that was better than either could achieve on their own. Their characters, contrary to popular belief, were very similar. Both were attentive to the needs of working people. Both had a kind of wry sense of humour. When together or in a family situation they were relaxed and full of fun — sometimes behaving like two overgrown schoolboys, playing football on the beach or swimming or going on picnics. My father was more gregarious than his brother who was of a slightly more reserved nature. In a work context, both were more serious, they discussed almost every issue without ill feeling and, at no time, did I sense an air of rancour between them. They were as close as twins. Their understanding of each other's views was uncanny. I have heard it said that, in the complementary way they dealt with issues, in the time they worked together, they were likened to different parts of the body, Uncle Jim to the head and Dad to the heart.

As far as my late mother, Anne, is concerned, I am fully aware of the wholehearted support she gave to my father throughout their married life. She had been a member of the Labour Party and of the Unity Drama Group before they met. In fact, she knew her future father-in-law before his son. Some people still living will be aware that Big Jim used to refer to her as "the little one", as she was barely 5 feet tall. Needless to say, he never called her that to her face as she was a strong, determined character.

In the last years of Denis's life he had a very difficult time as he lost his brother Jim, a working partner of almost 40 years, in 1969 and his beloved wife Anne in 1970. Both died from cancer.

Finton and Edie Larkin, Ramsgate

Denis and Anne Larkin on their wedding day

Political Beliefs

My grandfather and two of his sons, Jim and Denis, all had the honour, at different times, of being President of Congress (ICTU). The three of them also had the privilege of representing constituents in both Dáil Eireann and Dublin Corporation. In addition, Denis, in 1955-6, was Lord Mayor of Dublin.

To chronicle their participation in the various posts they held would require two or three volumes on their own. Suffice it to say, that, in whatever arena they operated, either private or public, they never did other than represent the best interests of the weaker elements in society. The areas they concentrated on were, all industrial relations issues, housing, health and social welfare problems.

Denis Larkin speaking at Fairview Corner

I intend, however, to cite a few examples of areas they had of common interest and the depth of conviction demonstrated clearly, not solely by their words, but followed up by practical action.

An issue I would raise with a number of commentators on my grandfather's life and work is the impression that some put across of a man whose effective contribution to the Labour Movement ceased in the mid-1920s. This is far from the truth. Jim Larkin's industrial record started when he was 9 years of age, and finished within a week of his death in 1947. During that period he was also involved, as I mentioned above, as a public representative in both Dáil Eireann and Dublin Corporation. He added greatly to debates on housing, health, and social welfare. In a sense, this was a reversion to his earlier links with the Labour Movement in Liverpool which were more involved with political rather than direct union activity.

His work at that time of life, was fully in accord with his oft-repeated statement that, "A union man who was not involved in labour politics was akin to a prize-fighter boxing with one hand tied behind his back."

As a youngster he told me that and explained, that while it might be possible for Unions to secure improvements in conditions of employment, it was equally possible for Governments to strike down the gains that had been made at the stroke of a pen.

The motivation affecting my grandfather's political life and that of his sons, Jim and Denis, had the same origin as their trades union activities. The original basis was the difficult times they all, but particularly Jim, had to undergo.

Big Jim and Jim Jnr flirted briefly with Communism. They were both attracted to the idealism that was evident at the early stages of the development of that particular political philosophy. Big Jim, however, while representing Ireland at the Commintern or Communist International, fell out with the practice, when it became obvious that delegates were bound to accept dictate on the operation of policies, from Moscow. As I am certain you will realise, my grandfather would not accept instructions from anyone. Big Jim's main concern was to improve the conditions of the workers of Dublin and he would face up to any authority that prevented him from carrying out his own philosophy like only he could. What must be remembered is that he did get astonishing results. Reference to this is noted in police reports included herein. This correspondence supports the argument that he was subjected to a major international conspiracy.

2nd December 1924

My Dear MacNeill,

The activities of one James Larkin in this country more especially in the capital are most prejudicial to good order and unless he can be restricted he will seriously injure the social and economic life of the country. Already he has on several occasions held up the trade of the country and he is doing his very best to create unrest amongst the workers and to sow the seeds of revolution. Fortunately, measures of various kinds have been taken against him which look like being successful. It is important, however, to find out precisely how he is connected with revolutionary organisations as it may be necessary to deal with him as a dangerous revolutionist.

Sometime before the last English General Election when Mr Arthur Henderson was Home Secretary in England the Minister for Justice was speaking to him on the question of Larkin's international activities. Mr Henderson said that the English Home Office had a good deal of stuff about Larkin and that he saw no objection to our having the benefit of it. The Minister has instructed me to ascertain from you whether Mr Henderson's successor is willing to grant the same facilities. If you find him of the same mind as Mr Henderson, it is thought that the most practicable way to arrange matters would be to secure facilities for Colonel Neligan of our Detective Branch to see the appropriate officer in Scotland Yard. Colonel Neligan could go to London with credentials and you could introduce him.

The Minister will be obliged if you see that the matter receives early attention.

Yours sincerely,

J. MacNeill, Esq.,

High Commissioner of the Irish Free State,

York House, Regent Street, London

SAORSTÁT ÉIREANN

(IRISH FREE STATE)

TELEGRAPHIC ADDRESS:
"SAORSTÁT" PICCY LONDON.
TELEPHONE NO. REGENT 6755

YORK HOUSE,
15 REGENT ST.,
LONDON. S.W.1

OIFIG AN IONADUÍ
(OFFICE OF THE HIGH COMMISSIONER)

8th December, 1924.

My Dear O'Friel,
        Yours of the 2nd.
        I saw the Home Secretary to-day. If a
responsible officer such as Colonel Neligan is sent
over all the information available will be given by
Scotland Yard. Colonel Carter would welcome an
opportunity of referring to other criminals as well as
Larkin.

Please ask whoever comes over to let me know at
least a day, preferably longer, beforehand.
When he reaches me I shall have arranged it all.

                    Yours sincerely,

                    James Mc Neill

H. O'Friel, Esq.,
Secretary,
Department of Justice.
Dublin.

By 1926 he had become disenchanted with the practice of Communism which, not only in Russia, but in other countries, was altering in the direction of totalitarianism. His son, Jim, at a later stage, although having spent a year studying in Russia began to see the flaws in the system. My father Denis, at no time supported the Communist Party, albeit recognising that some of the practices were beneficial. Nonetheless, when he stood for election in 1950, at some churches in his constituency I personally heard parishioners being advised not to vote for Denis Larkin because he was a Communist. This was untrue.

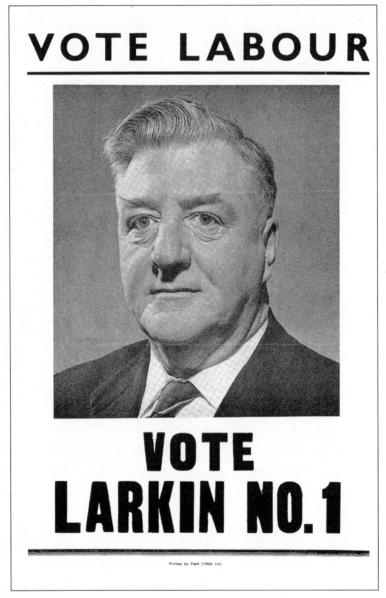

Poster for the local council elections

Whilst the members of the family, both in the Dáil and in Dublin Corporation, represented the Labour Party they saw another political philosophy as a major danger to working people. This philosophy of untrammelled capitalism they saw as a system which was far more open to corruption and abuse than almost any other political philosophy ever dreamed of. The results of following that form of lifestyle led to greed, the manipulation of people without any care or thought for their personal needs and, even more so, showing no interest in the development of people's moral sense.

Jim Jnr Stephen McGonagle (ITGWU), and James Dunne (MPGWU) in Moscow, 1960

Public Representation

Referring back to my grandfather and his sons, but as public representatives, it appears to me that their approach to the representational role was almost totally pragmatic. When issues arose regarding conditions of employment they were ideally fitted to argue any point. Likewise, in respect of conditions of life generally. I have quoted before that specific areas of politics were of great interest to my family. Housing was number one, arising both out of personal experience and a realisation that reasonable housing is a basic human need to support the idea of a comfortable family life. The next area that was very high on their agenda was the matter of healthcare. Their common view was that healthcare should be provided through the State system and that it be given in very strict priority and that those most in need be treated irrespective of the depth of their purse

Another major area that was dear to my family's heart was that of education. This came about partially because my grandfather had little formal education. It may have been influenced by the fact that Denis, my father, and his brothers Jim and Finton were unable to secure a place in any primary school in Dublin, and if it had not been for Patrick and Willie Pearse providing places for them in St Enda's, Rathfarnham, they would have been denied formal education too. Other doors were not opened to them was because their father was an agitator and reformer. Despite the Christianity shown by the Pearse Brothers I can say, with certainty, that my father and his two brothers disliked St Enda's intensely. The regime in the school was strict, the living conditions were spartan and the food was scarce. During the winter heating was kept at a minimum and there was a great belief in much physical exercise to keep oneself warm. Denis played one game of hurling for the school in Croke Park. He was hit on the left elbow with a hurley, he was taken to hospital and the elbow was set in rigid splints. As a result, for the rest of his life he was never able to touch his left shoulder with his left hand.

Another area of keen interest for the family has always been Social Welfare. It always has been regarded that the Social Welfare System should take into account that very many people are in need of help. Where this has happened through chance it is understandable. Where the problems arise directly from the implementation of economic policy it becomes a tragedy. The effect of widespread unemployment touches very many families. It affects families at all levels in society. Dare I say it, it can even be visited on the immediate families of those getting the most out of the capitalist dream, which is becoming more and more of a nightmare. In respect of Social Welfare, governments have to recognise that the problems are not only monetary. They touch the spirit, the morale, and the heart of families. To have no hope is a real indictment on the shape of current society.

It would have been impossible to include, in detail, copies of speeches made by my grandfather, Uncle Jim and my father, Denis on these topics. Suffice it to say, that the Authorities in Dáil Eireann and in Dublin Corporation are most helpful and if any reader wishes to pursue specific debates it is possible to do so on application to the appropriate source.

Other areas of involvement have included transport, in all its forms; with specific reference to internal transport and also sea and air transport; Power, manufacturing industry and the operation of State enterprises.

My grandfather, when speaking on the Transport Bill in 1944, talked about the involvement of private concerns interfering in the control of public utilities. With the State paying large amounts of tax-payers money to private individuals, (pp 2204-2244 of the official report of Parliamentary debates). Jim Larkin said the following in answer to a rebuke from An Leas-Cheann Comhairle:

"Whom was I referring to, Sir? I dare say that most deputies knew the man to whom I am referring, but I am not putting a label on him."

An Leas-Cheann Comhairle: "The Deputy is going very near it. He is referring to a particular organisation and I think, that the man who controls that organisation is being clearly indicated by the Deputy's remarks".

Mr Larkin: "Well, Sir, I always say that the nearer the bone, the sweeter the meat. However, my contention is that we have no right in this House to submit public utilities to the control of any private concern."

One of the best of Uncle Jim's contributions to debate in Dáil Eireann was a masterly exposition of problems associated with the cost of living. This took place on the 15th March 1944. In the official report of Parliamentary debates it is on the 1994–5 vote on account. Although it is too long to reproduce here it is worth looking up.

My late father, Denis, made frequent contributions in the same general areas as his father and his brother. In Dublin Corporation he followed his father directly in becoming Chairman of the Housing Committee for a considerable period of time — over a decade. In that position he was held in great esteem by his colleagues, of all parties, as a result of his impartiality. In 1955 with the support of Bob Briscoe, leader of the Fianna Fáil Party in the Corporation, he was elected to the mayoralty of Dublin. For a man who was born in Rostrevor in County Down, to be elected and serve as the 1st Citizen of Dublin, Denis considered this to be a signal honour, all the more so, as he expressed on the day of his election, that he appreciated the support of Fianna Fáil as they had not been the party who had denied the mayoralty to his late father.

Election of Lord Mayor

It was moved by Alderman McCann and seconded by Alderman Senator Clarkin, P.C.: " That persuant to Section 38 of the Local Government (Dublin) Act, 1930. Councillor Robert Briscoe, T.D., P.C., be, and is hereby elected Lord Mayor of the City of Dublin for the period from this day to the day of the Quarterly Meeting held next after the 22nd of day of June, 1956, and until his successor shall have accepted office":

It was moved by Councillor Cowan and seconded by Councillor Sherwin: "That persuant to Section 38 of the Local Government (Dublin) Act, 1930, Alderman Alfred Byrne, G.C.S.S., T.D., be and he is hereby elected Lord Mayor of the City of Dublin for the period from this day to the day of the Quarterly Meeting held next after the 22nd day of June, 1956, and until his successor shall have accepted office';

It was moved by Councillor James O'Keeffe and seconded by Councillor Conway: "That persuant to Section 38 of Local Government (Dublin) Act, 1930, Councillor Denis Larkin, T.D., be, and he is hereby elected, Lord Mayor of the City of Dublin for the period from this day to the day of the Quarterly meeting held next after the 22nd day of June, 1956, and until his successor shall have accepted office":

Councillor Briscoe, T.D., P.C., having stated that he did not desire to be a candidate for election, Alderman McCann as mover and Alderman Senator Clarkin, P.C. as seconder, withdrew the motion that Councillor Briscoe, T.D., P.C., be elected Lord Mayor.

A poll was then taken, and the Clerk to the Council declared the result as follows:—

For Alderman Alfred Byrne, G.C.S.S., T.D., ... 22 votes.

For Councillor Denis Larkin, T.D. ... ... 23 votes.

Lord Mayor of Dublin, Denis Larkin
and his wife Anne, 1956

In 1956, while Denis was Lord Mayor of Dublin, my parents went to Rome. They were shown round by Father Ronan Cusack who was, at that time, at the Irish College. He assisted them in getting an audience with the Pope Pius XII. My parents assumed this would be a general audience but the went through different security checks and were finally shown into a very small ante-room by the Pope's private secretary, who informed that the Holy Father was arriving immediately and that Father would have to leave. At this point my mother said, "But we never see anyone without our chaplain". As you can see from the photograph Father Ronan Cusack was allowed to stay.

Denis Larkin, Anne Larkin and Fr Ronan Cusack meet his Holiness Pope Pius XII.

At the conclusion of my research many reasons came to me as to why the appelation "Big" was given to my grandfather:

1. His stature.

2. His care for anyone in need and his generosity.

3. Whilst being irrascible he bore no personal ill will towards anyone, whether they were William Martin Murphy, Bill O'Brien or any other whose methods he might deplore.

4. His hope for the future of mankind.

All these factors made him stand out among men.

Just before I received the proofs from the publisher I had a phone call from Ms Bernadette Byrne regarding my grandfather. She told me that he had been of great help to her late mother on the death of her husband James Patrick Byrne. Her mother's name had been Elizabeth Nolan. The names Nolan and Byrne are significant in the Labour Movement. Two of her relatives, James Nolan and James Byrne, were the young men batoned to death in the area of Beresford Place and Abbey Street on the 30th August 1913. Big Jim continued to repay the loyalty of his members, in whatever way he could, right up to his final days.

Big Jim's Last Weeks

*Big Jim speaking at meeting early
January 1947*

In late 1946 the Thomas Ashe Hall was undergoing refurbishment. Some of the flooring needed replacement. My grandfather was watching ongoing work when he fell through the floor, sustaining injuries that effectively, brought his life towards its end. When he had the fall he refused to have hospital treatment for a couple of weeks. He continued with his work until the very beginning of the last week of his life. The picture included is of one of the few occasions when he addressed a public meeting both sitting down and using a microphone.

He was taken to the Meath Hospital, finally, where he died on the 30th of January 1947. His remains were brought from the Meath Hospital to the Thomas Ashe Hall where he lay in state for two days. It is impossible for me to forget those times. A man who had looked after workers for almost his entire life lay in state with a guard of honour formed from members of the Irish Citizen Army and old members of the Union at each corner of his casket. Thousands of people paid their respects including all the great and good of the time, as well as the people who had been of the underclass but were no longer due to his efforts.

On 2nd February, 1947 Requiem Mass was said for Big Jim in his Parish Church, St Mary's, Haddington Road. Early February of that year was bitterly cold with a very heavy fall of snow but that did not deter the many thousands of people who walked after the hearse from Haddington Road, past Thomas Ashe Hall, Liberty Hall, towards Unity Hall in Marlborough Street.

Right up to the present day any time I walk along Marlborough Street towards Parnell Street I am conscious of hearing the scuffling of thousands of feet in the snow and slush. The parade then proceeded to Glasnevin Cemetery where Big Jim was laid to rest. Although, at the time Stella and myself were still young the scene left an indelible impression in our memories. Each year, since 1947, there has been a memorial service in Glasnevin.

> *There is a time in every life*
> *for joy and sorrow, this I know*
> *but I could hear my grandad say*
> *look to the sun, not the shadows*
>
> – Stella McConnon (née Larkin)

I am certain that Big Jim would have appreciated the erection of the statue in O'Connell Street, as it is effectively a tribute to the Irish Labour Movement generally, as well as recognising his own contribution to the Movement, being, as it is, the only monument to a Labour leader in the main thoroughfare of any capital city in the world. I feel very strongly, that he, more likely, would have appreciated the recognition afforded to him by Dublin Corporation when they named the seafront road at St Anne's estate after him. He had put to the Corporation that the estate be purchased by Dublin Corporation, and set out thus: one third for housing, one third for playing fields and one third for a public park and gardens. He did not live to see the fruition of his proposal, however, certainly he would have appreciated the developments in the estate which came out fully in line with his ideas. He would have been happy with it, particularly the Rose Gardens which are of a very high standard and are well-known internationally. The reason why I have mentioned that area is in thinking of Sean O'Casey's remarks about Big Jim, when he said: "Jim Larkin was a man who would put a flower in a vase as well as a loaf of bread on the table". Jim saw beauty in the world as well as misery. He thought of the human spirit as well as the body.

On a few occasions I heard my grandfather repeating the following brief poem at the funerals of colleagues. This verse by Ralph Chaplin from North America, seemed a fitting way to complete this section:

> *Mourn not the dead that in the cold earth lie,*
> *Dust unto dust as all men must,*
> *But rather mourn the apathetic throng,*
> *The cowed and the meek*
> *Who see the world's great anguish and its wrong*
> *And dare not speak.*

129

Jim Jnr and Denis
as Others Viewed Them

Once again others have spoken about my father and uncle and they have spoken for themselves. Some of these pieces are reproduced here.

JOHN DE COURCEY IRELAND

In 1935 I met young Jim Larkin at a meeting in Manchester where he spoke about the dangers of war in Europe and of fascism.

On the 18th of July 1945 Jim Larkin Jnr speaking in a debate on External Affairs, raised an issue that showed his consistency in opposition to fascism of all kinds. The occasion was that of the courtesy call paid by the Taoiseach on the German Minister on the occasion of the death of Herr Hitler. Jim, in the debate, put forward his views and that of many others in saying:

"For my own self-respect, I feel that, on the occasion of this Vote, I must make my position clear. I do so because on a number of occasions recently it has been emphasised from the Government Benches that Ministers act on behalf of this House, having been elected by the House. Therefore, the Minister for External Affairs, in his capacity as such, calling to make that courtesy visit to the German Minister might, in certain circumstances, be regarded as speaking for all the members of the House. I do not want to dwell upon the position during the last six years. My attitude goes back much further, and much further than Deputy Dillon's goes. Because of one aspect, and one aspect alone, I want to record myself here as dissociating myself from that courtesy call. I do so as a trade unionist, as a member of the Labour Party and as one who for many years had deep fraternal relations with men, women and children who were butchered by that individual.

I do not want to say any more than that, except that I can understand, because of the mentality of the Taoiseach, because of his very correct and, if you like, exact, approach to certain problems, why he took that decision and carried out that particular act. At the same time, without commenting on the events of the past few years, I feel that, from the point of view of many of those who associated themselves with the Taoiseach and the movement he led in years gone by, men and women of the Irish working-class movement, Irish trade unionists, to whom he has in the past paid tribute for their services to the country, it might have been better if that call had not been made."

I was given the privilege of asking Jim Jnr if he would stand for the leadership of the Labour Party, we were walking near the top of Bray Head. He was on one side of the stile and I was on the other. He thought about the proposal, his response was:

"John, there will only be one Jim Larkin in history and that's my father".

Some weeks later I met him and congratulated him, saying, "I think you were probably right, because, as things stand, building up the Trade Union Movement is probably the vital thing now."

Young Jim said, "Thank God, somebody agrees with me because everybody criticises me for not going forward."

Jim Jnr, Denis, and Finton

DONAL NEVIN (FORMER GENERAL SECRETARY *ICTU*)

I met Jim Larkin Jnr in 1949 working for Congress and as Parliamentary Officer for the Labour Party, I also met him at quite a lot of meetings. I met him at the Dáil frequently. Often, for some years, Tom Johnson, Jim Larkin, Luke

Duffy and I had lunch together.

I remember Jim, when he got talking could go on and on. He was not boring or tedious but he had much to say and in a hurry, that in a period of an hour or so, there was no need for anyone to keep the conversation going. He used to probe deeply and get to the root of issues. Whether they were world or local problems he had a tremendous analytical ability to break it into its constituent parts. His analysis would be a scientific one.

Now I would never have thought for a moment of either questioning or indeed contradicting — or looking for any fallacies or any faults in his reasoning; I would start off by saying his reasoning must be right and therefore I was more concerned with benefiting from the fruits of his reasoning to be able to come to a conclusion or make up my mind in a matter. It wasn't as if I was pitting my understanding with his — I was assuming his was the correct understanding. And, of course, in due course in time I came to realise it was.

He was (which I think was of great benefit to him over the years) a Trade Union negotiator who was recognised by employers as being honourable in a way negotiators may or may not be. Some are not. Secondly, that he would deliver, and thirdly that he would not go back on his word. So he started off in a sense after the early years with a great advantage. The other — now in that case he may have been bluffing — but I would say generally an employer would not regard Jim Larkin as a type who would bang the table and said 'or else" or a person who would bluff and go to the brink in the expectation that he could pull back, like so many other colleagues over the years tend to and still do it. So that he started off with a great deal of advantages. And the other advantage he had in negotiations with employers, whether it was Guinness or Aer Lingus or anybody else, was that he knew that the employer knew that he wanted a settlement. One thing always struck me — I remember it was a remarkable statement for a General Secretary of a Union to make, I think it was in the introduction or the preface to the Book of Rules, where he wrote that 'a strike is an admission of failure on the part of the Union official.

MATT MERRIGAN SENIOR (FORMER GENERAL SECRETARY ATGWU)

"In the 1960s, the Government introduced an Emergency Powers Act to preclude disputes and picketing in the ESB. An unofficial dispute took place, first day workers, then supported by shift and general workers. A number of workers were jailed, there were over twenty. A crises conference was held in the Dept. of Industry and Commerce because the strike was escalating and the Government took fright and were prepared to concede that the legislation was unworkable. Young Jim and I were at the conference amongst others, we were looking for a formula to deal with the release of the guys who were in jail, as the Government had caved in.

"The men wouldn't pay fines, so that became the issue. Young Jim then intervened and said to the Management of the ESB "Well, you were the people who created the situation of those lads being in jail, OK, the strike was unofficial, but putting workers in jail is not the solution. Now they are not going to pay the fines, so the people who should pay the fines, are those who created the dispute in the first place by their tardiness in negotiating and that's the ESB. So the ESB paid the fines for the men, about midnight on the third day of the strike, and taxis were provided to bring the men home from jail. I was very much impressed by Jim as a negotiator."

TOM CREAN (BRANCH SECRETARY FWVI/SIPTU)

"A Joint Industrial Council was set up in the Gas Co. Young Jim was largely responsible for its foundation. The Principal of Rathmines College of Commerce, Sean O'Ceallaig, was chairman. Dermot Doolin from Actor's Equity was the worker's representative. The Council worked reasonably well over a period of a decade. "Jim Jnr also had a habit, first noticed in his father, and latterly independently, in his brother Denis and in the author too, of when conferences became difficult a request was made to the management to provide tea and biscuits. This enabled a heated atmosphere to cool down and allowed for rational thought and an acceptable resolution to whatever was the problem.

DONAL O'SULLIVAN (INDUSTRIAL ENGINEERING)

"I knew Jim Larkin Jnr and Denis and Anne Larkin extremely well. I was working in ICTU in the Sixties. Jim was marvellous at finding solutions to complex problems. Few Trade Union leaders had that ability and skill, he was extremely interested in building the Labour Movement as all the Larkin family were. We became friendly because they realised I was active and I was Treasurer of the Labour Party at the time. The Labour Party had little money then, there was no proper organisation. They were very supportive and Anne particularly was trojan. She was amazing when we ran fund-raising campaign called 'the million shilling campaign'. "Anne did most of the background work. It was quite a successful campaign. Above all, the family were most helpful in dealing with TDs and others who did not want interference from a Head Office. They helped in laying the foundations for the much more vibrant movement which we now enjoy.

"In South-west Dublin Hilda Larkin ran as a candidate. She and her late husband Sean Breslin were all part of the team in Dublin. In 1965 there was one Labour seat in Dublin, after the election there were 6. In my view one of the main reasons was the influence the Larkin family had in encouraging young people like myself, at that time, to get involved. They were important years for the growth of the Labour Party and the wider Larkin family were greatly involved.

In the two years from July 1952 to July 1954, my Uncle Jim edited the Workers' Union of Ireland Report, monthly. Apart from editing each issue, he wrote a personal column entitled, "It seems to me". That column reflected on the past as well as the future of the Trade Union Movement. It laid out signposts for us to follow, in seeking the path leading to the future of the movement, that the founders sought and sacrificed to achieve.

I have included a number of excerpts from his column, as it appears to me that very many of the ideas he expressed are as valid today as they were over forty years ago.

Workers' Union of Ireland Report
No. 1 July, 1952

It seems to me that on each every opportunity members must be given to clearly understand that the Union is a living organism of thinking men and women — that the members are the Union and the Union is what they make it. Therefore, the task is to get them to know the Union in all its strength and weakness, to know themselves, their power and limitations and by knowing more to achieve more. Unity is strength; organisation is power; but education and intelligence is the driving force. Let us therefore learn that we may think and think that we may act.

No. 2 August, 1952

In all cases the amount of the wage claim has been decided by the members concerned with the advice of the Union officials; the negotiations have been carried on by the Union officials accompanied by the direct representatives of the workers in the particular job or trade; and where a claim has been settled the decision has been made by the members themselves. That is trade unionism as we in the Workers' Union of Ireland understand it.

134

No. 4, Oct/November, 1952

It seems to me... at least let us think about unity with the intention and determination to not only think but act, because the price that has to be paid for disunity is too big. We cannot afford disunity any longer, but unity will not come through wishful thinking, but only through action.

No. 7, February, 1953

This Union is now making a start in the sphere of recreational social and sporting activities, and if we all pull our weight we can achieve success and then go on to wider efforts. But ultimately if the trade union movement is to serve its real ends these tasks must be undertaken by the movement as a whole on a national basis. One immediate obstacle stands in the way — our failure to even act together as a single national movement.

Jim Larkin Jnr with Keating's portrait of Big Jim

Report No. 8 March, 1953

It seems to me... unemployment is not only an evil in itself, with its horrible, soul destroying waste of human beings, but it is a menace to the level of wages and conditions of every man and woman still in employment, to the trade unions and their organised bargaining powers and above all it is a morass, a bog in which the whole economy of the nation, and the well-being of the nation's families can be smothered.

Report No. 10 May, 1953

It seems to me... Let's decide we are going to have democracy in this Union, not from the top downwards, but from the bottom upwards. Democracy is not a gift, it is a right and they have rights who alone maintain them. The members of this Union must maintain their democratic rights by making full use of them in the control and direction of the Union; and not by leaving it to officials or to the other fellow! Let each of us carry our share of the responsibility and let us begin by understanding and making full use of the parliament of our Union — the Annual Delegate Conference.

Report No. 13 August, 1953

It seems to me that the tribute we owe to those Dublin workers of forty long years ago requires more than the momentary pause, the half spoken word of praise. Rather should we appreciate and cherish what they gave to us. Not merely a nation re-born, a vital flame rekindled to burn away the dross of national servility, but more than all this, the emergency of the Irish working class in all their power and strength on to the field of Irish history to carry through and complete the historic national social and economic tasks of the Irish people.

Report No. 15 Oct., 1953

Unlike the older trade unionist the present generation of trade unionists cannot of their own experience and knowledge recall the days when nearly all working class families in Dublin lived in tenement rooms or small box-like cottages, insanitary, vermin-ridden and dark, with the only security of tenancy the goodwill of the landlord. They never knew the heartbreaking struggle of the family of a casual worker to keep above the line of dire and desperate poverty. They cannot look back on the working week of seventy or more hours, or the morning start at 6 o'clock. Those who today hold the right to rest on public holidays and to enjoy two weeks annual holidays with pay cannot remember when the few public holidays granted carried no pay, and the annual holidays did not exist except for the unemployed. They never were unemployed without any unemployment insurance, or sick without sickness benefit. They cannot look back to the time when old age or widowhood brought no pension but only the workhouse. They have never had to feel they were the hapless servant of the "boss" to whom they must raise their cap and say "sir" if they wished to work and eat.

Report No. 16 November, 1953

There is a simple test for newspaper editors and government ministers who advocate increased production. Let it be made a legal obligation on employers that where production is increased no worker will be laid off and they will get a share of the increased prosperity flowing from increased production. Better still, make it compulsory by law that employers must in advance consult with and secure agreement with their workers on any measures to increase production. Make the illegal partnership a partnership under the law. It can be done by government ministers and it can be advocated by newspapers. It is a test of the sincerity of their professed concern for the welfare of workers and if the law is passed it will be a test for employers also when they pat the workers on the back and declare "Work more efficiently, produce more and your job will be safe".

Report No. 23 July, 1954

If they are to give more by producing more then they want their share of that added wealth. The workers as much, nay, more than any other section want to see the industrial strength and capacity of this nation increased; they want a greater flow of goods; and they want Irish industries to be able to hold their own against other producing countries; above all they want the wealth of the nation made greater. But they are going to ask and get an answer to the question "What about our share of the wealth we produce?". The trade unions are the most effective medium through which the workers will get an answer to that question, an answer which will be in keeping with the needs of workers. For so long as that question must be asked will the trade unions have a job of work to do.

INTERVIEW WITH DEPUTY BEN BRISCOE, LEINSTER HOUSE, FRIDAY 12TH NOVEMBER 1993

BB: *"Well, of course, your late father, Denis, God be good to him, was on the Corporation many years with my father and also in the Dáil here and I spent a number of years in the Corporation with him as well and on the Dáil, but my father and he always enjoyed a good personal friendship and, also of course with his brother Jim, but in 1955, I think it was, when my father was nominated by his party to become Lord Mayor of Dublin and Denis was nominated by the Labour party to be Lord Mayor, my father, who was pretty good at mathematics, had worked out that if he stayed in the race neither he nor Denis would be elected Lord Mayor, and as Alfie Byrne had already served 9 terms in a row as Lord Mayor and then had a further 10th term and was looking now for an 11th term, my father felt it was time to share the office out a bit more equitably. So, having been formally nominated and seconded, he asked his Party's permission to withdraw his name and asked them, as he was the leader of the group, would they support Denis Larkin's name for Lord Mayor, which they agreed, on the spot, there, without any pre-planning, there was nothing premeditated about it; that was as much a surprise to them as it was to Denis, who as you know, didn't expect to be Lord Mayor. I was present in the Council Chamber when this election took place, so I remember it quite vividly and in the event your father won by one vote and became Lord Mayor of Dublin. Of course, that is in the Minutes of the Council meeting of that time and confirms the veracity of what I'm telling you.*

"Then there were other times of course, when Denis and my father would have had a lot of dealings at various levels and I think Denis was also, was he leader of the Labour Group? Yes, so my father was the leader of the Fianna Fail Group which was the largest group in the Corporation in those years, and always had a lot of dealings with your father. But he always found him a very fair man — very straight and his word was his bond. And that was a wonderful thing about those people of that time. I suppose maybe people are like that today too but, if they gave their word, they kept it. And when mutual trust builds up, that was important.

"My father had hoped that the following year your father might do the same for him but there was no deal on it so it didn't happen and, in the event, my father's name came out of the hat in the draw."

JL: *Getting back to the question of morality. Was there any further effect on your own family, say, in your own case?"*

BB: *Oh, yes, indeed. Well the rewards came many years later, unforeseen by my father of course, but a good turn can sometimes be visited upon the children, because when I was running for the mayoralty in 1987, Carmencita Hedderman was elected Lord Mayor over Ned Brennan who had won the nomination from me and he couldn't attract the support from the opposition that I knew that I could, but in any case Michael O'Halloran said to me in the same month of July that Carmencita was elected that if I would be candidate the following year he would support me but if one word of this leaked back to him he would withdraw that support. So I wasn't going to tell anyone that I had Michael O'Halloran's vote in the bag, as it were. But just shortly before the election, Michael called me and said to me: 'Didn't your father have something to do with Denis Larkin becoming Lord Mayor?' And I said, "He was the cause of him becoming Lord Mayor," and I told him the story, showed him when I met him a copy of the Minutes and he said to me 'Well, I told you that I was going to support you and I can assure you now there is no way I won't be supporting you.'*

"And he was absolutely firm, because of course Michael O'Halloran absolutely loved James Larkin, Big Jim, and I would say was very much a disciple of him. But it paid back in a way I never expected — or should I say my father would never have expected, but as I say, one good turn deserves another, it came a generation later, and I know my father would have been very grateful."

JL: *"I think your father also had dealings in the trade union front with my late uncle."*

BB: *"Yes, he did indeed. When the Leaf Chewing Gum Co. came to Ireland my father had managed to persuade them to come to Ireland when he was Lord Mayor and he was visiting Chicago, he met people from the Leaf Chewing Gum Co. who were looking at seven different locations in Europe, none of them Ireland; and my father persuaded them to come over to Ireland, he told them all the various grants that were available. At that time, Cotts of Kilcock had just gone out of business and Kilcock would have become literally a ghost town but for the fact that the Leaf Chewing Gum people came out but the one thing my father insisted on was that, when we came to labour relations, he would handle them for the company. He was appointed a director of the people and he looked after that end of things so whenever there was any dispute over wage increases — but, yes, your uncle Jim was the man who was in charge of the Workers'*

139

Union at that time. Founded, of course, by his father. But I remember talking to your father about the fact that whenever there was anything to do with wage increases, my father would be on the phone to your uncle Jim who would say, 'I'll leave it to you Bob, because I know whatever you agree on will be fair.' And of course that was putting another pressure on my father because, instead of settling for maybe a penny an hour in those days, he made it a penny-halfpenny just to show that he would be more than generous. But when I was talking to your Dad about this he said, 'I don't think that Jim would have ever sort of left it to anyone!' I don't think my father would have any reason to not be speaking the truth to me when he told me this story, but it was a token of, first of all, his admiration for Jim Larkin, it was a measure of the respect that both men had for each other and irrespective of what political parties that people can belong to, if they have integrity and if their word is their bond, then everything else falls into place.

"On another occasion, when one of the American directors, who has since passed away, Leslie Shankman — he was a bit of a goer — was going to get tough with the workers because production wasn't high enough from his point of view and he said to my father 'I'm going to get those workers and I'm going to tell them if they don't start producing more, we're going to close the factory and we're going to fire them', or something like that. My father said, 'Look, Leslie, the British tried that in Ireland and they got thrown out; now you'd better stay away from labour relations because you know nothing about it, you leave it to me.' I remember they had a very good manager in the Leaf Company who came over afterwards and he had a very good labour relations man called Jim Willie whose own mother had been Irish. His father was German, but as he said 'The Irish will be lead but they won't be driven'. And this was always the philosophy, I think. That more or less would cover the mutual respect which Jim and my father had for each other.

"... And of course my father served with your grandfather Big Jim Larkin on the Corporation as well. I don't know how well he got on with him: but I'd say that at the end of the day, they had respect for each other.

"... But I knew when I became Lord Mayor, that what was very near and dear to Michael O'Halloran's heart was the question of Mandela and his release from prison and his interest in the Anti-Apartheid movement and, so when I was doing my courtesy calls, without discussion with anyone, I called on the then Taoiseach, Charlie Haughey. I told him that I would like to give the freedom of the city to Mandela. Now at that time in the Dept. of Foreign Affairs, a lot of people were a little bit ... they didn't quite want this, because there was always this question mark of whether he was in jail for terrorist outrages, bombings, and there was this sort of question mark and with the IRA, would this be misunderstood and that sort of stuff. But anyway, I said to Charlie "I'd love to

140

give the freedom of the city to Mandela. He said, 'Would you not just pass a resolution calling for his release?' I said, 'Sure, we've done that, that's been done by the City Council, but I'd really like to do something like this'. He said: "It's a matter for the Corporation, but I've no objection.' So I went back to the leader of our group, Vincent Bray, who was of course the Chief Whip and I told him that I had spoken to Charlie about it and that he didn't have any objection. So we had a meeting of our group and it was agreed that the leaders of each group would meet with the other leaders to put the proposal to them. Because as you, when we're discussing the freedom of the city, it is always done behind closed doors. You get agreement and then you announce it rather than doing it publicly and causing embarrassment to the person if there is an argument over them. So in that event anyway they all agreed, one or two people decided they weren't going to turn up on the day, anyway I had won. I then called Michael. I told Michael what we were doing, and he was absolutely thrilled and he called in Donal Nevin who prepared the script for me for the speech to award the freedom. Now, Mrs Tambo came over, Oliver Tambo's wife, and Bishop Huddleston, and some of the Anti-Apartheid Group. In fact, we were a little bit worried that the Anti-Apartheid people were going to take over our show and we made sure they weren't. But the input of the Irish Labour Movement into that, and as I say indirectly as a result of my father's support of your father to make him Lord Mayor, that a generation later when Michael O'Halloran supported me because of what my father had done for yours, and then my reciprocating by springing it on Michael."

JL: *"I think the point you made earlier about industrial relations is very interesting and if you would be kind enough to expand on those relationships, I'd appreciate it."*

BB: *"Yes, we were talking about common courtesy — the importance of please and thank you. I know the most important word in any language is thank you — never forget to say thank you. In fact, any time I ever start a speech on anything, or I'm a recipient of something, whatever it is, I always start by saying thank you. It's so important because if you forget to say thank you afterwards you're punishing yourself for a long time. And I finish up by saying thank you. I still remember after having dealt with the other problems. There is no need in business or in commerce, or whatever it is, for people to be treated other than with dignity. I am a great believer in the dignity of the human being and when somebody treats another person and takes away from their dignity — they don't take away the dignity of the person they are addressing, they themselves, take away their own dignity. Now, having been with Marks and Spencers from 1953 until 1961, I know very well the great respect that they had for people and it didn't matter whether it was the lowliest member of the staff, the person in those days who would be regarded, not as the lowest form of life. The lowliest position* *in the store, might be the cleaning woman. I think I was telling you before, but a store manager would not have the authority to fire a cleaning woman if she 'd been employed for longer than two years because of the fact that if she was all right for the two years, what had suddenly gone wrong now, and there would be an investigation. The Welfare would investigate it to see if there was some domestic problem at home, and who had members of their family who were ill and they needed to convalesce, Marks and Spencers would organise for them to go into convalescent homes and pay the costs. If families needed money to help them they would give them no-interest loans to help them over their difficulties. Once you joined Marks and Spencers you were there virtually for the rest of your working life because they looked after their people.*

"Everybody must have respect for human beings and it is an interesting thing that my father and myself had the longest unbroken service in the history of this State in the Dáil. Now in the Oireachtas, Neil Blaney would have with his father — I think his father lost office for one term in the 30s. But my father was a member of this House for 38 years uninterrupted; I've been a member of it just as I say about 28 years this year — 66 years without a break. But I think it's because we've always had respect for people and people recognise that. We work for each other. When I went into the Mansion house and I had the staff around me and we were talking to the staff — now I didn't send for the staff — I said to them 'Listen, I'm not a boss here. We all have a role to play. I have a job to do, you have a job to do. We're all representing Dublin and we want to all help each other and I represent the citizens of Dublin. And if anyone makes a mistake, you need never worry about me screaming or shouting. All you have to do is let me know, so that I can correct it.'

"I've always said never be afraid to tell me if you've made a mistake, because we can always work it out. But, in industry today there are people who have been for so long looking down, now people have education and I always used to say that you must never equate education with intelligence. Some people do and they make a terrible mistake. Now I know some very well educated people who have very little intelligence and I know some very uneducated people who are highly intelligent. Today of course, not everyone, has the opportunity of education. Unfortunately in our inner cities the pressures on people not to carry on to higher education are greater very often and there can be problems at that level of people saying 'O look at yer man, thinks he's a great one, gone off to university,' and that puts pressure on him. But nevertheless people today are more educated. The trade union people today are highly skilled, highly educated and are more than a match for management who can't any more run around with figures. Many years ago, when education wasn't as freely available for people, people in the Trade Union Movement very often might have found themselves (now I'm not a historian on the Trade Union Movement I might be talking a load of

balderdash) but I have a feeling that a lot of people were throwing out figures saying we can't do this. And maybe the trade union official at the time mightn't have had as great a formal education in order to argue the figure she was being shown. Today they have all that, they have all sorts of expertise. So management now I think has a far greater respect for the trade unions and I think they are working more as a team. I mean, when we have these PESP talks this is a partnership, this is getting down to what is possible, which is ultimately what everyone is concerned with, keeping people in their employment. We don't want to give people such a huge increase that they are going to be out of a job or someone else is going to be out of a job. Everything relates to another."

TOM CREAN

"From October 1975, I worked with Denis till he retired. I found him to be an excellent man to work for. He was a great supporter when your neck was on the block and in the Gas Co. the official's neck would be on the block frequently!

"My predecessor, Hugh Montgomery, was instructed to go and see Denis, this was to put him under pressure. Having completed their business, they were walking down the stairs, Denis was wearing large horn-rimmed glasses, as he took them off they fell down the stairs. Denis bent down, picked them up, perfect, no damage, whatsoever, turned to Monty and said, 'Well, Monty, we're both indestructible.'

"Denis had great qualities in deciding how to deal with problems and the methods to employ. Ruairi Roberts, former General Secretary of the ICTU, used to refer to him as the Master Strategist! At his retirement dinner they were talking about National negotiations in which Denis had run against everyone else and told them what to do, a very high risk strategy, which paid dividends. Ruairi wrote back a note to Denis addressed 'Dear Master Strategist!'

"Denis was involved in the negotiations for the 1974 Wage Agreement, it was the 1st Agreement that had an anomaly clause and it should be recognised as one of Denis's achievements.

"The Workers' Union had a reputation of being a good organisation to work for. Access to the General Officers was easy. There was a great fraternal spirit. From the point of view of staff, no matter what issues regarding pay and conditions of employment, it was always settled in house. There was a kind of a bond that we sorted our problems in that way, basically because working for a trades union was not the same as working for any other employer.

"It is all our hope that this method will remain in SIPTU as it should also in every other trade union."

MATT MERRIGAN SENIOR

"I knew Denis and Young Jim well, we shared membership in a number of jobs, particularly Cadburys and Irish Biscuits. We had a good relationship, sometimes we had differences on how to proceed but I always found Denis very courteous and committed to his work.

"I also think Denis was much more pragmatic than Jim. No less effective, but more pragmatic."

DONAL NEVIN

"I was involved with Denis in the negotiations in the 1970s with the National Wage Agreements, where he was always superb. On one famous occasion he walked out and went to the pictures. It brought the employers to their senses. Within a few hours (the rest of us stayed on) the employers began to move. Denis was back again the following day and took it up from there."

BRENDAN HAYES (REGIONAL OFFICER SIPTU)

"Denis asked me to his office. It was full of paper piled all over his desk. I knocked and went in and he said, 'I have a letter here from a hospital secretary, I think you should read it.' I read it, it was highly critical about my performance at a meeting. I started explaining to him, in a couple of minutes he stopped me and said, 'Brendan, you don't seem to understand. This is the kind of letter that I like to receive about Branch Secretaries, because it means you are doing your job. You have nothing to worry about. I will write back and deal with him.' I later got a copy letter where he cut the legs from under the hospital secretary. He was very supportive.

"Soon after I joined the Workers' Union I was just leaving Parnell Square with Paddy Cardiff, late one evening and I had a brand new briefcase, because I thought that was the thing to do. We met Denis Larkin and he said to me 'That looks very well, where are you going?'

I said, 'I am going to a meeting.' He replied, 'What is the meeting about?'

It was something minor but I was all the business, dressed up, new briefcase and all. I said to him, 'Where are you off to?' He put his hand in his pocket, took out an envelope and he said, 'I'm off to do the National Pay talks.'

'I had a new briefcase for a minor meeting, he was doing the National Pay talks from the back of an envelope. With no disrespect, he did a better pay agreement than I in my negotiation.

"The next thing that stands out in my mind was, we were doing negotiations in the Eastern Health Board, Gerry Barry and myself. Gerry was the Branch Secretary, I was the Branch Assistant. It was a major productivity deal following out of the Corporation settlement that had arisen out of a strike in the Corporation back in the mid-70s. And we were trying to set up a meeting with the Chief Executive for quite a long time and then he turned up to a meeting that wasn't arranged. He eventually gave me a phone call and said to me 'Do you realise we're supposed to be up in the Eastern Health Board?' Now we didn't arrange that meeting at all. And when we went down Denis ate us for being late which I thought he had some cheek for us being late for a meeting we didn't know was on. We eventually went up, and the Chief Executive walked in and he made a few comments and then, without a note Denis just turned around and gave the history of the old Dublin Dispensary Service — gave the history of the pay relationship and the pay developments from the 1940s to the 1970s, dealing with all of the pay rounds, all of the pay adjustments, all of the pay movements and all of the Ministers for Health that had been in office. By the time it was finished, (the Health Board had been refusing to concede the position totally) the Chief Executive of the Health Board just turned around and said 'Well, I agree with you, Mr Larkin and I think we will let the officers sort out the details..' So it was just a masterful display, brilliant, simply brilliant.

"I always found Denis Larkin to be a gentleman, to be helpful, not critical. I never heard him say a bad word about anyone."

PADDY CARDIFF (FORMER GEN. SEN. FWUI)

"I believe the contribution of Big Jim Larkin was backed up by total commitment. He had a deep and sincere feeling for human beings, which affected his work in their interest. He faced the most tremendous odds and difficulties throughout his life. He was a man of great courage, resolution and singlemindedness."

"Jim Jnr helped people articulate, he inspired people and he was very committed to the education side of the Union, while he clung to the fundamental beliefs of his father, he knew the trade union movement was ending and he played his part. He was largely instrumental in the setting up of the Labour Court. He set the pattern for presentation of cases. In fact, he was the first Union official to present a case, that was in a case involving the ESB group of Unions. He prepared the case and led the argument for the Union's side. This was in late 1946.

"In negotiation he was formal. He never used first names, he used the person's title, discussions were therefore kept at an impersonal level. When he gave a commitment it was honoured. When he received a commitment he expected it to be implemented.

"In the Dáil, Mr Sean Lemass remarked that, 'the most famous man in the Dáil from a procedural point of view was Jim Larkin, because he never stood up unless he had something useful to contribute, well thought out, well reasoned, beautifully argued, a tremendous orator."

"I'm quite hot-tempered. I remember rushing upstairs to see young Jim. Denis waylaid me, 'Where are you going?' he says, he knew the problem.

He took me into his office, made me 'sit down, cool off and choose your words very carefully.'

"Anyway when I had relaxed I went to see Young Jim and told him the bones of the problem. Jim said to me, 'I worked with a man for years and years who was never wrong, he just had such a strong mind I suppose'.

"If there was anybody I would want by my side in a tough situation with an employer it was Denis. He acted more out of the heart than the head, than Jim. He was similar to me in the respect that he would never let go or retreat under the most difficult circumstances.

"Twenty-five years ago when the trouble started in the North, Denis played a great role in stabilising Congress. Denis's tolerance, and insistence on placing the interests of the Trade Union Movement first was a major factor. His family came from the North originally. His reputation and that of his father was absolutely critical.

"Denis had a fine political brain, his political analyses were always accurate. He could forecast political change in a remarkable manner. When he was fired up, he would make a speech off the top of his head showing complete mastery of the subject and without a note tremendously effective. He could do it at the drop of a hat.

"Denis was a far better judge of people's character than his father or his brother Jim but Denis would rarely comment about people. He would show his feelings by his manner, he never criticised anyone behind their back no matter what had occurred. He was extremely human, he was always solicitous of people who were ill.

"Denis took an important part in the National Agreements. In 1964, I recall, Denis and Charlie McCarthy were largely responsible for securing a 12% increase. Sean Lemass took 6% of it back within six months, through taxation changes."

BREDA CARDIFF

"I went to work in the Workers' Union of Ireland when Big Jim was still General Secretary. It was about two years before he died. We were never afraid of him — he was very nice but kind of remote. He had no idea of running an office. In giving me dictation he would go at a rate of knots and he used to drop his articles. He would dictate twenty pages of shorthand and we used to leave pages out and when you would bring it back to him he would say, 'Did I say all that?' — and you after leaving about eight pages out of it!

"He had many housing cases to deal with. Women would come in with their children and he'd say, 'Where's your husband? Send him in to me'. He was

Taken in Thomas Ashe Hall: Breda Cardiff puts up a portrait of Big Jim as he was in Sing Sing Prison

147

always very sympathetic to women and would not tolerate bad language where women were concerned. The same also applied to his two sons.

"On the death of Big Jim, Jim Jnr took over. At one time he told me that if he had a choice he would have loved to have been a surgeon but he had to continue his work in the Trade Union Movement.

"Jim Jnr would meet anyone who called — I said to him often, 'you should really see are they paid up members,' But he wouldn't refuse to see anyone and some of them were not even members of the Union.

"The Union got a Work Study Expert in who said he (Jim Jnr) was doing too much and he was offered an increase in his wages, twice, by the Executive Committee, he said he had enough. He was not interested in the money, only what he could do for people.

"While Jim Jnr was a great Dáil debater he disliked going round at election times. I used to say to him, 'You'll have to shake hands with the kids and hug the babies.' His response was, "I'm not going forward at all if I have to do that".

"Now Denis was different, more gregarious. He was Lord Mayor of Dublin. His brother as Lord Mayor would have been a dead loss! It just shows how different two brothers can be."

Denis Larkin pursuing his favourite pastime

149

My Father Denis

In the course of his retirement Denis continued to be active in the Labour Movement, as well as, on the boards of some State bodies such as CIE and AnCO. He also continued with his hobby of photography. As my sister Stella and I found out after his death, contrary to popular belief, Dad actually had film in the camera! There was a drawer full of unprocessed film in his bureau and we are convinced that he enjoyed using the camera and taking the photographs rather than seeing the actual results!

By nature he was full of life, and possessed an infectious spontaneity that frequently led to unusual adventures. Quite often he would get up early on a Sunday morning and announce that we were going for a "little run" in the car. A number of times he took us as far as Wexford or Waterford before realising that we had to get back to Dublin before the Sunday dinner that we had left in the oven was ruined.

Denis Larkin, just like his father, feared no human foe. However, my sister Stella and I were aware of the dread he had of developing the same disease that two of the people he loved most, his wife Anne and his brother Jim, both succumbed to. In the course of his last few years of life he did develop cancer but the family kept the nature of his illness from him. The year before he died, however, his working life was crowned with a round-the-world trip in the course of which he went with AnCO apprentices to an International competition in Osaka, Japan. He revelled in the trip, meeting a number of old colleagues in the course of the journey. As usual, he had taken many photographs of which we only saw a fraction. His health deteriorated in the latter end of 1986, so much so, that at Christmas he wished to visit his family grave in Glasnevin and that of his mother, Elizabeth, in Mount Jerome cemetery. As we were walking back to the car he said, "You know, Jim, no one will visit my mother's grave again." I promised him that I would do so.

His last public appearance was on the occasion when it was announced that shortly May Day would become a Public holiday. A reception was held afterwards in the Royal Hospital Kilmainham.

For the last few years he had lived with my sister Stella and her husband Michael McConnon and their family. Stella's family in the very late years were extremely supportive. An amazing thing happened in the last week of his life, the family had support from many friends and there was a nurse from the Irish Cancer Society who remarked to us that she had seldom seen a patient where the disease had spread so much, and where the patient in his last days, suffered no pain. He died in July 1987.

His funeral took place in Dominic Street church and from there went to Glasnevin cemetery where he was buried with Anne his wife, and her mother. Denis and Anne's third child, Vivian is also remembered there. Beside him rest Big Jim, Delia and his uncle Peter.

The funeral was effectively a celebration of the ending of a full and rewarding life, which had been of great benefit to working people. It was attended by the then President Patrick Hillery, who postponed a State visit to be present. There were also colleagues from the Labour Movement, a wide variety of employers representatives, public representatives from all parties. A particular Senior politician did not attend but sent his aide-de-camp. It is my hope and belief that the politician who was not present stayed away because he showed on that occasion, the sensitivity to realise that he would not be welcomed by the family.

Bishop Kavanagh gave the oration. This was most appropriate as his own mother, Tammy Kavanagh, had been active in the Workers ' Union of Ireland for many years — serving on the executive of the Union at one time. Bishop Kavanagh himself is an expert on industrial relations and carried out a number of important surveys in this area, including a very detailed examination of the production department at Aer Lingus. The Fire Brigade manned a guard of honour.

He very kindly gave me a copy of his sermon which I have included here, unabridged.

"Death is always a sad and sorrowful occasion. On the parting of a loved one, it is natural to feel great pain. Our Lord himself wept at the graveside of his friend Lazurus, seeing the grief of Mary and Martha, the sisters of Lazurus. We sympathise deeply with Stella and Jim on the death of their dear father Denis and their grief is shared by nieces and nephews and other close relations. The presence of so many of Denis's friends here is a source of great consolation to the family.

"I knew Denis and his father Jim very well. Jim Jnr was more reserved, somewhat shy — Denis was more outgoing, less introverted. If I were to use a football analogy, Jim Jnr would be likened to a very clever forward, good at scoring goals often in difficult situations, Denis could be likened to a sound full-

back or centre-half, a very useful stalwart on any team. But they had one great thing in common, no doubt springing from their father Big Jim, a man of charisma in the affection of Irish workers, what they shared was a tremendous concern for social justice.

"Denis succeeded Jim as General Secretary of the Workers' Union of Ireland. Many honours as you know were conferred on him over the years — President of the Irish Congress of Trade Unions and an executive member for 30 years. he was a city councillor for 30 years and he had the great honour of being Lord mayor there in 1955 and 1959 an office which he appreciated enormously and an office which he filled with great distinction. Denis was also a TD for Dublin. He was very effective in fronting the interests of the poorer sections of the community, especially in his advocacy of housing development.

"Denis was a man of great personal charm, always with a ready smile and he enjoyed conversation with unfeigned delight. In spite of the important positions he held in public life, he always retained the common touch. As we say in Dublin: 'He never lost the run of himself'.

"Denis was a great family man. One of the great dangers for Union officials is the time consuming nature of their work: so many meetings, so many people calling with problems. Few appreciate the sort of demands made on trade union officials. They really have a hard life. But Denis never allowed his duties to take him from his loving care of his family.

"I always remember with affection his attendance in Kilkenny for the first poverty conference held by the Council for Social Welfare in the early seventies. He made many telling contributions, because he knew what he was talking about. His cheerful presence was always a tonic, because he combined common sense and humour.

"To know Denis was to love him and that is why he will always be remembered with great affection by the people whose lives he touched with his own special blend of humanity.

"We pray now for the repose of his dear soul. We know he will comfort and sustain those he has left behind, particularly the members of his family. For us all his death reminds us of the passing nature of temporal things. As scripture reminds us: 'we have not here a lasting city, we seek one which is to come'.

"I feel sure that Christ who has told us that: 'Blessed are those who hunger and thirst after justice, they shall be satisfied', will welcome him home to join all those who are especially dear to Christ who also said: 'whatever you did to one of these least brethren, you did to me'.

"May his gentle, humble, cheerful soul rest in peace. Amen."

On the way to Glasnevin my youngest nephew, Eoin, said to my wife Brenda and I, "Isn't this a happy funeral?"

He was right because, in spite of our own personal grief, the thousands of people present were there because they admired, respected and liked Denis Larkin. It has been said also that it is unlikely there will ever be a similar funeral in Ireland again.

The following note was sent to me after my father's death.

Denis Larkin

When Denis Larkin was Lord Mayor of Dublin he was very involved with our centre for mentally handicapped children in St Augustine's, Blackrock, which is run by the St John of God Brothers.

He collected funds in the United States for uniforms for our boys band and attended all the functions which the handicapped were involved in. He and his wife, Anne, gave generously of their time to help in any way they could.

Many times he invited the children for afternoon tea in the Mansion House and then organised trips for them around the City. He was also instrumental in sending them on holidays to the seaside. This was at a time when the handicapped person was largely forgotten about in society and Denis and Anne Larkin were the forerunners in opening up the minds of many people to the needs of the mentally handicapped people of Ireland. There were no Parents and Friends Associations in the country at that time and he advised the Brothers of the need to start an organisation which was done within his lifetime.

The Brothers owe a debt of gratitude to the many endeavours that Denis and Ann Larkin were involved in with the order of St John of God.

Prior, St. Augustine's

Michael Cox, former Gen. Sec. of NATE on Denis Larkin

"At any ICTU conferences, when Denis Larkin introduced himself — 'Larkin, Workers' Union of Ireland' — immediately silence would fall so that you could hear a pin drop. His contribution to any debate was always worthwhile."

MATT MERIGAN SNR ON DENIS

I worked on Denis's election campaign, Anne, his wife was his agent. She was a smashing organiser, she had the campaigns mapped out from A-Z. They ran like well oiled sewing machines. She was the boss, she laid out the strategy and that's the way it was and rightly so. Those were days when there was some life in the movement, and it had a philosophy about life. They recognised the social problems that underlay the issues that affected industry and had a great feeling for both social and civil justice. They were the heart and soul of the movement. They were an inspirational family and gave the movement a perspective that was not related to careerism or self-serving. They understood the primacy of politics as a means of forwarding the development of the Trade Unions Movement and raising living standards of working people. People don't make that connection anymore and its a great pity.

I believe the movement has lost quite a lot of impetus since the pioneering days of Big Jim; including Young Jim, Denis and Anne's role and your own role up to retirement. Your family gave the movement an idealistic heart that seems to be gone out of it at the moment and I think that cannot be gainsaid.

The split in Labour in the early 1940s was not just a personal vendetta between Big Jim and William O'Brien,, it had a political base too because Jim made reference to the fact that, during the campaign against the Wage Standstill Order and the 1941 Trades Union Act. that O'Brien's fingerprints were on the legislation, that he advised the Government on the general shape of the Bill. The architects of eventual unity between Congresses were, Young Jim and John Conroy. Norman Kennedy of the Amalgamated Transport had a big role in ensuring that six county trades union membership retained their integral part of the reunited trades centre.

My Family Life

Anne, Stella, Jim, Denis Larkin, Marino, 1948

The Fair Hills of Ireland

A plenteous place is Ireland for hospitable cheer,
Where the wholesome fruit is bursting
From the yellow barley ear;
There is honey in the trees where her misty vales expand,
And her forest paths, in summer, are by falling waters fanned,
There is dew at high noontide there, and
springs i' the yellow sand
On the fair hills of holy Ireland.

Curled he is and ringleted, and plaited to the knee,
Each captain who comes sailing across the Irish sea;
And I will make my journey, if life and health
but stand,
Unto that pleasant country, that fresh and
fragrant strand,
And leave your boasted braveries, your
wealth and high command,
For the fair hills of holy Ireland.

Large and profitable are the stacks upon the
ground;
The butter and the cream do wondrously
abound;
The cresses on the water and the sorrels
are at hand,
And the cuckoo's calling daily his note
of music blend,
And the bold thrush sings so bravely
his song i' the forests grand,
On the fair hills of holy Ireland.

by Sir Samuel Ferguson, (1810-1886)
translated from the Irish.

My Mother's Parents

My mother's parents were James Moore and Annie. They married in Dublin and had two children, Anne, my mother, and a younger daughter who died very early in life. James (Jem) Moore came from a Dublin family. He worked in the building trade but when he reached 16 years of age, he joined the Connacht Rangers. He served with them in South Africa, India and other locations. On finishing his tours of duty he returned to Dublin and secured work with McLoughlin and Harvey, builders. He worked on a number of major projects including the Pigeon House Fort for the ESB and the construction of the headquarters of the Royal College of Surgeons.

He was about 5' 10", and stocky in build, with a well-trimmed bushy moustache. Annie Moore, his wife, had been born in India, daughter of a British Army officer and an Indian lady. She was very slightly built and never, in all her years in Dublin, became accustomed to the climate. Even on the hottest summer's day she would insist on the fire being lit and would also be wearing a cardigan or two. She would sit by the fire toasting her shins. Many people today might find my referring to hot summer days incredible. I can assure you that during my childhood they did exist.

When Annie was in her mid-teens she acted as companion to Lady Mary Guinness, the widow of the poet Sir Samuel Ferguson. She was Lady Mary Guinness. They had married late in life and I remember Annie telling me, when I was young, that on their wedding day Lady Mary and Sir Samuel had promised each other that, whichever of them passed away first, they would return from time to time to find out how the remaining partner was coping. She also said to me that the housekeeper had told her not to mind if she saw an elderly gentleman in a smoking jacket and hat going into the library, as it was only Sir Samuel — he had been dead some years. During Annie's six or seven years in the position she saw Sir Samuel over twenty times. She said he never spoke but sat in the library listening to his wife.

About 1910 my mother's sister, who was about 4 or 5 years old at the time, told my grandmother about a horrible scene in O'Connell Street with men pointing sticks and making loud banging noises over the

James Moore, in the uniform of the Connacht Rangers, with his wife Annie and daughters Anne and Elizabeth, 1915

body of a horse. When my grandmother Annie heard the story she told, she took her to the Pro-Cathedral. She left her daughter with a priest. About two hours later he brought the child home and said to my grandmother, "Look after the little one, she won't be with you for long." She died about a year later and no medical reason could be found for her death. After the funeral, the priest told my grandmother what her young daughter had said " There is a lovely lady who came to me when I was asleep and wanted me to come home. I am very happy". It is not difficult to see that the vision seen by the little girl was of a well-known picture taken during the Easter Rising, four years later.

One abiding memory I have of my Grandmother, Annie, is from when I was about 5 or 6 years old. I was having a bath, when she came into the bathroom and spotted that my back was very brown. She immediately got out the scrubbing brush to remove the offending "dirt", but it was actually sunburn! The pain of that incident still sticks in my mind.

Annie Moore, Marino, late 1940s

When I was 14, at our house in Marino. Annie was sitting by the fire, reading a book and I asked her if she would like a cup of tea and went out to the kitchen to get it for her. When I came back she was lying back in the chair, the book had fallen from her nerveless fingers and she was at rest. For a child of my age to meet death in those circumstances was not difficult. In the latter years of her life, she had suffered very badly with arthritis and rheumatism. Her face had been lined and drawn with pain. When I saw her no more than a minute or two after her death the lines had smoothed out and she was smiling. She looked like a young girl in her twenties. I will always remember her with great affection.

When we were small Jem Moore used to amuse us by telling stories of campaigns in South Africa. From what I remember, he was in the Ambulance Corps and therefore a non-combatant. He refused to use a gun but when his regiment was attacked I understand he wielded his rifle as a club to good effect.

While Jem was working on the building of the Pigeon House in Dublin he had an amazing accident. He was walking on the top course of bricks carrying one end of a plank, a mate carrying the other. As they approached a corner he shouted to his mate to be careful because of the breeze, the other man dropped his end of the plank and Jem was knocked down to the cobbles about 80 feet below. He got up and walked to the Foreman's hut and reported that he was going to Sir Patrick Dunnes Hospital. A similar accident happened to my wife's father, Thomas Riding, who was a steeplejack in Birmingham before the Second World War. He too walked away from it.

Whilst working on the final polish for the foundation stone for the Royal College of Surgeons building, Jem had the stone dropped on his left hand by the crane operator. This had the effect of crushing all the nerves in that hand. When we were young he used to amuse Stella and I a number of ways, one of which was that he could pick up a glowing ember from the fire with his bare hand and light his pipe. We could smell the flesh singeing whilst he had no feeling.

Jem also had a hole in his tongue but where that came from I do not know. From time to time he would pass a piece of twine about 6" long through the hole in his tongue and tie it into a knot!

Before I was born there was an incident concerning my mother's father Jem Moore, which arose directly out of antagonism to our family by some people. There were threats made that my sister Stella would be kidnapped on the grounds of a false allegation that my father Denis was a Communist. The Gardaí took these threats seriously and advised my parents to carry firearms for protection. My father refused to do so as he a lifelong pacifist. The Gardaí, however, insisted that my mother carry a pistol.

Jem Moore, who had been in the British Army, said one day that he would clean the pistol for her. The story goes that he put the muzzle of the gun up to the palm of his hand and squeezed the trigger in order to clean the barrel. Unfortunately he forgot to check whether or not there was a bullet up the spout. The bullet was discharged and passed through the palm of his hand. I understand he was not best pleased and expressed his views with feeling! I was told by my mother that he called for a bucket of water, a packet of salt and a clean handkerchief. Using a technique he learnt on the battlefield he put the salt in the water, put his hand into it and then, when the bleeding had reduced, he pulled the handkerchief through the hole in his hand, tied it up and went off to Sir Patrick Dunnes Hospital — yet again!

To those of you of my generation, you will appreciate that for our parents and grandparents the visitation of a clergyman to perform the Last Rites immediately heralded, in most cases, the rapid demise of the person visited. Jem Moore was tougher than most. Over a period exceeding 10 years, he received the last sacraments on at least fifteen occasions. Jem Moore was quite a character.

My Arrival, Childhood and Youth

My entry into the world on 2nd January 1936 was dramatic. I arrived in the course of a thunderstorm, weighing in at just over a stone. My mother was in a nursing home on the southside of Dublin. When I was born my parents were concerned as I showed no signs of life for over 15 minutes. I understand that I was wrapped in a blanket in front of a fire, waiting for an ambulance to take me to hospital. Before its arrival, the blanket caught fire and the shock of the burn started my heart beating. What an entrance! I still have the scars on the right side of my face, my arm, chest and leg, all on my right side. As can be seen, I started life the hard way and many people have said that I have done most things the same way ever since!

My sister Stella and I were fortunate to have very supportive parents who made sure that our childhood was both happy and interesting. We did have a baby brother who was born a few years after me, in 1939. His name was Vivian, and unfortunately he died in infancy. His oesophagus was not properly formed and consequently he could not eat at all and died of starvation. Medicine was not sufficiently advanced in those days to deal with his condition. Now it would be possible to carry out an operation that could have saved his life. I have often wondered how our family life would have altered should our younger brother Vivian have survived.

Our homes over the years included a basement flat in Merrion Square, Kitestown Cottage, and houses in Howth, Killester, and Marino. When I was born we lived in Merrion Square. Whilst I was still in a pram we moved to Kitestown Cottage, on Kitestown Road near the Summit in Howth.

It was a thatched cottage beside a hotel called the Waverly. It was here that we got our first dog, Pal, a cross between an alsation and a collie. I was told when I was five or six that Pal had taught me to walk. I didn't believe it until I saw him with a neighbour's infant. He lay down on the ground until the child held on to his coat, then stood up very slowly and paced along quietly. My mother used to lend him out to neighbours to take with them when they were shopping. He would lie under the pram and allow passers-by to talk to the baby. If, however, they attempted to touch the child he would "talk" to them, as he was most protective of children. The last I heard of him was that he had been knocked down by a train whilst escorting children home from school.

The news report below tells of a fire at Kitestown Cottage. From what I remember the thatch caught fire. The retained fire brigade attended the blaze but there was no water pressure at the fire hydrant and only a dribble came from the hoses. The men, I was later told, had watered the flowerbeds as they did not want to waste the little water they had!

> ## COTTAGE DESTROYED BY FIRE
>
> The cottage occupied by Mr Denis Larkin, second eldest son of Mr James Larkin, TD, and his wife and two young children, at Kitestown Road, was destroyed by fire on Thursday afternoon.
>
> Neighbours assisted in removing the furniture and the Howth Fire Brigade was also promptly at the scene. Mr Larkin was at work in the Unity Hall at the time.
>
> Over £1,000,000 has been paid in settlement of claims — Fire and Accident — by the Hibernian Fire and General Insurance Company, Ltd.

As a result of the fire in Kitestown Cottage we moved to Howth Village. Many of the people in the village were most helpful and became firm family friends. The recent accident when the SS Kilkenny with a German boat in Dublin Bay took the life of one of those people, Dave Harding, whose family we know well. It was ironic that a man who had fished out of Howth in all weathers and far across the sea, should lose is life in an accident in Dublin Bay.

The McNallys were also friends of our family. They lived in St Mary's Terrace. Mrs McNally was a lovely lady, extremely hospitable, she always left her front door open. I remember her homemade bread and jam as if it were yesterday. She made a particular "medicinal" jam with rhubarb and ginger and other secret ingredients. It was known locally as "Margaret's Jam" and she kept it in a large stone jar on a shelf in the kitchen. On one occasion a visitor asked if he could have some homemade bread and jam. In Mrs McNally's absence he helped himself to the bread and applied "Margaret's Jam" liberally without being aware of its "secret". He was unable to leave his house for the following couple of days.

Furry Park in Killester was our next base. This was round about the time of the "Emergency". My wife Brenda, who is English, has never understood we Irish using that particular appellation for the Second World War. At the time of the North Strand bombing my mother was in the St John's Ambulance Brigade and my father was in the A.R.P.

At that time, the Government recommended that people build Air Raid shelters and gas masks were widely issued. We had such a shelter in our back garden, which was very well built with built-in beds, seats and a table, as well as food and water. It was just as well that we never had to use the shelter as I well remember on one occasion when it was checked, it was found to be full of water to roof level.

Killester was our first experience of school and it was a pleasant time for Stella and I. Stella went to the local Convent school and I was in infants. In my class there were tiers of desks on either side of the room — the boys on one side and the girls opposite. As a form of punishment if a child behaved badly they were made to sit on the opposite side. That happened to me from time to time and on one occasion I was sitting behind a girl who had a long pig-tail. I couldn't resist dipping it in the ink-well on my desk. That was not the thing to do — as I found out rapidly!

I do remember, with great affection, a nun called Sister Carmel who I always thought must be at least the grand old age of twenty (a very old age to a boy of four). In fact, I found out later that she had been almost sixty at the time. I well remember her giving us sweets, and at Christmas being asked by her to go into a senior class to take a present from the Christmas tree there. Sister Carmel loved children, was very quietly spoken and was happy and content in her vocation.

On reflection life at that time was far less complex and, for the majority of children, much safer than it is today. There was a general atmosphere throughout the city that adults had a kind of collective responsibility for the well-being of everyone's children. On the other hand children who misbehaved would be chastised by any passing adult, without the parent rushing to their offspring's defence without question as to the circumstances.

In this respect I can recall, that in Howth, the Garda Station was manned by a Sergeant and a Garda. These men were frequent visitors to the local schools, also to lone elderly people. Should they apprehend a child engaged in anti-social activity such as "boxing the fox", raiding apple trees, cycling without lights, or other serious crimes, the wrongdoer would be given two choices — one was to be taken to the back of the Forester's Hall to be chastised, the other, far more terrible, would be to be taken by the Garda to one's father. The latter option was never taken! It's been over a half a century, I know of nobody from Howth who grew up in that atmosphere who found themselves in serious trouble with the law.

In the early 1940s our family moved from Furry Park Road in Killester to Marino Park. Being quite young at the time I wondered why my grandfather, Big Jim, never visited the house for the remaining years of his life. It was not until I was about 16 that I found out what had happened. Marino, at the time, was a corporation estate. The large family who lived in the house got into serious arrears of rent, and were going to be evicted. They pleaded with my father to pay the arrears and take over tenancy of the house. He did not want to but in view of the straightened circumstances that that family found themselves in, he reluctantly agreed. As Stella and I were our parents' only living children my grandfather was against our moving because, in order to qualify for a Corporation house, at that time, prospective tenants had to have more children.

Although Big Jim did not visit Marino park he did retain a very close relationship with my parents and my sister and I. We normally met him at least once a week either in Thomas Ashe Hall or in 41 Wellington Road where he lived with his sister Delia.

Some years later when the scheme for tenant-purchase became available to Corporation residents in Marino my parents purchased the house. Whilst in Marino my parents had a difficult time because, as I found out in my late teens, Dad had gone bail for the son of an old member of the Union. He immediately decamped and left my father to pay bail of several thousand pounds, which was equal to a few years wages at that time. Despite this, Stella and I never went without food or clothing, but other treats were few and far between.

As with any family, Christmas and birthdays were times of additional stress on the family purse. Not to the extent they are today though. For example, last Christmas I heard a man who was unemployed talking about the pressure of Christmas, because he had to give his six-year old son a present of computer equipment and games valued at over £500. The toys in my youth were simple and basic — a football, a clockwork train set, and in our house, books. Memories of those times are still happy. With many toys today, it is not necessary for a child to use their imagination to play. We however had to use our own minds. A camán (hurley) could be used to play hurling, cricket, rounders and also cowboys and Indians.

Christmas particularly was a magical time. It started in early December, unlike like today when last year I saw, in Dublin, a Christmas Sale in August! The fact that Christmas was not a four-month festival allowed it to be a special family occasion.

When I was about 10, we had a glorious Christmas. Our house, in Marino Park, was lit up throughout with candles, lanterns and nightlights. No electric light at all. Over the holiday we had many visitors calling and they thought it was a lovely idea. In the evenings sitting round an open fire in candlelight listening to ghost stories was very stirring. It was not until the day after St Stephen's Day that my mother found a cheque for the ESB in my father's pocket, and then told us why we had had candles over Christmas! Stella and I asked if we could have it every year.

Another outstanding Christmas happened when I was about 17. Some of my friends from school (Belvedere College) decided to sing carols for St Vincent de Paul in O'Connell Street. The first evening we had about fifty people singing and about four collecting the money. That did not work out well financially, so it was decided to change the numbers round and four of us were left singing with the rest collecting. Such was our enthusiasm that some of us decided that we should extend our collecting area. We had a brainwave — we left the group singing in O'Connell Street and hopped on the train to collect money outside Dublin as well. After a couple of days we were labouring, a gentleman came along and said, "Could I help you?"

I was given the job of asking, "Can you sing?"

He could sing. It transpired later that the gentleman's name was Marion Nowakovski — who, at that time, was Bass singer with the Covent Garden Opera Company. He was over in Dublin on holiday but he came back to join us on a couple of other evenings. With his magnificent voice the income increased immensely. Thereby rests my only claim to fame in the singing world.

The following year I helped a mini-bus driver who was taking some children from St Augustine's in Blackrock to see Dublin and the Christmas lights. We had a very enjoyable day going round seeing a number of Santas in different stores. We wanted to get some tea for the boys and sad to say, particularly at Christmas, there was no room at the inn, with the exception of Clerys whose restaurant provided goodies for the children. It was about time to go home and we went to look at McBirneys window (now Virgin Megastore) and the display there. We were there almost a half hour when it was time to go. From the crowd we collected the boys and loaded them into the minibus. At that moment a lady with an umbrella started belabouring the driver while shouting "What have you done with my son?"

In the minibus was a quiet little lad sitting amongst the boys from St Augustine's keeping his mouth shut, so as not to be discovered mother. The problem was then resolved.

I mentioned the financial difficulties my parents had and consequently there were few holidays. As a matter of course, up to and in my early teens, I used to spend about a month each year with my Uncle Jim and Aunt Josie in Bray. I found it very enjoyable. Most of the time I either went hiking round Bray Head or swimming in Bray Cove swimming baths. It was in that pool that I won my first medal which was for under-14 50 yds breaststroke. It was a little embarrassing as I was at least 6" — 8" taller than any other competitors.

Jim Larkin, 13 years old, at the Hole in the Wall, Sutton

Summertime then consisted of very long days. Apart from swimming I played football, joined Dun Laoghaire Children's Theatre group, sang in a couple of choirs, hiked a lot. There was never sufficient time in the day to do all I wanted to do.

During the summer months much of my time was spent going to Clontarf, Blackrock and Bray Cove Baths. In the winter both Tara Street and Iveagh Baths were my home from home. I was also a member of North Dublin Winter Swimming Club and I spent most Sunday mornings and some other days swimming in Clontarf Baths and at the Bull Wall. In the Club a number of us played waterpolo and swam, not only in Dublin, but also in the Ormeau Road and the Falls Road baths in Belfast; sometimes too in Pickie Pool in Bangor. Those days were very enjoyable. A number of these baths are now sadly defunct.

Swimming was definitely my favourite past time and I was lucky enough to win a few medals in local galas, Leinster Championships and at waterpolo. The latter game was possibly the dirtiest game ever invented! It was one of the ways I had of breaking my bones. Travelling to galas in other locations was interesting. In the early 1950s the National Championships were held in the Lee Baths in Cork and I remember a prominent hotel in Cork, in MacCurtain Street, gave us great sport.

A member of our club booked into the hotel but about a dozen of us stayed in the room! One of my colleagues actually slept in a linen cupboard and when the chambermaid came for the sheets, he fell out on top of her, much to her surprise! We played small pranks during the night like changing room numbers, and reallocating shoes outside the doors. On the next day it was fine and some people got up on the roof of the hotel and sprayed the fire-hoses up in the air so that a gentle rain fell on passersby in MacCurtain Street. The only problem we had was we were unable to all get breakfast the following morning!

That winter we had a visitor to Clontarf Baths — it was a female seal with a damaged flipper. As I have mentioned, North Dublin was a club where races were arranged every Sunday morning. The hardy boys would line up on the sea-wall and swim in towards the dressing rooms. That year, when we found the seal, some of us used to go down during the week with fish for her. When the races were on she would take her place lining up at the wall until the race started and she would then swim along with us. She always won. At the end of the winter season her flipper had mended and she headed out to sea. The following winter she returned briefly with her pup. I like to think she was thanking us for our help.

Like all sports clubs there were competitions, and the hardest of the lot was in North Dublin. To win a medal for consistency a member had to attend each Sunday during the winter and swim in a race. Placement in the race was not important, but absence for even one day, no matter what the reason, illness, death in the family, would mean the loss of that highly-prized medal. In about ten winter seasons I was awarded one. Other members over the same period might have got two or three. No other sporting trophy was more eagerly sought after and harder to achieve.

On one occasion our club was playing in the final of the Leinster Schools Cup for Waterpolo in Blackrock Baths. After the game we went to a café at the top of the town. There were about ten of us, and the lads all gave me their money to pay for their fish and chips. Just before we left, I saw the referee of our match having a meal. He was from England and I went over to ask him how the standard in Dublin compared with that of England. We had a very interesting chat but then I noticed that the lads had left without me so I rushed out the door to catch up with them. I was halfway down the street with the gang when I remembered I still had the money in my pocket. I looked round and the manager and waitresses were standing in the door shouting and waving their fists. We all took to our heels and fled. Would you believe the others asked for their money back! Then the price for fish, chips, tea and bread and butter was about one shilling (5p). Should the café owner wish for repayment after 40 years, I will gladly forward him the money plus interest!

Clontarf Baths, in the mid 1950s, introduced a juke box sited in the shop, for the enjoyment of the baths denizens. For the first week or two it was alright but one day a young lady came to the shop and had a lot of change in her pocket. Now I liked Mario Lanza but this young lady proceeded to play the record of Mario Lanza singing "Be my love"— not once, not ten times but fifty times in succession. The music was played by loudspeakers over the pool area. After fifty plays, alas, the juke box played no more as it was manhandled down to the pool and thrown in the deep end. There were no tears at its passing!

I was privileged to represent Ireland at the International Student Games in Manchester. The organiser of the swimming team was a man called Seamie Hatton, formerly of Bray Cove. I had the pleasure of renewing acquaintance with Con O'Callaghan and Eoin MacCrae of Clonard Swimming Club in Belfast and Sean Nolan of Dublin Swimming Club. Our team was complete with the addition of a few athletes and others from different sporting disciplines. The most well known member was the pole-vaulter, Ulick O'Connor. Although the team was small in number we all had a go at everything. A couple of the athletes who were unable to swim but could play waterpolo. Some of the swimmers participated in athletics and cycling. Our team, however, was ejected from the basketball tournament as the referees objected to tactics such as rugby tackles. Altogether we had a great time.

My own return to Dublin was delayed for a couple of weeks. When I reached the pier head at Liverpool it was to encounter pickets on the B & I boat. My conscience was wrestling with a dilemma — to travel or be stranded without money. The decision was taken out of my hands when one of the men on picket duty said, in a Dublin accent, "Hello there, Jem, how are you doing?"

My dilemma was noticed by a policeman to whom I explained my plight. He explained he had left his digs a couple of weeks before and he did not think his landlady had got a new tenant. It was then I first came across the generosity of Liverpool people. His landlady and her family took me in and kept me for the two weeks without any thought of regard. I wanted to send them money on my return to Dublin but they would not hear of it, so I sent over some Irish linen. Unfortunately, in the intervening 40 years I have lost their address but would be delighted to hear from them or their family.

Clontarf baths was also the home of the Clontarf Water Safety Club. In the early 50s the Club was successful in winning the Leinster Championship of the Red Cross Water Safety Competition. They also won the President's Trophy, which was competed for in Blackrock Baths. Water Safety can be a very dangerous occupation! One year our group gave a display of Life Saving at the finishing point for the Liffey Swim, a barge was moored between O'Connell Bridge and Butt Bridge. Before the event we had decided that having a couple of people pulling a couple of other people out of the water had no drama. It was arranged that one of us would dress in old clothes and sit on the edge of O'Connell Bridge. When the atmosphere was becoming tense he fell into the river, the plan being we were going to rescue him. We never realised how brave the people of Dublin were. A number of fully clothed bodies followed our colleague into the river bent on rescuing him! Discretion proved to be safer than the valour of informing all those present that it was part of the display.

Another sport I became involved in was rugby. I had gone to Belvedere College and it was one of the games played there. My only claim to fame in donning the hooped black and white jersey at Belvedere and later in Old Belvedere was that I had been in the same class as Dr Tony O'Reilly, but not in the same league of rugby! The form of rugby I played was very ably written about in a book *The Art of Coarse Rugby*. In Anglesea Road the third Bs or Cs could be seen playing on an irregular shaped pitch beside the river with an equally irregular shaped ball. The rules we operated under were that, if the ball was lost in the river the match was over. Sometimes, however, when we needed a rest or a smoke the ball would be propelled into the river!

Positional play was a mystery to us. We seldom played 15-a-side — sometimes 14–12 or 9–11 which made the course of the game very confusing. Many occasions required either team to borrow or lend players, for the course of the game. There was no transfer fee! A knowledge of drama was essential, not only to impress the referee, but also to bewilder the opposition. A standard rule was, when playing a leading team, we would normally not shave for a day or two, and we would also use old jerseys. If there happened to be old, tattered representative jerseys, Ireland or Leinster, lagging the pipes in the dressing room, we would wear those! We would attempt to look ferocious and to appear as if we knew what we were doing. Should our opponents be a junior team we would wear clean jerseys and shorts that had been ironed, and we would trot out on to the pitch attempting to look fit. Seldom would we pass the ball to one another before the game started because we knew we would drop it and reveal our lack of skill. Enthusiasm definitely did not win representative honours! We had a great time!

Having spent a number of years in Belvedere. What I learned from the Community and teachers was to be critical of life in general, to look at how people behaved rather than listen to what they said. There were a lot of decent fellows and there was a reasonably strict regime, where any of the boys who misbehaved would be given a note by their class teacher to take to the Prefect of Studies who administered punishment. The couple of slaps on the hand with a leather strap were not really painful — the worst punishment was standing in a line outside his office waiting to hear the dreaded words, "Come in". The time spent waiting was intense and full of whispered conversation about the efficacy of application of spit, hair oil or vinegar to the palms of the hands to lessen the awaited pain. I certainly never suffered any ill effects from these punishments and nor, to my knowledge, did any of my school mates.

Whilst in Belvedere, I learned a method of coping with the pressures of exams, even though, in those days, the problems were not as great as they are today. Judging by the many of my former classmates who have gone on to succeed in professional and academic careers, the system we were taught obviously works.

In recent times, I have heard, with horror, of children being unable to face life because of their fear of failing their exams. So strongly do I feel about this that, fully in accordance with my family's views, I knew it to be imperative for me to share this technique with anyone facing exams of any kind, at whatever stage in their lives.

Stage 1
To recognise the power and capacity of the human brain. (Greater than any computer.)
Stage 2
To build up one's self-confidence so that information can be readily retrieved from the memory when required.
Stage 3
On-going Revision of subjects in the months before is necessary.
Stage 4
A day's rest before the exams is valuable.
Stage 5
Bring no texts to the exam hall, on the day, last minute revision can imprint on the brain fresh information which could block earlier learned data – unless specific texts are necessary requirements.
Stage 6
On entering the exam-hall take two, slow, deep breaths, this oxygenates the blood and stimulates the brain.
Stage 7
Read the questions and instructions slowly, twice.
Stage 8
Allow your brain to decide which questions should be answered first.
Stage 9
The amount of paper given in answer books is normally the optimum for correct answers.
Stage 10
Picture the examiner in your mind, so that your answers will be concise and to the point.
The examiner will be:
a) A day before retirement
b) Suffers badly from migraine
c) Has a gastric stomach
d) Has already corrected 500 papers
e) Has become irritated by the same questions.

I am sure that if the above formula is applied diligently a lot of the stress of exams can be alleviated.

When we were in Belvedere the pass mark in all exams was 40%. The honours mark was 60%. There was no points system for different disciplines. In too many subjects now an unfair points system is used where, from year to year, the number of points may alter significantly.

Points will give an idea of theoretical knowledge, however, where much of the skills required in a particular profession involve dealing with people the points system is of little value.

During my years in Belvedere, amongst the classmates I became most friendly with were Phelim Donlon, Tony Prendergast, Peter Vale and Tom Cullen, all of whom, as well as others, had visited our home in Marino as I had visited theirs. (Amongst our group, also, in school we formed a 'secret society' which carried out a number of attacks on the establishment. The society was called "the Alpha Triangle". Some of the major disruptive activities we engaged in included, removal of all the seats from a number of classrooms and putting them all into one room; wetting the chalk so that it would not make a mark on the board; there were other similar depredations!

Phelim Donlon and Jim Larkin, Marino 1950

I particularly remember Phelim's parents who were very hospitable and his sisters, Sheila and Eileen, both of whom went to Loreto, North Georges Street. It was only recently that I heard of Eileen's death some years ago.

Another family that I met in my late teens were the McSweeneys, Paddy, Sean and Imelda and their parents as well as their cousin Olive. With the McSweeneys, and a number of their friends, I used to regularly go to Croke Park. On the occasion of an important match the group of us went along, except Olive who had had her appendix out in the Bon Secours Hospital the day before. After the match, six or seven of us went along to the hospital to see cousin Olive and cheer her up. She was in a small ward with four beds and we decided that rather than tell her about the match, we would replay the game in the ward! So we pushed the beds back to the corners of the room, we found a potty and the replay commenced. The game had been going on for ten minutes when Olive, who was laughing uproariously, called for assistance — her stitches had burst! The game came to an abrupt end, matron confiscated the ball/potty and we were all given the red card and sent off the pitch never to return! Happily, Olive recovered.

As far as the McSweeneys were concerned, with going to England and subsequently working for the Union I lost touch with them as with many other friends from earlier years. I do understand that Sean McSweeney became a very able artist.

Croke Park, in the mid-50s, gave me my introduction to American football. Two US service teams were playing an exhibition game. There were very few spectators and I was invited to sit on the bench with a number of cheerleaders. The girls were friendly and explained the rules of the game to me. My wife cannot understand my interest in the game. With the development of plays I regard that game very simply as 'chess with muscles'. I still have an interest in the game, albeit on television.

Since I left Belvedere there have been two reunions, the 25th anniversary of our leaving school and also the 40th. At that latter event our colleague, Tony O'Reilly, invited us all, with our partners, to his home at Castlemartin. The evening was very enjoyable and we were extremely grateful for the opportunity to meet our former schoolmates again. As Brenda and I were leaving Tony, in accepting our thanks, suggested we should look in his study and we would find something of interest. We did, it was a painting by Sir William Orpen of William Martin Murphy leader of the employees in 1913. At this point, I would wish to thank Tony for his great assistance in my research on this book. In some way, he made good some of the differences between William Martin Murphy and my late grandfather.

Whilst I was at Belvedere my sister was going to school in Loreto, North Georges Street. I went with her in the bus to the bottom of North Georges Street and then I would walk about 20 yards behind her up the hill. It was not the done thing for a teenage boy to be seen walking with a girl, even if she was his sister. That time led to the most embarrassing day of my life.

When I was 13 and there was a sale of work in Loreto school. I was persuaded to attend by my mother and Stella on the basis that all the girls' brothers, fathers and uncles would be present. When we arrived there, there were about 700 girls and mothers, about 2,000 aunts and 40 members of the Community — not one other male in sight! I was mortified. Could anything be worse? Yes! I won a leg of mutton in a raffle! I hate mutton, but I had to go up on stage to receive my prize from the Mother Superior who congratulated me saying, "Well done, aren't you a nice polite little boy." At 13 I was almost six foot tall and could be seen by everybody which added to my embarrassment.

Although when Stella and I were in our teens, we were invited to Butlins, Mosney, for a week in 1955. That was the year Dad became Lord Mayor. The camp, at that time, had room for about 2000 people. It did not have many of the amusements, including the indoor swimming pool, and Bru na Boine Complex, that have been more recently added. However, what was available suited us and we had a good time. In 1958 we returned and it was the year that Stella met her future husband, Michael McConnon.

One of our favourite places to visit when we were younger was Dublin Zoo. At that time there was a female Indian elephant named Sarawathi who was patient enough to allow children to clamber aboard her back. She had a special talent for finding hidden chocolate bars in your pockets and removing the wrapper with her trunk before eating it.

As far as general entertainment was concerned both Stella and I would go to

Stella and Jim Larkin on Sarawathi,
Dublin Zoo 1948

174

the cinema. I generally went to the Fairview cinema. The prices at the time were 4d for the front of the stalls, sitting on wooden benches, seven pence for the rear of the stalls which had padded seats. I think the balcony seats were ninepence, but I never had the money to find out. The four-penny rush on a Saturday morning had a showing of cowboy films normally with a "follier-upper!" — the adventures of Smiling Jack, Bulldog Drummond and Buck Rogers (the original one). If the particular film was not to the liking of the patrons, perhaps it was too soppy, a boxing ring would be made out of four benches and matches would take place, sometimes with the usher refereeing. For young patrons who were 'skint' the management would allow payment by way of accepting empty jam-jars — 1lb jars were worth one penny, 2lb jars were twopence.

All our family were inveterate cinema-goers, time permitting. My grandfather, particularly, liked the escapism offered by old-style cowboy films. Apart from the cinema, I can recall many visits to the theatre with my family. These included the Gaiety, the Olympia, the Queen's, the Theatre Royal and the Capital. The latter two having stage shows as well as films. We also went to the Gate and the Abbey when possible. Over the years it has been my privilege to see most of the leading artists of the last 50 years. Our affection for the theatre started with my mother's involvement both in amateur variety shows and amateur drama. This had been encouraged by her participation in the drama group in Unity Hall, in Marlborough Street.

My own direct involvement with the theatre started with Dun Laoghaire Children's Theatre Group. Amongst the shows produced was a production of *The Tempest* by William Shakespeare in Wexford. I played Caliban who was a deformed villain. The highlight of the play, however, was when a group of young ladies, who played the roles of elves and fairies, were instructed that their marvellous costumes made out of butter muslin would be spoiled by the wearing of any undergarments. When they appeared on stage the effect was startling, it was as if the Folies Bergeres had reached Wexford! The parish priest was not amused and the company were asked to leave the town!

A year or two later, we moved up in the world. A performance was given, in the Olympia, of *An Inspector Calls* by J.B. Priestley. My contribution to the show was to perform the task that came under the title "noises off". With the detective story it was necessary to get a starting pistol to simulate a shot being fired. It proved impossible to hire a pistol and I was asked to generate the appropriate noise. I found that hitting the top of a soft suitcase sharply with a school cane gave a good sound. In the course of the play coming to my big moment I was

175

watching the stage from the wings and as the detective made to give the gun I brought the cane down sharply on the suitcase but there was no sound. Still watching the stage, I repeated the blow. There was an agonised gasp — the stage electrician had placed his hand on top of the suitcase and got two stripes of the cane across the back of his hand. I was never asked to provide "noises off" again!

Claude Hall in Drumcondra was another venue for amateur drama. There were two performances I remember very clearly from my teenage years. One was a pantomime *Ali Baba and the 40 Thieves*. The specific memory I have arises out of the stage being quite small — insufficient space for 40 thieves was available even if the company had been that large. Any time the 40 thieves had to appear there was a backdrop around which the 10 thieves had to run 4 times changing hats, etc. en route. On the first night one of the thieves was unlucky enough to fall on the stage in full view of the audience and for his four laps round the backdrop he was greeted by raucous cries from the audience of "Get along, Hopalong!" or similar remarks.

The other memorable performance was a Passion Play. The passions it roused both amongst the cast and the audience were inappropriate to the theme. For that production the costumes were excellent. There were a couple of men dressed as Roman soldiers and on their feet they wore insoles tied round their feet and legs with bias binding which looked extremely good. A problem arose however, the design for the Crucifixion scene was most impressive with pictures of the three crosses at Golgotha projected at the back of the stage as a screen. At the crucial moment one of the roman soldiers picked up a counterweight which held scenery in place. Unfortunately it slipped out of his hands and landed on his unprotected foot. His cry of "Jesus, Mary and Joseph!" was a prayer from the heart! It brought the house down.

Of the amateur dramatic groups we were involved with the Crofton Players were the most accomplished. Though, like all such groups, they were faced with the occasional set-back. The leading lights of the company were Jack Maxwell and Winifred McConnell who were the producers, and motivators. They produced a wide range of things from comedy to serious drama. One particular event remains with me. A production of *People at Sea* which was given up as an offering in a three-act drama competition. We expected to do well as:

1. The adjudicator was English.
2. The other twelve companies produced versions of *The White-Headed Boy*.
3. We were the final group to perform.

The play itself was based on a storyline where a number of people,

176

of different walks of life, had serious accidents and the action took place on an ocean liner, which was in fact the state between life and death. It was a very good and dramatic play. The final action was when a radio officer came on, just before the curtain to make an announcement that a message had come through. This was the nub of the plot in that the characters were about to find out whether they would join the living or the dead. The drama was marred, somewhat, when the radio officer had great difficulty in opening the door to the room he was entering. He had so much difficulty that the door to the room he was entering came off in his hand and he walked on stage holding it. It spoiled the effect rather. We did not win. At the same festival a year before, my mother had won the Best Actress award playing the part of Elvira in Noel Coward's *Blithe Spirit*.

While my father never participated directly in the acting he provided a trophy in my mother's name to the drama society in Howth. That was competed for for a long time as I was informed by a former colleague, Brian Hoey.

Another activity I became involved in when I was about 17 was Irish dancing. I was asked if I wished to join the Irish Folkdance Society which was organised by Lily Comerford, who incidentally had taught my mother Irish dancing when she was in Primary School. I think the only reason why I was asked to join was because they needed someone to carry the flagpole! My attempts at the noble art of tempiscore, whether ethnic or not, were at about the same level as my expertise on the rugby field. I found it impossible to learn individual step-dances, but I did manage set dances where I could hide amongst the multitude. My participation was punctuated with "What do we do next?". The Society had a number of performances at the National Stadium. One year something odd happened. When we got to the Stadium we found a couple of Gardai in attendance. At the break they were still there. The following day they were there again. I asked one of the Guards whether they were expecting any trouble, it seldom happened that a Folkdance Festival turned into a riot, but you never know! He said, "The Sergeant sent us up because he thought there might be trouble with the British flag on display".

I said, "Where?"

He replied, pointing to the Dutch flag with the red, white and blue parallel bars, "That's it."

I had to inform him that that was the flag of Holland from which country there was a team participating.

Apart from the Irish Festival, which also went to Cork, the team travelled to a number of European countries. In England we appeared at the Royal Albert Hall. I can recall one event, whilst waiting in the foyer of Euston Underground Station, dressed in saffron kilt, saffron socks, black jacket, green shawl and white shirt, carrying a 16 ft flagpole with a furled Irish flag, I think I was taken for an employee of the Underground Railway as I was asked directions by many travellers!

On a couple of different years I was privileged to join the team in going to Holland. At different times we stayed in Arnhem, The Hague. Our experience was very happy, our hosts were most helpful and obliging. Two things happened that will live in my memory.

The first was in The Hague. I was late for a rehearsal and my host loaned me his son's bicycle. I accepted the loan gratefully until I went outside the house and found that the "bicycle" was a 1,000 cc motor bike! I had never rode a motorbike before. With trepidation, I climbed on top of the beast (I was wearing my kilt). I started the bike, which had the flagpole strapped along the tank. I had gone about a mile when the kilt blew up in my face, the flag became unfurled and I noticed a number of drivers flashing their headlights and sounding their horns. It was only then that I realised that Dutch drive on the right! When I got into The Hague I rang up my host and asked him to tell his son to come and collect his "bicycle". I have never ridden a motorbike from that day to this!

Hospitality was the cause of my reason for opposing sexual harassment in all its forms. The troupe were giving a show in Philips in Eindhoven. After the show, as a special treat, we were asked if we wished to go round the factory. Seamus, the fiddle-player and I accepted the invitation. Still in kilts and very innocent we set off. After seeing some of the factory we came to a very large workshop where many hundreds of ladies, from 16 to 60, were assembling television sets. In the course of walking the hundred yards or so Seamus and I were subjected to numerous pinches as we passed by. Our need, over the next week, to eat our meals off the mantelpiece has underscored my objection to such harassment!

Starting Work

As you will know by now my childhood and teenage years were happy, busy and left no time for boredom. I was now approaching the time to try to earn a crust of bread. Being Denis Larkin's son and Big Jim Larkin's grandson was of no assistance whatsoever in my search for employment. The treatment I received at the hands of employers, including those whose employees were members of the Workers' Union, led me into a lifelong dislike, I could say hatred, for discrimination in employment on any basis, whether it be race, colour or creed. To be told by many employers "don't call us, we'll call you", after polite requests regarding my family background, led me to believe that few employers in Ireland would be prepared to look at my abilities or lack of abilities, rather than judge me or my parents. It was almost two years after I left Belvedere before the possibility of employment came about. What happened was that my Uncle Jim asked the late Brendan Corish who was then prominent in the Labour Party, if he could arrange an interview for me. Deputy Corish was kind enough to ask one of the Staffords in Wexford, who had an interest in Liffey Dockyard, to give me an interview. I was successful in that and started work in the costing Department of the Yard.

I worked there for about two years. The people who worked in the Yard were very co-operative and helpful. About three months after I started work I recruited the clerical staff into the Union, became Shop Steward and a member of No. 15 Branch Committee. I remember one of my colleagues Dick Whitter said to me that paying the union subscription was worthwhile just because: "I now realise that the General Manager is working for his living just as I am."

In 1955 I was a delegate from the Branch to the WUI Annual Conference. The Branch Secretary was Tommy Doyle. I was given the task of proposing that a section of the Annual Report on Ireland's entry to the European Community be referred back to the Executive Committee for further consideration. The next working day I had a phone call, a gruff voice said, "What are you doing at lunchtime?" I tried to make an excuse but my Uncle Jim, whom it was, said, "After stabbing me in the back over the Annual Report you're coming up to have lunch with me in the Dáil."

That lunchtime, with trepidation, I made my way to Kildare Street. Uncle Jim was not harsh with me, that lunchtime and many others during the following three months, we spent discussing the arguments I had made in the debate and what their foundations were. No conclusion was ever reached but I am certain that he wanted to ensure that I could hold my own in an argument. I learned much from the encounter. A year or two later Uncle Jim warned me that it would be impossible for me to secure a job as a Branch official in the Workers' Union as long as he and my father were still living. Sadly, that proved to be true.

During the years from the mid-50s I worked in England. I spent approximately the first year as an Area Organiser for British Actors Equity. The area covered was the North of England, North Wales, the Isle of Man and Northern Ireland. In the function I performed I received immense support from the then General Secretary, Gerald Croasdell and his deputy Peter Plouviez. However, being just 20 and single, whilst finding the work most interesting, I overdid my working hours and resigned with great regret. The work gave me a much better insight into the lives and work of members of the acting profession, together with a knowledge of some of their difficulties.

After that time I worked at a number of occupations, clerical, semi-skilled and manual. The work, including a wide variety of shift-patterns, proved to be of great benefit later on. One of my first jobs was with a company called Barlow and Jones, Princess Street, Manchester. At the end of six-months work the large number of employees were informed by a letter in their pay packets, of impending computerisation. We were all informed that the purpose of computerising was to ensure proper protection of our jobs. We were told our jobs were safe.

Some three or four weeks later almost 200 of us received a week's notice of redundancy. My first thoughts were how had I deserved this treatment? Living far from Ireland I was feeling depressed. Wandering back to my digs on a chill, damp Manchester evening, I was feeling sorry for myself. I was approaching Piccadilly where the buses left from when a man asked me if I would help him across the road. I did so, of course. His parting remark to me was to thank me and say, "It's a beautiful evening". I then started thinking. If someone with such a serious disability as blindness could rise above it, what had I to complain about? I then realised that the redundancy was not my fault, it is never the fault of the employee. I thought rather of people who worked in Barlow & Jones for thirty or more years being treated in that way too.

I also worked in the costing Department of Sid Abrams who were main Vauxhall dealers in Cheetham Hill in Manchester. A few events that come to mind in the course of my employment there are told here.

The first one relates to an attractive, curvaceous young lady. She had been employed to work on the petrol pumps. In her first couple of days she had made understandable errors like introducing oil into the hole that normally held the dipstick and also filling the radiator of a car with petrol! Those errors were not her responsibility as no one had given her any directions and girls were not as knowledgeable about cars then as they are now — it was always "man's work" (I am an exception to this). I may as well look into a bush as under the bonnet of a car! The next week suddenly traffic jams began and grew in Cheetham Hill Road. The young lady was dressed in hotpants, thigh-length boots and a brief tank-top. The road was choc-a-block with cars nose to tail all calling for a half a gallon of petrol! This sales gimmick did not last long as the police pointed out the danger to road-users.

Another time an apprentice mechanic had been asked to move a car from the car wash, he could not drive. He came out, in reverse, at high speed, damaging all the cars on the forecourt. His employment was short-lived.

The company General Manager figures in my last story. He had been given the first Vauxhall Victor Automatic that came off the assembly line. It was his pride and joy. He took it down to that year's Motor Show at Earl's Court in London, parked the car and went in to the Show where he stayed for a few hours. He returned to the car, tried to start it and was unable to. He opened the bonnet and found that the engine had been switched. The car park attendant told him that two men had come with a break-down truck carrying a replacement engine. They proceeded to exchange engines and went off with the original one. I was informed that the manager's sole comment on his misfortune was, "I wish I had mechanics who could work as fast!"

For another year I worked for a company called Roseman's on Moston Road, the owner of the company was Jeff Roseman and they were involved in the fruit and vegetable trade. They supplied vegetables to the School Meals Services in both Manchester and Cheshire. They were a fair company to deal with. I particularly remember on one occasion we received a visit from The Little Sisters of the Poor. Jeff told me then that when they called they were to be given a large cheque. I asked why because it appeared that the firm were not of the same faith as the Little Sisters. Jeff told me that his uncle who, like him, was of the Jewish faith, had collapsed in Cheetham Hill and had been taken in care by the Sisters. He subsequently passed away. They had respected his faith and ensured that he had visits from a Rabbi. That was the reason for the donations.

Another firm I worked for gave me the task of mixing, bagging and loading fertiliser — bonemeal, fishmeal and ammonia. While it was a hard physical job it had one major advantage, at the end of the working day, travel home in the bus was made easy as other passengers, no matter how crowded the service was, would give me a very wide berth due to the extremely noxious odour emanating from my clothing. I could not smell anything as the sensitivity of my nose was deadened from five minutes after starting work!

My last term of employment prior to returning to Ireland was with Courtaulds in Droylsden, North Manchester. The work there consisted of dyeing cotton and synthetic fibre, mainly for carpet production. it was an interesting job. With certain acrylics it was necessary to use acids to burn colour on to the fibre. One day a Staffordshire bull terrier from the local pub strayed into the works. Someone had left a pool of acid on the floor and the dog walked through it. The animal let out cries of pain, most of the staff working went into the office for protection, I did however approach the dog who stayed still for me, while I got a fire hose and hosed its paws. The dog was grateful for the attention, and because it had only been a second or two the acid had not done serious damage. I then took the dog back to his owners, and in the rest of my time in Courtaulds he never visited us again.

In the last few years I have been saddened by the deterioration of that area of Manchester mainly as a result of the massive Hulme Re-development Scheme. When that was mooted I was deeply involved in Moss Side Constituency Labour Party, particularly Moss Side West Ward and can say with certainty that the area was an honest working-class one, like everywhere else, there were problems with a small number of people. The town planners took over an area which was effectively a large village, with back to back houses and people who co-operated one with another, and supported each other in times of trouble. It was developed on the grounds that the estate should be a symmetrical one but which ignored the social needs of people. The new design left the area open to intrusion of the drug-culture, which made it difficult for ordinary people to live safely. I noticed recently in the newspapers, for example, that ambulance drivers going to certain areas of Hulme had to wear flak-jackets in order to perform their missions of mercy.

My other main interest at that time was the United Nations Association. The Manchester Central Committee organised public debates on a number of contentious issues, with speakers from both sides of the argument participating. These debates were most enlightening.

Through UNA I became involved in UNICEF, the United Nations Children's Fund — assisting in fund raising. This was a continuation of helping the same charity in Dublin in the early 50s. I now have the honour of being a member of the Executive Council of the Irish National Committee for UNICEF. With this change in activity little did I know what the future held for me as a result. On Saturday 3rd May 1970 a charity walk for UNICEF took place at Oulton Park Motor Racing Circuit in Cheshire. I was one of the stewards who had to sign cards for some of many thousands of men, women and children who had been sponsored for walking a number of laps of the track.

Amongst the thousands of participants was a young lady who had come along with a group from Cheadle 18 Plus Group. Her name, as I discovered later, was Brenda Riding. She, however, was not having her card signed at my table, but the next one. I had worked out that it took the walkers over 40 mins to cover a lap. Before that time was up I suggested to the person manning the adjoining table that he should go for a cup of tea and I would sign on his clients. In 4 or 5 minutes Brenda arrived, and much to her surprise, found herself sitting down resting and drinking a glass of orange. Before the end of that day I had arranged to meet her and her friends the following Saturday, the 10th

---

UNITED NATIONS CHILDREN'S FUND

U N I C E F

This is to Certify that

Brenda Riding

has walked

Fifteen miles (/5)

in my "Double Your Money For UNICEF" Walk

Date _3 MAY 1970_

UNICEF walk certificate

of May. We all went on a car treasure hunt round Cheshire and Derbyshire. I was amazed to find that the only way to get decent directions, was to wend ones way from the King's Arms to the Dog and Duck and then to many other licensed premises. Even so, as an abstemious person, it did not put me off asking to see Brenda again. We met on the following Saturday, 17th of May, and after having a meal we went to see a film *Butch Cassidy and the Sundance Kid*, in Manchester. I then left Brenda home to Heald Green, we went into the house about 11.45 p.m. I got a tremendous shock when a striking clock struck 13 terribly fast at midnight. That must have been a sign, because I talked from then till 3.30 a.m., when Brenda agreed to marry me. I had worn down her resistance thoroughly. People have often said that I have excellent negotiating skills. It is my view that I reached the peak of those skills on the 17th May 1970, which culminated in our marriage five months later on 17th October 1970.

Before we were married Brenda came over to Dublin and stayed with us so that she could see the sort of work and hours of a trades union official. They are totally anti-social. Even with that obstacle, she agreed that we should share our lives together. Early in October she went back to England and I negotiated that she would have the pleasure of making all the arrangements for our wedding.

Elizabeth Riding, Brenda Riding, Florence Smith, Thomas Riding.

Wedding of Brenda Riding and Jim Larkin 17th October 1970
REPRODUCED BY KIND PERMISSION OF STOCKPORT EXPRESS ADVERTISER

Working for the WUI

I had started work in the Workers' Union of Ireland in August 1970. The first branch that I was connected with was the Civil Aviation Branch This Branch dealt with all grades and categories of staff connected with civil aviation. We had members in Aer Lingus, Aer Rianta, British Airways and many other ancillary employments. They were based mainly at Dublin but also Shannon and Cork Airports. The Branch Secretary when I started work was Joe McGrane. About three weeks after I arrived he secured employment in Independent Newspapers and left the service of the Union. In case anyone is interested, having the name I do did not prove to be an advantage — rather the opposite, as quite a number of activists expected me to perform at the same level as my forebears. You will realise, however, while everyone inherits talents through the genes of those who have gone before, these do not produce clones and each one of us is different.

In thinking of the union movement my life from youth to the present is the best example I know for people to join unions. It underscores the need for collective action. Why say this? Simply because I have seldom, if ever, been able to make a case for myself in an argument, and I have been unable to blow my own trumpet. Nonetheless, I have had no difficulty at all in arguing against injustice or poor treatment, for others whether individuals or groups. The record of the work I have done is well known to the majority of members I represented over the years.

It would be reasonable to say that I had a friendly relationship with the majority of the many thousands of members I dealt with over almost 25 years. There were a few exceptions but these were mainly people who failed to understand my method of negotiation. I tend to be totally lateral in my thought, which meant that, in the course of negotiation while I was aware of the ultimate goal of negotiation, I could not explain to different negotiating committees the many steps to that goal. This annoyed a number of people.

Occasionally, committees took decisions that I found hard to understand. In the Airport Branch, about six months after I started work, the Civil Aviation Group of Unions, of which I was Secretary, arranged a trip to the United States, over a threat by the USA to remove landing rights from Aer Lingus at New York. The Committee, following a request from me, to advise me on the arguments to be made, in America and elsewhere, decided that they would give no advice of any kind. I viewed that as most unhelpful in the context that our national airline could have been seriously damaged had the USA proceeded with their threat. As it transpired the result of our endeavours was satisfactory.

Jim Larkin, August 1970, Dublin Airport

Members of Delegation

Group Chairman: Stephen Tracey, National Union of Sheetmetal Workers of Ireland

Group Vice-Chairman: Tony McCormack, National Engineering and Electrical Trades Union

Group Treasurer: Leo Gibson, Workers' Union of Ireland

Patrick Thewlis, Automobile General and Mechanical Operatives Union

Eamonn Griffin, Irish Transport and General Workers' Union

James Somers, Irish Transport and General Workers' Union

Group Secretary: James Larkin, Workers' Union of Ireland

It seemed strange that our visit to America was following on a similar visit in which my late Uncle Jim, participated some years earlier, though the subject matter was different. It is appropriate at this time to comment briefly on trips and conferences abroad. Since my uncle and my father's time it has been the practice for us, on return from any such trips, to submit written reports to the appropriate committees. With the recent controversy over trips for public representatives, it appears that one of the obligations on any such representative should be the need to provide a written account of their stewardship, whether to the houses of the Oireachtas or local authorities. Simply to demonstrate to their electorate that they are getting value for money. I know it was my father's position, when he was Chairman of the Housing Committee in Dublin, that deputations to housing conferences should be the minimum possible number, preferably the committee chairman and chief officer of the appropriate section, who should have a requirement of a written report on the completion of the visit.

Two aspects of the visit deserve special mention. Firstly, the courtesy and hospitality with which we were received, no matter with whom we were talking, our colleagues in the American Labour Movement, the Representatives of State of the United States Government, and the Public Representatives of the United States.

Secondly, I would like to place on record our appreciation for the co-operation and assistance we received from the Irish Ambassadors both to the UN and the USA and their staff – also the Irish Consul General in New York and his staff. There are many other friends we would like to mention but the list is a very long one indeed.

The following letters give some indication of the process of negotiation that was successfully undertaken.

Mr Bertram W. Rien   January 21, 1972
Department Assistant
Secretary of State for Economic Affairs
Department of State
Washington, D.C.

Dear Mr Rien:

On January 19, 1972 I met with Messrs Gibson, Larkin, Tracy, Sommers, Griffin, Thewlis and McCormick of the Irish Congress of Trade Unions — Civil Aviation Group of Unions. Our host for this informal meeting was Mr Ernest Lee, Director-International Affairs, AFL-CIO.

These representatives of Irish Civil Aviation Unions aggressively seek a negotiated solution to the Dublin landing rights question.

They have discussed their particular suggested solutions with members of the Irish Government.

I am convinced that at this time positive movement can be made in negotiations.

I submit that the United States Government might like to indicate its willingness to reopen bilateral discussions on the Dublin question.

Sincerely,

Errol L. Johnstad

President

Mr Errol L. Johnstad
President
Flight Engineers' International Association
905 16th Street, N.W.
Washington, D.C. 20006

Dear Mr Johnstad:

Thank you for your letter of January 21, 1972, with regard to our civil aviation relations with the Republic of Ireland.

I, too, talked with the Irish trade union leaders, and found them a group of articulate and dedicated men. As I explained to them, we are prepared at any mutually convenient time to reopen bilateral negotiations on the landing rights issue. The problem has been that the Irish Government has been unwilling to grant U.S. airlines access to Dublin under any conditions. We have in formal negotiations tabled our proposals; the Irish Government has offered none. It was this impasse which led us to issue to the Irish Government a notice of termination of landing rights at New York. That notice in particular expressed our willingness to reopen negotiations and to withdraw the notice of termination if, as is our sincere hope, a new agreement on an exchange of landing rights could be concluded before the notice takes effect on August 18, 1972.

I trust that this information has been responsive to your inquiry. However, if you have any additional views or comments on this problem, please let me know. In the meantime, I have enclosed a background paper which I hope will be of interest.

Sincerely yours,

Bert W Rein

Bert W. Rein
Deputy Assistant Secretary
Bureau of Economic Affairs

Paddy Thewlis and Jim Larkin outside UN Building,
New York, 1979.

A number of other conferences took place under the aegis of the Branch including an airline cabin-crew conference in Amsterdam, and visits to English and European airports to examine cargo facilities.

Many issues were referred, after direct negotiations were unsuccessful, to the appropriate body whether the Labour Court conciliation was followed by a full hearing if necessary. Individual cases would be dealt with by reference to Rights Commissioners.

There was also a form of internal conciliation with an independent chairman and representatives of the employer. Whether Aer Lingus or

Aer Rianta, together with a representative of the Union. Many problems, both group and individual, were resolved through these channels.

The Branch also supplied evidence as well as attended the first Commission and the Status of Women, chaired by Dr Tecla Beere. There were representatives from the Branch Committee as well as women members from all sections of the Airport. The chairperson commented favourably on the practical attitude presented by the deputation to the Commission.

Quite early in my stewardship, as a result of suggestions from my wife Brenda, I put to the Branch Committee and the Company the need for properly equipped rest-rooms for women staff at the Airport. At the commencement of negotiations I was accused, by a senior manager, not from the Personnel dept., of discriminating against our men members. When I told him directly that should I receive a note from him telling me that he had had his first period, I would then serve a claim for him and any other men who go through the same trauma as women. He took no further part in the discussions, which ended up positively.

Whilst we had many difficult arguments with Aer Lingus and Aer Rianta a considerable amount of progress was made for all grades of staff. Like both my father and uncle, I made it a practice when a meeting with the management became heated to look for tea and biscuits which meant that arguments, whilst still vigorous became less personal. The reason for this simply was to ensure that the management would not take any action against voluntary officials. They could do nothing to me that would create trouble for me in my employment. I regarded the protection of reps as being a responsibility on me as well as any union official.

The five years I spent at the Airport were challenging. I met very many people whom I would like to mention but the book would be just a list of names. Amongst the sections that I got most satisfaction from representing were those at the bottom of the pile. Many representatives and committee members gave freely of their time and effort for their colleagues. One group that gave me frequent bruises were the Women Cleaners in Aer Lingus and Aer Rianta. Emily Barr was the rep. in Aer Lingus and Mrs O'Riordan in Aer Rianta. Both ladies, when there were problems for the women were very vocal. Meetings I had with them, on occasion, almost came to blows. They would fight with anyone to get a fair deal for the ladies.

I am happy to say that their rates and conditions improved during the five-year period long after I had moved on from the Airport I was told about a mass for a former member, Mrs Eileen White, who had been killed in very brutal circumstances. On arriving at the Church I was told by Emily Barr that I was to read a lesson. After the very moving service I was chatting with the ladies in the canteen, when a thought came to mind. That sad occasion was the only time that I was able to talk to Women Cleaners without any answering back. Even when I retired I was touched by the fact that, almost 20 years after I first met them, the Women Cleaners at Dublin Airport presented me with a portrait of myself by Paul Kavanagh which will always have an honoured place on our wall.

Many other groups have been supportive since I left the Aviation Branch. In fact, for 15 or 20 years, any time I have gone to the Airport I have been asked by a lot of individuals, "when are you coming back?"

The answer to that is I'm retired now but I still have a keen interest in the future well-being of our national airline and Airport Authority. At this time I believe it is worthwhile to look at the position of Aer Lingus in some depth.

Stating the obvious is sometimes necessary, this is one of those times. Ireland is an island nation and since the digging of the Channel Tunnel, between England and France, it is currently the only country divided from all other EU countries by the sea. This, of course, means that for international transport airlines and shipping lines are necessary for the transportation of both people and goods. It is also a factor that Ireland is a small country compared to its neighbours. With the proliferation of the market economy and the down grading of social needs it becomes obvious that there is a necessity to have a nationally owned and controlled airline as also applies in Shipping. Otherwise this little island becomes open to exploitation by the major world airlines and shipping conglomerates. Insofar as airlines are concerned we have seen that when deregulation occurred in the USA there was major growth in the number of small airlines. These either shrivelled and died or were gobbled up by the large predator airlines. Without a state airline which, apart from providing great service to the travelling public, also employs many people in Ireland, England and world wide. It also faces competition from a private airline to which some of its profitable routes were handed over by the Government, which Government also refused to licence Aer Lingus to operate into Stansted Airport, whilst allowing the private airline to do so. These two decisions are decisions about which the question 'why' must be asked.

It requires an answer, particularly as I understand the same private airline has pulled out of routes it was granted because they were not considered profitable. I believe it to be most likely that these decisions, which in the long run, could threaten our national airline, would have been opposed most vigorously by my grandfather and his sons, Jim and Denis.

In my time working in No. 12 Branch I recall seeing aircraft from PAN AM, TWA and Seaboard World (freight). These were large airlines which, when the draught of the market economy hit them, one of their first moves was out of Ireland prior to their total collapse.

Unless our country has its own national airline for air transport it will be totally dependent on the whims of the market economy — International carriers not controlled by the Government will only operate on routes they think viable. Ireland's experience of service by airlines other than Aer Lingus have proved this point over many years. A strong and vibrant national airline is necessary to guarantee proper service to the Irish people.

In another form of international transport, Ireland is similarly disadvantaged. Some years ago the nation's shipping line, Irish shipping, ceased trading. It is not possible for me to lay responsibility for its closure, but when one thinks of the service given to this state by the company and its seafarers, many of whom lost their lives in providing much needed cargo on the Atlantic run particularly during the course of the last World War, it gives a clear picture of how an island country without its own shipping line can be affected by decisions taken elsewhere in Europe, as to whether or not particular services shall be provided and at what cost.

During my next twenty years I had the privilege of representing members in almost all areas of work — Health Boards, Local Authorities, Forestry, Public utilities and private industry. As far as the claims and negotiations were concerned, the needs of members, irrespective of jobs; were almost exactly the same. A few brief comments, I think, would be useful.

My work with the Union gave me the pleasure of going to almost every town and village in Ireland. A specific claim, one that I feel is worth a mention, is a claim for equalisation of pay-rates for women attendants in Health Boards outside Dublin. This was satisfactorily resolved in the early 1980s. Prior to this women working as attendants in hospitals were paid approximately £25 a week less than their male colleagues. The equalisation was achieved in three payments over 18 months.

Meeting at Cavan County Council, 1980, Jim Larkin speaking.

In general terms the relationship I had with employers, with the exception of three, tended to be polite. With members it was somewhat different because to become friendly with members could call into question our integrity, should they be promoted, etc. While I have said, that employers were polite this was not true when their relationship was with members. Sadly, I found that in virtually all employments I had to deal with over a period of almost 25 years, good manners were at a premium. After about a year with the Union when I met a new group of members I would ask them about their personal relationships with their own supervisors and managers. Invariably I was met with a stony silence. I would then ask whether the words "Please" and "Thank you" formed a part of their own employers vocabulary. Their answers in all cases was hysterical laughter. It would be my wish that employers learn that by being polite they can make more money by increasing productivity and creating a better atmosphere for working in.

From some of the things I have said I am sure it will be appreciated that a trade union official's life is not particularly easy, in the sense that family and social life take a back seat to the needs of union members. For my own part, without support and encouragement from Brenda the work I did over the last quarter of a century would have been well-nigh impossible. It is also true that no Union official can achieve any progress without the wholehearted help and assistance from voluntary officials. In 25 years I have met many thousands of men and women. It is impossible to name them all but there are two I do wish to mention, both of whom have gone to their last reward — Maura Doolin, who was a shop steward of the WUI. in Irish Hospitals Trust and Alex Fogarty, who was also a shop steward in Dublin Fruit and Vegetable Market. The work they did on behalf of their members was a great inspiration. They are missed.

The Labour Court

My experience in dealing with the above body, including the Conciliation Rights Commissioners and also the Employment Appeals Tribunal, was that the officers of the Court proved to be very able in their function of assisting in the resolution of disputes. At some stages during my work I felt that I should actually move house and live there such was my workload. In the last few years they moved from Mespil Road. The new location is called Beggar's Bush. I wonder was the move deliberate and is the appellation pointing the finger at anyone in particular! There were occasions when I will admit to wearing the sackcloth and ashes in negotiations!

The first Hearing of the Court at which I presented a case was early in 1971. My late father, Denis, who was then General Secretary of the Union, attended also. When the Court members came into the room I received a shock — the employers representative on the panel was Mr Hugh Lennox, who had been General Manager of Liffey Dockyard, my first employment 20 years before. My father had not warned me, we still did reasonably well and the final results were accepted by an overwhelming majority of members.

Many people had difficulty with the Labour Court. For my own part, over the period of years problems and claims made for members were resolved in almost 95% of cases. In the area of unfair dismissals my record was even better. At this time I would like to express my thanks to all the officers of the Court for putting up with my personal vagaries and verbosity.

An area of organisation I also wish to touch on is that of the Health Service. Since my retirement and the two heart-attacks I had subsequently, I appreciate more now the work performed by all grades within the service. Very many of our members work in different areas of health care. It appears that their labours in the interests of suffering humanity are not always appreciated by the powers-that-be. Pressures that are put on front-line staff are becoming extremely difficult. A group that we did not represent, junior hospital doctors, have been working under stress for many years. On a personal note should I require urgent medical treatment due to my heart condition, which thankfully is not as serious as many, nonetheless I would like to know that the junior doctor who attends to me has not been working for 15 or more hours without proper rest. I may be wrong but I am sure that when someone has worked for that period they are more likely to make a mistake than if working reasonable rosters.

A difficulty faced by the medical profession in general, and thus the community, is the ever-increasing number of legal cases being taken against the profession. This is not to say that anyone is not free to take a case of negligence against anyone, but the increase in the legal profession, when a patient presents with a medical problem, because the MD has their eye over their shoulder viewing the possible legal complexities, will refer people on to specialists and for extensive and expensive tests. Thus in court proceedings they can produce records of the procedures that were undertaken in order to protect themselves from the law rather than assist in curing the patient. This is my view.

With other grades in the Health Service there have also been problems arising out of short-staffing, part-time and contract employment. These inevitably lead to additional problems for staff and patients alike. Some years ago an examination of the Health Service took place. The thrust of that exercise was a look at the cost of services. To my mind, what firstly is necessary is a full examination on a demographic basis of the range of illnesses extant, secondly an examination of the services available currently and their location. The next phase would require an attempt to provide the appropriate services nearest to the point of greatest need. The slavish following of ideas from England — of charters, which are unrealistic — is unhelpful. Also unhelpful in the past, was the practice of medical, particularly hospital, services being sited on the basis of local political decisions. These did not necessarily provide the right services in the right place.

The Department of Health has a major problem particularly in psychiatric service with the development of Community Care. The ideals envisaged of long-term patients being put out into the community are marvellous. However, in the last decade, many men and women who had been in hospital for long periods of time, consequently becoming institutionalised, have been put on community care programmes. When I was working in Parnell Square, coming out after meetings in the evening I would frequently see people who had slipped through the net lying in the shop doorways of Dublin's inner city. These men and women need greater care than is currently being provided by Charities. Those organisations such as Simon, Alone, etc.

do magnificent work, If we look at the word 'asylum' — a place of refuge and protection, for people who need to be protected from 'normal' people, — that word starts to look good again. It was my privilege to represent staff in Hostels for those who needed help with the everyday things that we take for granted. Items as small as how to cope with simple shopping, public transport, looking after money, which is difficult enough for us all. These hostels provide as near a family environment as is possible. Many more such places are needed. Don't take my word on the present condition of far too many former patients — open your eyes in the evening and the bundle of clothes that you see in a shop doorway (not only in Dublin but in every city in Ireland and in England) may well be someone who has been left in the care of the community.

In mentioning areas I have dealt with I have briefly talked about some shop stewards but any mention of the work I did would be incomplete without due thanks being given to my colleague officers of the Union. These included Joan Fortune, Padraigin Ní Murchu, both at Dublin Airport, Paddy Trehy, Brendan Hayes, Tony Dunne, Michael Gogarty, all in Parnell Square, the late James Redmond of the Federation of Rural Workers, Bob Redmond of USEDU, Patricia King and Gene Mealy of the FWUI. Without the assistance of those, my colleagues, and the clerical staff, as well as all the voluntary officials it has been my pleasure to work with, little work would have been achieved. Amongst the clerical staff who had to put up with my scribble were Annette Mongey, Nell O'Brien, Peggy Rafter, Elsie Perdisatt, Mary Nolan, Margaret Shortt and Pauline Kerrigan. These ladies are all entitled to congratulations for their ability at translation.

As, during my working life, I made a practice of not disclosing individual cases I intend to continue that in retirement, as members are entitled to confidentiality.

The Local Authority Branch covered all grades of staff working for Dublin Corporation and County Council including the Fire Brigade, gardeners, etc. one of our stalwart shop stewards was Larry Sweetman whose birth was an historic event. the Union had bought Unity Park, which estate is now occupied by Whitehall Church. The estate was used as an area for social gatherings, including picnics, sports days and a range of other activities. Larry was born in June 1928 while his parents, Thomas and Jane Sweetman, were working and living in Unity Park. It is likely that he was the only child born from those premises for many years. It is certain that he was the last.

The last Union Branch I worked in was the non-commercial semi-State. This branch, apart from the obvious, had many members in a wide variety of organisations, charities, galleries, libraries, etc. Of the many groups that I shared with Patricia King and Gene Mealy, were the National Gallery, who had a noted member as shop steward, Alfie Murphy, who earlier in his career won a Scottish Cup Medal with Clyde and also represented Ireland at soccer. The NCSS branch was so large that again to mention everyone would be impossible. One of the areas though which was dealt with by the Branch was the Irish Trades Union Trust, which was a body set up by the WUI and ITGWU primarily to assist unemployed members. The senior officer is Eddie Glackin who, had amongst his able staff Ross Connolly, whom I had earlier dealt with in No. 3 branch. Ross is grandson of the late James Connolly.

For Big Jim Larkin THE BIG ISSUES *were Homelessness, Unemployment and Poverty.*
The same issues remain today.

Jim Larkin and his Stage Grandfather Jer O'Leary support the policies and aims of the Big Issues.

GAISCE Left to Right Front Row: J.T. Murphy, Jim Larkin Michael Carruth,
Catherine Kiely, Mary
Left to Right Back Row: Mark Carroll, Fiona Carroll, Susan Doherty, Francis Behan.
REPRODUCED BY KIND PERMISSION OF TOM CONNOLLY

In looking at unemployment I had to ask myself whether anything positive could be done to alleviate the problem. In the NCSS branch we had in membership GAISCE — the President's Award Scheme. The basic principle of this body is that people who participate set challenges for themselves in a number of areas, Community Involvement, Personal Skill, Physical Recreation and Adventure. The award grades are Bronze, Silver and Gold. In talking to the staff I also talked to many participants who found that the scheme had helped them in many ways. It helped to build up self-confidence, which is essential for anyone seeking employment. It assisted them in recognising that they could assign and reach personal goals. This again proved to be helpful. While getting the awards was a great achievement, a number of participants asked that they be provided with lapel pins that they could wear at job interviews. These have been provided. I believe that the thousands of people who have given time and effort to joining in the scheme, in whatever capacity, have spent their time wisely.

Sketch of Jim Larkin by Catherine Fitzpatrick

Retirement

My retirement from the Union took a long time, so much so that one of my colleagues, Bernard Brown, said, "I've said goodbye to you so frequently, Jim, please tell me when you are going to bloody go!"

The first portion of the wake/celebration, happened on June 6th 1993, when Joe Duffy and his crew from the Gay Byrne Show, arrived in 29 Parnell Square. This episode had been organised by Tom Gormley, I don't know whether to call him a colleague or an agent! It was a very enjoyable morning. I have included here part of the discussion. The music was provided by Eric Fleming another colleague, and the Work and Play Band. Tom Crean, also a branch secretary sang a bar or two. Despite being a stressful time refreshments were provided by the Larkin Unemployed Centre. The Executive Room was packed and included James Plunkett, Jack Harte, Francis Devine and many colleagues in the union. Joe Duffy organised his interviews with consummate professionalism. The crew were great in very crowded conditions. The morning proved to be a very pleasant experience for all those involved. Even almost two years after I am still being stopped by people who heard the programme. Immediately after the programme I got many calls and letters with good wishes as a result of the Gay Byrne Show.

EXCERPTS FROM THE GAY BYRNE SHOW (RADIO) 6TH JUNE 1993

Joe Duffy "There's 200 yrs clocked up between members of the Larkin Family. Jim Larkin how do you feel at this time on your retirement?"

Jim Larkin "I feel that it's an historic occasion in the sense that being a small part of the contribution to the Labour Movement and having to retire at this time — I'm sad in ways, but as you mentioned full-time employment I've been privileged by SIPTU to be enabled to continue with the education division of the Union."

JD "Obviously you remember your grandfather."

JL "I do indeed."

JD "When did you realise that Big Jim Larkin was different?"

JL "It was at the end of January 1947 — at his funeral. Before that he was my grandad. He was a lovely man, personally. We went to Thomas Ashe Hall when I was maybe 4 or 5 years of age and he always gave me 2/6d for myself and 2/6d for my sister. Now, I realised on that day it was his funeral and we'd walked through the snow and slush from Haddington Road Church behind his coffin. We were going along Marlborough Street towards Unity Hall, that had been the old Union headquarters. Passing by the corner of Nth Earl Street and Marlborough Street I saw a sight that I never saw before and probably will never see again. An old Garda Sergeant, maybe in his 50s or 60s, standing to attention and tears rolling down his cheeks as the coffin passed. Also I still get the feeling any time I walk down Marlborough Street of the silence, other than the shuffling of thousands of feet in the slush and snow. That's when I came to realise that Granda Jim was maybe a little bit different to other people's grandads."

JD "Do you remember sitting or standing at his knee and him giving his powerful voice at these open-air meetings?"

JL "I do indeed. I remember one particularly at the corner of Malahide Road and Griffith Ave. The chairman, and there were maybe 7 or 8 thousand people at the meeting, closing off the traffic completely. The chairman handed the microphone to him as you did to me, and the chairman said, 'Here you are Jim. Here's the microphone' and I remember Granda saying 'the day I use one of those I'll retire'."

JD "Gay Byrne says the same thing! But he was a powerful, powerful man and you are over 6 foot as well."

JL "Yes indeed."

JD "And to go to your father's generation, which would have been Young Jim, your uncle, and Denis Larkin who was your Da. Tell me, I want you to begin, if you can, with your mother please, because women played such an important role in the Larkin family. Annie Moore, she was a small woman."

JL "Annie Moore was small in stature but very big in spirit and I probably gave her one of the most difficult times in her life because she was 4'11" and slight in build and when I was born I've been told I was 14 $^1/_2$ lbs."

JD "Good heavens!"

JL "So that gave her a difficult time but there was one thing unique about my Mum. She was responsible for the only time Big Jim bought any alcohol for anyone. Herself and Dad were going on their honeymoon on the Mailboat from Dun Laoghaire. She ran down the gangplank jumped up at Grandad Jim —"

JD "This is 4'11" jumping up at 6'2."

JL *"She made it. She gave him a kiss and Barney Conway, rest his soul, one of Jim's greatest supporters, was telling me when I was very young — after she ran back up the gangplank Jim put his hand in his pocket, pulled out a £10 note and said 'Get a drink for the lads at the office'. The only time in his life that he had ever bought an alcoholic drink for anyone."*

JD *"Because all the Larkins, down to you are pioneers — is that true? I knew Big Jim was very strong anti-drink."*

JL *"Not pioneers but non-drinkers. Grandad Jim, Jim my late uncle, Denis my father and myself, mainly due to what all of us had seen though people's lives and families being destroyed by abuse of drink."*

Song from Tom Crean — *Dublin City in 1913.*

Gay Byrne Radio Show, June 1993

REPRODUCED BY KIND PERMISSION OF TOMMY CLANCY

JD Jim the story about —

Again going back to Denis's wife Annie and Sean Lemass and Fianna Fáil and the collection."

JL *"Well my mother was Secretary of the local branch of the Labour Party in Marino and she was late with the National Collection and she figured out that what she would do was go into Dáil Eireann and she approached TDs of all Parties, except the Labour Party because the members were too poor to contribute! What happened was, she approached a number of prominent Fianna Fáil people*

205

and they were kind enough to contribute. She spoke to the late Sean Lemass and she said 'Would you like to contribute to the Labour Party?' and he said 'Why should I?' She replied 'I was listening to you in the Dáil the other day and I heard you say you wanted to have an effective opposition and I'm giving your the opportunity to put your money where your mouth is.'"

JD *"So she got money out of him?"*

JL *"He went to give her a £10 note and she said she wouldn't insult him by accepting less than £20 from a man of his stature and he gave it to her."*

JD *"She collected money from others."*

JL *"From a local TD. A very pleasant man, Eugene Timmins, a decent man. Fianna Fáil. He worked well with my late father in the Dáil. She got £10 from Eugene and a few weeks later she was approached by Deputy Timmins outside Marino Church and he asked her to contribute to the Fianna Fáil National Collection. 'After all I contributed to the Labour Party Collection' he said. And she said 'Well, Deputy Timmins, I appreciated that but some of us have our principles!' She didn't contribute but she went back to Deputy Timmins the following year and got a contribution — he was a very generous man."*

Gay Byrne *"I want to move on to the phone calls. Billy Attley, joint President of SIPTU is on the line to pay a brief tribute to our guest of honour today. Billy would like to say what you have to say to Jim?"*

Billy Attley *"First of all, I regret I can't be with him to broadcast live this morning. I'm at a meeting and have just come out to take the call to pay tribute to Jim. I can recall vividly when Jim was recruited into the Union and of course there has always been great affection for him because of the Larkin name within the old FWUI but within the Labour Movement generally. He's been held in a very special position within the organisation for the work both of his father and of his grandfather and Jim came into the Union many years ago, and of course, everyone was delighted to see him coming in. He has become a great friend of every member of staff over these years and the very name of Larkin going out as a Union official to deal with ordinary people has had something magical about it. He certainly has been in the heart and affections of a vast number of members over the years and I think we're all going to miss him. Generally we're going to miss him because he never seems to be in bad humour. He always seems to have a smile on his face and even when those of us around seem to be depressed because of difficult situations he's always there with a bounce and we'll miss that. Now, he's only retiring — nobody ever retires out of the Labour Movement and we expect to see him around. As a colleague we just want to pay tribute to him for the work he did on behalf of working people. He has certainly lived up to the best traditions of the Larkin name."*

GP *"Thank you very much indeed, Billy. You heard all that Joe? It was very good."*

GB *"We are just paying tribute to Jim Larkin on his retirement and Ruairi Quinn we have on the phone now to pay a little tribute as well."*

RUAIRI QUINN *"Well, Jim is part of an extraordinary family tradition that is the Labour Movement. I don't think anyone can go up and down O'Connell St. without seeing the statute of Big Jim that Oisin Kelly did and not recognise the strength of that family and what they did for the working people of this country. I don't know Jim that well but I served a kind of political apprenticeship with Denis Larkin, the late Jimmy Molloy, who was much-loved City Manager of Dublin City, told me a story of when he first went on to the Housing Committee as a young official in the mid-1950s. There was a bitter row and everyone was arguing and the Chairman, Denis Larkin, started writing in the Minute Book. Jimmy Molloy asked one of the senior officials what he was writing. The official replied that he was writing the decision. Jimmy said "They haven't finished the debate yet". Yes, but when they do finish it, he'll read out the decision and they'll all agree to that!" Denis Larkin had this extraordinary way of taking a little of everyone's way so that they all felt they were part of the final decision, even though it was a carefully crafted compromise. That ability to find common ground and find a solution is something that the Larkins are particularly attributed with.*

The Larkin contribution to the Labour Movement and to the well-being of working people has been enormous and Jim is very much in that tradition and I would just like to pay tribute to him and to wish him the best in his retirement and, as, Billy Attley said, you never retire from the Labour Movement."

Music from the Work and Play Band.

JD *"Francis Devine of the Labour History Society — Larkin and his role and the perception Dubliners have of him —"*

FD *"Well it's quite unique. There's no other capital city anywhere that has in its main street a statue of a trade union figure — the famous Oisin Kelly sculpture — if you haven't seen it make it your business to. He represents the heartbeat and the soul of the city. Larkinism, in its various phases, raised the working class population of Dublin off their knees. He challenged depression, he challenged the golden circles of 1913. He gave a credibility and credence to working class people. He gave us a place at the table and we were in at the formation of the State. It was carried through by the socialist vision of Young Jim in the need for planning a responsible, democratically based Trade Union Movement negotiating as a social partner might through to the current day. I think it has become fashionable to criticise Larkin, academics have been doing it, pointing out his faults and so on and we had the Carey slur on the television and radio. I think people out there listening who have no connection with the Labour Movement have to realise the contribution that the Larkin family have made to the democratisation of the State — the fact that we have a society untouched to a significant extent by Thatcherism and Reganism, where, despite the problems we have we do have a voice at the highest levels through the social partnership programme. Everybody out there owes something to the Larkins and in this city in particular, the Larkin tradition is woven into the fabric and soul of this city."*

GB *"Beautifully said. Well said."*

Big Jim (Larkin)

Though not of this Land, yet a hero became,
In the hearts of all workers, he kindled a flame.
That burns every bright, at factory and bench,
That great fire of Freedom, nothing will quench.

With a voice loud as thunder, a heart of pure gold,
True friend of the People, the young and the old.
The watchdog of Labour, so massive of limb,
No time for ambition, his name, yes, Big Jim.

Now well I remember his great clarion call,
"United we stand divided we fall",
The words ever true, we learned down the years,
As we fought on undaunted through sweat and tears.

When I look back and picture the dreadful '13
Our spirit was strong, as our faces grew lean.
But we weathered the storm a we sang Labour's Hymn,
And there like a beacon, shone our friend Big Jim.

A Man of his Word, no boss tried to sway,
With his able lieutenant, Barney Conway
He toiled on unselfish his one great desire,
Was lifting the Worker, out of the mire.

We owe such a lot the valiant Big Jim,
He was our shining light, when hope seemed so dim.
Let's keep this before us what ere may befall,
"An injury to one" is the concern of us all.

I'll never forget that Day, that he died,
The strongest of men, just stood round and cried.
For the passing of Jim, was a far greater blow,
Then the sufferings and wants of the great Winter's snow.
We laid him to rest on the coldest of Days,
But somehow the Sun spared a few golden rays.
As if in salute, to a Warrior Grand,
Who sacrificed all for the dreams he had planned.

Written by Peter A. Keenan

Formal Retirement, Liberty Hall, John Fay, Miriam, Brenda and Jim Larkin, Tom Garry, Damian Daly

The next formal event was a presentation from SIPTU itself. I was asked by the Staff Committee if I wished it to be held in Parnell Square. I expressed the desire that it be held in Liberty Hall, as a gesture of my belief that my grandfather and his sons, Jim and Denis, would have welcomed the uniting of the FWUI and ITGWU into SIPTU. The officers and staff were most generous and Brenda, Miriam and I had a most enjoyable evening.

As my retirement was fast approaching I decided to invite colleagues from the union, from congress and shop stewards I had dealt with over the previous 23 years. I was honoured by the couple of hundred people who turned up from all over the country, may of whom I had not seen for 15 or 20 years. To share in an evening with those I had worked with was a pleasure. I brought back many happy memories — the sad ones had no place on that evening. I would recommend this approach to any impending retiree. The venue was the Larkin Hall in Parnell Square, which formerly had been the AOH Hall. The former owners might not have been pleased at the occasion, I was.

My last month or so at the Union was interrupted by a number of local celebrations, Brendan Hayes my immediate superior was most understanding!

Life After Retirement

North Wales has always been a popular place with Brenda and myself to take our holidays. On one of these holidays, while I was sitting on a beach in a well-known coastal resort, I started thinking of the power of the natural elements and the really tiny effect that man has against the forces of nature. I got out a pen and for the only time in my life, wrote a poem.

Colwyn Bay

Cliff face marked, man's needs affect a change in nature.
With pick and shovel soft beauty take
from one place to beautify another.
Below, the sea smiles
What treachery
Even in repose, her white foam teeth
devour the land
pebbles, satin smooth, mingle with sand,
Where once, on either hand, stood mountains.

For those of you who do not know Colwyn Bay, the first lines refer to the old quarries. While writing the poem I thought of, and dedicated the little piece, to those, over the centuries who have worked on the sea and given up their lives for others.

On our last visit we went to Ty Mawr Holiday Park a few days after my retirement in 1993. On the fourth day we were there I had an attack, which, but for the staff, in the camp, the ambulance service and the staff at Bodelyddan Hospital, could have been much more serious. Some months later it transpired that it was a mild heart attack. Over the last few days of the holiday Brenda and I were helped tremendously by Brendan and Ann Hayes who were staying in North Wales with their family at the same time. We hope to visit North Wales again.

Although we have managed to visit places both at home and abroad, our life has not been one long holiday – this is far from the truth. It was only the insistence of my late father, when he was General Secretary of the Union, that Industrial officers must take 3 weeks holidays a year in order to recharge their batteries. Brenda and I denied ourselves of many treats in order to be able to afford trips to the Continent.

Our latest holiday so far took place prior to my writing this book. We went to Jersey in the Channel Islands for a fortnight. I went overland, because after that holiday I intended to do some research in England prior to returning home.

After our holiday in Jersey in 1994 I went to London where I stayed with my cousin Lorian and his wife Hillary whilst doing some research for this book. I was assisted in this by Christine Coates Librarian of the TUC and also Regan Scott of the T & GWU. I also spent some time in the Newspaper Library at Collinwood.

From London I went to Manchester where I was given shelter by my wife's cousin Bill Barber and his wife Marilyn.

Prior to going to Manchester I had telephoned the Museum of Labour History there and Stephen Bird, Archivist. When I informed him of my interests he said he would see what he could find and for me to call when I was in Manchester. When I arrived at the Museum he had already sorted out those files in which I had shown an interest. The Director of the museum Nicholas Mansfield, was also most helpful and interested and I had the enjoyable experience of visiting their centre at the Pump House. Ken Coates, MEP for Derbyshire, and his wife kindly entertained me one afternoon. He had earlier written a history of T & GWU and presented me with a copy.

Tammy, Kelly, Andrea Maguire – Emigrants to Oldham.

212

When in Dublin I had met the Maguire family from Ballyfermot fairly frequently, as one of the daughters, Marty, had been a shop steward of ours in the fruit and vegetable trade. Three of her sisters, Kelly, Andrea, Tammy, emigrated to near Oldham, north of Manchester. I met them briefly and had a cup of tea and a yarn. Wherever I go somebody who knows me knows somebody.

Back in Dublin I had help from many friends. Special thanks must go to the following people: Shirley O'Keefe, Jean McGrane, Kim Jenkinson, and Patricia Donlon.

On the last lap of my research trip Bill kindly dropped me in Liverpool. My journey around had been affected by signalmen's strike, which very clearly had been the responsibility, firstly of the British Government and secondly of British Rail management.

Shirley O'Keefe

My host in Liverpool was Tony Birtill. I am greatly indebted to him. Through him I met with E.J. Roberts of the T & GWU who was very co-operative. John Nettleton who works on the Mersey ferry took me round the docks where it all began and Alan has been most obliging in assisting my search for my great-grandfather's and mother's graves. Robert Parry, Labour member of Parliament for Liverpool, Riverside and his secretary Sheila Coleman both were of great help to me. I also met Mary van Helmand, Curator of Merseyside Maritime Museum and Teresa Doyle of the Walker Art Gallery. The latter is the sister of someone I met in Dublin.

Eric Taplin, had written an article on the Dockers' Union and I had the pleasure of meeting him and discussing it with him.

In the course of my stay Tony Birtill introduced me to many people and he took me to Toxteth and we located the house that my late grandmother, Elizabeth Brown, had married my late grandfather from. The main impression I was left with was the warmth of feeling for my late grandfather who had died nearly 50 years ago and this feeling came to me from, not only people of my own age group and older, but

Jean McGrane

also from teenagers upwards. My grandfather's working life in Liverpool had been a few short years at the turn of the century. The affection that came through to me told me much about his worth.

I have been involved in writing this book and giving talks to schools on the need for trades unions and on the social history of the early part of the century. I also retired undefeated from going to Pelican House with a total of 64 donations. My reason, in the first instance, for giving blood was, when I saw the effect of a blood transfusion on a friend of mine from North Dublin W.S.C. It had a miraculous effect on him so I started donating blood when I was 18.

I also became more involved in UNICEF and am currently a member of the Executive Board of the Irish National Committee. The reason why I and many others, have worked for UNICEF, is because of the manner in which it works.

The Irish National Committee for UNICEF, together with other National Committees, have signed recognition agreements with UNICEF HQ. This lays severe strictures on the spending of monies for other than direct aid. One other unique aspect of UNICEF's operation is, in the case of long-term and structural assistance, the receiving country must agree the programmes. They must also contribute to the cost of carrying out the programme. This latter requirement clearly underlines the necessity for receiving governments to be committed to whatever programme. Quite a number of international celebrities have given freely of their time in order to espouse the cause of

Patricia Donlon

214

UNICEF. Amongst those who have passed away are Danny Kaye, whom I had the pleasure of seeing in the Theatre Royal many years ago, Audrey Hepburn, a particularly lovely lady who gave much time and effort on behalf of needy children throughout the world. Placido Domingo, the Spanish tenors Roger Moore, star of many films and Nana Mouskouri whose interpretations of modern Greek songs are acclaimed throughout the world, are Goodwill Ambassadors. Ms Mouskouri was elected as a Member of the European Parliament recently. I believe that she will have much to say regarding the health and welfare of children.

Kim Jenkinson

I have also had more time since my retirement to use my expertise to give advice to local community associations.

Brenda was the prime mover of our residents association over a decade. This body, together with many others nationally, became defunct due to the appalling application of public liability insurance. Local communities throughout the country have been seriously affected because they cannot afford the enormous premiums. Often these simple activities are children's sports days or outings or similar events.

The only dangerous events that take place are the Bonny baby Competitions where poor unfortunate judges' lives may be at risk from outraged mothers!

In an agricultural context the same form of insurance means that farmers have to insure against trespassers having accidents when they should be protected against intruders.

There are many other instances of the law being an ass.

Drawing by Niall Parkinson

A Changing World

In order to give some idea of the time span covered by this book I would just like to briefly refer to some of the developments and achievements in the world which occurred after my late grandfather's death.

He did not live in the age in which the first man reached the moon nor did he see the development of the supersonic plane, Concord. Personal computers had not yet been developed. The Chinese had invented the abacus as a mechanical form of computer but the electric and electronic computers had not been developed.

My grandfather also did not see a hovercraft, a colour television or a CD player. He died prior to the first transplant surgery carried out by Christian Bernard. There were no electron microscopes, CAT scan equipment or Ultra Sound. He did not see the breaking of barriers in Eastern Europe or the crumbling of apartheid in South Africa with the election of Nelson Mandela as President of that country. Within his own direct sphere of interest, none of the following were within his life experience: the 39-hour-week for working people; the establishment of May Day as a National Holiday in 1994, the amalgamation of the Workers' Union of Ireland and the ITGWU into SIPTU, and finally, the coming of peace to Northern Ireland.

While commenting on a number of events and developments my grandfather did not see in his lifetime, it might well be appropriate to comment on a number of developments I believe he would not have welcomed.

Firstly, the widespread nature of unemployment with its consequential damaging effect on the morale of those affected, and on their families. The despair that affects very many people when the efforts they make to seek work turn out to be fruitless. One of the most damaging effects is a loss of the ability to recognise one's own personal value and talent.

Secondly, the opposite side of this coin arises out of the antics of the 'golden circle' in Ireland, also the behaviour of senior executives in privatised industry in England with their acceptance and futile attempts to justify their massive pay rises and share options worth a fortune. This, at a time when many workers had been made redundant.

217

The wages needed to support families were thus transferred to those who in no way could be considered to have earned the obscene salaries. They and their clique paid themselves. For very many working people in those industries the munificent salary increases they were allowed to receive were of the order of 1–3%. I saw, with interest, that the British Prime Minister, John Major, said he regarded these massive rises for the executive levels as 'distasteful', this definition of monstrous greed is being very much over polite. It is typical of conservative thinking and it shows clearly that, whilst some action may be taken to redress a major social wrong, it seems it will be too little, too late. It does nothing to change my view that the Conservative Party effectively got their title from their actions in conserving privilege, to the extent that, over their period of stewardship, the gap between the greedy and the needy has grown immensely. This particular section is written out of the beliefs that has come to me from my grandfather, uncle and father, who devoted their lives to those who were disadvantaged and needed someone to talk for them. They did not pursue a policy of envy, instead they gave to, rather than took from, those in need.

A clear example can be given: when my grandfather died, apart from a very few personal possessions, he left an estate of £4.50, at the end of his life's work. In the case of my Uncle Jim and my father, Denis, both men, at different times, refused pay increases that they had earned, in the interest of Union members.

Thirdly, my grandfather would have looked askance at something that had grown through working life, related to redundancy. While sympathising in genuine cases of redundancy, he would be against the idea espoused by a small number of people, when faced with difficult choices. I can only use the phrase "don't be a chump, take the lump" to express one of the problems that sometimes arise. His view would have been, a job held by someone is not theirs to sell. That job may be the one that a person's son or daughter or other relative or friend, may aspire to.

The next area that he would look at dubiously is the recent development of short-term contracts, for many reasons. They provide lack of security, which leads inevitably to less than the best work being done which also damages their employers firm. Couples thinking of getting married find it very difficult to get any kind of mortgage. The effect of short-term contracts has a devastating result on deferred income by way of company pensions. For young people this does not appear important, but they will find that having to rely almost solely on State pensions is very difficult. Don't take my word only but talk to any pensioner you know who is existing solely on State Benefit.

Another recent development that I believe my grandfather would not have been pleased with is the proliferation of counsellors to assist in circumstances of individual tragedy or grief. The reason why I think he would not welcome this is because it shows a symptom of the breakdown of people caring for each other within the family, neighbourhood or group. In past generations when death occurred in a family the bereaved could count on their extended family and people in their neighbourhood for morale and practical support. This appears to be lessening and a situation is produced where people's isolation brings about reliance on counsellors. One recent example I read of, in England, was where members of a local fire brigade attended an appalling incident where a number of people lost their lives. The first thought of the particular local authority was to get a team of counsellors to talk to the firemen involved. While being aware that fire-fighters have very stressful incidents to cope with, it surely is more effective for the members of the brigade to support one another in those circumstances. A Dublin fire-fighter, the late Willie Bermingham, responded in a very practical way to tragedy when he had to turn out on a call when a very elderly person died alone and unwanted in their flat. Instead of being disabled by grief he was responsible for setting up ALONE which is a charity assisting elderly people with no direct family support. This organisation is still being supported by many members of the Fire Brigade.

My grandfather had a great interest in the problems faced by pensioners. While seeing that there was a reasonable State pension scheme, he saw the necessity for occupational pensions also. He would not have liked the trend in employment that reduced the availability of such schemes.

Another aspect of life I recall him talking to me about was the function and worth of the Stock Exchange. While he was prepared to accept that when that august body was raising new money to invest in employment it had something on the credit side. However, his general view was, the organisation was nothing more than an upper-class bookie's shop. However, the idea of a Common European Currency would have been supported by my grandfather. With the existence of a common currency it would make it far more difficult for individual and corporate speculators to increase their private wealth at the expense of undermining their own and other national currencies. This type of currency, while difficult to organise, would be likely to stop the fat cats from getting fatter. As we have seen, over the last decade, many attacks were made by speculators which, effectively, took money out of working people's pockets.

Big Jim would have regarded the growth of computerisation as being a possible barrier to human relationships. This to a lesser degree would equally apply to television. The development into the sphere of virtual reality would be an avenue I feel he would have been loathe to travel. He would have recognised that there is no realism whatsoever in such an approach but rather it is a pale imitation is devoid of all emotion and which is inhuman in concept. However, he would have recognised how the use of a format of that kind to examine medical problems or similar problems in engineering could prove useful.

The final area I wish to refer to is my grandfather's care of children. He saw a need for parents to look to the future for their children. In his day it meant a hard and difficult life. He saw that children who were spoiled found it more difficult to achieve reasonable goals. He would have been extremely upset by the change in the city of Dublin, as well as all other cities, world-wide, with increasing violence on the streets, the need for shops to be shuttered up each evening, as if they were banks. He would have thought deplorable the introduction of aggression to children at a very young age, through television and films. Had I been seen attempting to kick a playmate my father would have taken immediate remedial action.

A lesson that many parents learn too late is that children who grow up with aggression find it extremely difficult to obtain suitable employment in later life due to their inability to relate to people. Big Jim believed in the development of everyone's personal talents and thus was opposed to intoxication of any kind whether by alcohol or drugs.

My late grandfather was honoured in many ways in his lifetime. Later there have been many public acknowledgments of his contribution to society. In 1976 to honour the centenary of his birth, An Post, issued two stamps in his memory. The photograph included here is of my late father, Denis, and his two surviving brothers Finton and Barney and myself on the occasion of the stamps issue. The city of Dublin agreed that a statue in his memory be erected in O'Connell Street. The statue was commissioned by the Workers' Union of Ireland and was designed and executed by Oisin Kelly. It was unveiled by President Patrick Hillery. Both Dublin and Liverpool Corporations paid the honour to him by naming streets after him. The Workers' Union called their Hall in Parnell Square The Larkin Hall. He would have appreciated this greatly as it had formerly been owned by the Ancient Order of Hibernians.

Dublin City University have also named their lecture theatre after him as also a block of flats in North Strand have been.

Over recent years there have been a series of Larkin Memorial Lectures given by a range of prominent scholars and politicians. The lecture in this year, 1995, was given by Dick Spring, Leader of the Irish Labour Party, Tanaiste and Minister for Foreign Affairs, and member of SIPTU, as he informed us. The lecture was held on 22nd February. That was the day that the Framework Document was presented to the

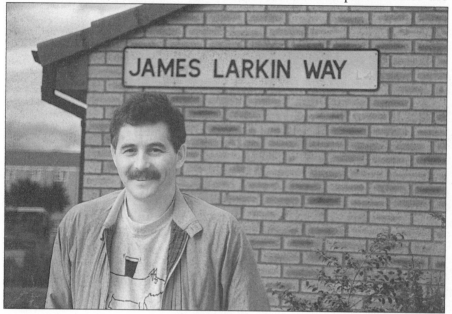

Tony Birtill, Liverpool, in front of James Larkin way

people of Northern Ireland. Deputy Spring gave us an outline of the contents of the document. Knowing my late father's views, particularly, as well as those of my grandfather, I am certain that both of them would have welcomed the end of violence in the North and the prospect for lasting peace.

At the time of the cease-fires in the North I felt compelled to express to the N. Ireland Committee of Congress the gratitude I believed that my three forebears in the Union would have wished me to pass on to the members of the Committee and shop stewards throughout the North for their courage and determination in ensuring that violence did not, at least, visit workplaces throughout the North. I expressed this view in my father, Denis's, own words which he uttered as President of Congress in July 1974.

The launch of An Post's stamp commemorating Big Jim Larkin. From left to right: Barney and Finton Larkin with Denis Larkin and his son Jim

The unveiling of Big Jim's statue in O'Connell Street. In attendance were: Frank Clusky TD, Denis Larkin FWUI Gen. Sec., President Hillery, Michael Mullen ITGWU Gen. Sec.

Mr Terry Carlin
Northern Ireland Officer
ICTU
3 Wellington Park
Belfast BT9 6DJ13th October 1994

Dear Terry

I couldn't let today, October 13th, go by without expressing my admiration for the Northern Ireland Committee of Congress, together with the many Union Committees, Shop Stewards and Union members throughout the province, whose unceasing efforts during the last 25 years saved many hundreds of lives in workplaces.

Their courage has been of the highest order and is a living example of the Trade Union slogan — "An injury to One is the concern of All".

I know that my late grandfather considered that his greatest achievement was helping to unite Protestant and Catholic workers for a brief period in 1907.

My late father, too, was unstinted in his praise of you all, as I'm sure you are aware. At the conclusion of his Presidential Address to congress in July 1974, my father said the following:

"This Congress of Trade Unions has repeatedly made its position clear on the terrible events which have cost the lives of more than a thousand fellow human beings — men, women and children.

It has repeatedly expressed its opposition to the violence, the bombings, the senseless murders and the injury and suffering inflicted on many thousands of human beings. During the last few years, pamphlets have been issued setting out distinctly Congress policies and programmes on the essential issues.

These pamphlets represent the mature contribution towards healing the divisions that so tragically divide our community."

May I ask in conclusion for your co-operation ... and for an expression of your determination to make this Island of ours not a land fit for heroes but a land and a society which as workers we shall be proud to be part of."

As a direct result of all your efforts, many families were spared from mourning and the needless loss of many souls was avoided.

When I hear any reference to Peacemakers, you will all be in my thoughts.

Yours fraternally

Jim Larkin

I had also written to Mr Jack Jones, former General Secretary of the T&GWU in Britain, Now the guiding light of the T&GWU Retired Members Association. I was delighted to receive a letter in reply as I had always found Mr Jones to be a lifelong advocate of working people.

Jim Larkin
Swords   **19 May 1994**
Dublin.

Dear Jim Larkin,

Thank you for your letter and good wishes for you project. My father was one of the rank and file supporters of your grandfather and worked as a docker at T & J Harrison's berth at Toxteth docks in Liverpool when your grandfather was active there.

My father was a great admirer of your grandfather as a trade unionist but also his political campaigns in Liverpool. He often mentioned 'Big Jim' and told me he had named me after him. I guess it was a bit nostalgic as he was not a close associate but simply a working member of the NUDL who had been tremendously impressed by your grandfather. He was, for example, highly critical of Jimmy Sexton over his attitude towards 'Big Jim'.

Like your grandfather he went to sea as a youth and experienced some rough times abord ship. So there was some affinity there.

I'm afraid there is little more I can tell you. Unfortunately for your project many of the older members whom I knew when I personally worked on the docks at Liverpool, some of whom knew your grandfather, have passed away. That is also true of old members of the TGWU staff who had formerly worked for the NUDL and had contact with your grandfather. In one or two cases they were critical of 'Big Jim' because of their loyalty to Sexton. You will know of course that the NUDL old Liverpool area office of the TGWU was formerly the headquarters of the NUDL.

With Fraternal regards,
Your sincerely,

J L Jones

Sketch of Big Jim's statue by Miriam Larkin

The ICTU

The centenary of the unity of the Trades Union Movement in Ireland was in 1994. It was celebrated in a number of ways. To commence the year a parade that rivalled any other in Dublin took place in May and that parade formed a dual celebration, firstly it was a 100th birthday party and secondly it honoured the granting of May Day as a Public Holiday. Many organisations took part, Macnas from Galway played an important role in the format of the celebration. The floats were very imaginative and a number of bands, including the Artane Boys and SIPTU, took part. Our family, along with many other Dubliners, had a splendid day out. Big Jim was also there, along with the unemployed in the shape of Ger O'Leary.

UCD hosted a Centenary Workshop on aspects of the Trades Union Movement with contributions from a number of eminent speakers. The Irish Labour History Society was the prime mover in the event which was extremely interesting, with delegates from all of Ireland, England and Wales and North America.

ICTU Summer School 1994, Pat Daly, Jim Larkin, Ross Connolly

I was honoured, as the grandson of Jim Larkin, to be asked to have my photograph taken with the grandsons of two of the other major Labour leaders from early in the century. One was Ross Connolly, whom I had met when he was working in Irish Hospitals Trust and latterly the Irish Trades Union Trust. Ross is the grandson of the late James Connolly. Pat Daly was the other, and he is the grandson of P.T. Daly, whose contribution to the Labour Movement has never been given the recognition it deserves. P.T. Daly also served as President of Congress in 1939.

The Irish Congress of Trades Unions, in conjunction with RTE, produced a book to mark the occasion of the centenary. It is called "Trade Union Century" and was edited by Donal Nevin, former General Secretary of ICTU. The book comprises of a collection of reports from the RTE Thomas Davis Lectures, a selection of Congress Presidents' addresses, a selection of articles of historic interest, details on trades union membership and Congress views on important aspects of working life. The President of Ireland, Mary Robinson, launched the book in the Radio Studios in RTE. In her presentation she was as ever most articulate and knowledgeable on the subject matter. Her comments were all extempore. I found that the book is a very valuable addition to anyone's library and does Congress and the editor great credit. I can say this with some family authority as my grandfather was President of the ITUC in 1914; Jim Larkin Jnr. my uncle, was President of the ITUC in 1952 and also President of the ICTU in 1960; my father, Denis Larkin was President of the ICTU in 1974.

In July 1995 the ICTU biennial conference was held in Tralee. As I was an observer I had the pleasure of renewing acquaintance with many of my former colleagues. I also met Joe Jameson, Research officer of the AFL/CIO, New York and he provided me with a good deal of information. Ms Noreen Moore, administrator of Counteract and Terry Carlin, Northern Ireland ICTU officer are in the photo included here.

Brian and Patricia Johnson had a small stand at the Conference reminding people of the foul treatment meted out to employees of GCHQ in Britain. This organisation has been one of the main intelligence gathering bodies in Britain for many years. Former British Prime Minister, Margaret Thatcher, failed to recognise that trade unionists were capable of integrity. As a result, the campaign of the Conservative Government in Britain, Brian Johnson and a number of his colleagues were dismissed solely on the grounds of refusing to deny their trades union principles and leave their unions.

Noreen Moore, Joe Jameson, Terry Carlin.

Brian and Patricia Johnson.

How many more trade unionists are facing the same from the current, but hopefully not the next, British Government.

The day before the conference ended, whilst going through Tralee, I saw a picket outside Dunne's Stores. I heard shortly after taking this photograph that the dispute was resolved and that the talks were commencing. It has been my belief through my years in the Movement that when talks can be arranged, progress is possible.

Mary Morgan, Lena Aherne – MANDATE
Kevin Monaghan – SIPTU

The Future

L ike my late grandfather I tend to be a short-term pessimist and long-term optimist. Having lived through times that have seen major changes on the world stage, the lessening of international tension, the end of the Cold War, the fracturing of the bonds of apartheid and other similar movements, I can see real hope for the future. The use of force for political reasons appears to be based mainly on greed and personal self-aggrandisement, and should be shunned. Ultimately, it fails. The use of force for so-called 'religious' reasons is the total antithesis of the tenets of all the major world religions and must be the promptings of devils. This should be abhorrent to all reasonable people. In this latter case religion is used purely as an excuse to gain worldly wealth and domination over others by force.

My late grandfather, while caring for all Ireland and its people for whom he had great affection, told me on a number of occasions the following: "I believe Nationalism is the ultimate form of egoism. Why should one country be better than another because I happen to have been born there. That is why I have always been an Internationalist".

He lived up to his words in spending his life working for those who were oppressed wherever they were, Ireland, England, America.

To illustrate clearly the reason behind this thought, one only has to think of his own father, Jim Larkin from Lower Killeavy, and his mother, Mary McAnulty from Burren. Effectively, had it not been for their accidental meeting Jim, his brothers and sisters and their descendants would not have existed. In thinking of those circumstances, had the meeting not taken place the Labour Movement would have been denied the services of a great advocate. Every family, over four or five generations will have been subject to similar co-incidences.

Considering the above I began to think of life and its ending. Every family have been touched with the sad loss of a dear one. Where this is by accident it is difficult enough to cope with, however, when a life is taken by a deliberate act of another person, it is appalling. The effect of the latter act is not only to take one life but also to deny the person who has been killed any descendants for the rest of time.

In the above context I thought of the people of Rwanda who have suffered horrific slaughter where almost a third of complete families have been wiped off the face of the earth forever. All for personal greed.

Having been given almost 60 years of life, and a happy life at that, and being an individual who, during that time, has not found it possible to speak for myself, I reckon my experience demonstrates clearly the continuing need for an active and effective trades union movement. I would also contend that there is a necessity for a vigorous political party working together with the trades unions in the interests of working people. People may say that problems are now different than they were in my grandfather's time, but I don't believe this to be the case. The differences are in scale rather than substance. The needs of people will basically never change — sufficient food, clothing and shelter, which go back to prehistory. The ability to raise a family and to care for them. The need also to develop intellectually and to be able to see the beauty in the world as well as the sorrow and pain. This seems a strange way of being cheerful about the future. I am hopeful that people will begin to realise their potential to do better than past generations. It is obvious to me that very many younger people have begun to realise the need to take care of this planet of ours. That first step is essential to a bright future. I believe that this trend will continue.

In conclusion, I would express the wish that, in the not-too-distant future, I will live to see both in Britain and Ireland, the election of the respective Labour Parties to Government. I believe they offer much for the future of our countries.

My last expressed wish is that peace will remain in this island of ours throughout the world.

The last words are those of my grandfather taken from *The Irish Worker*, 12th August 1911. These are as true today as they were when he wrote them.

"It is good to be alive in these momentous days. Reader, have you ever got up on a box or chair, physically and mentally tired, perhaps suffering from want of food; amongst strangers, say a mass of tired workers, released from their Bastilles of workshop or factory; and then suffering from lack of training, want of education, but filled with the spirit of a new gospel. You try to impart to that unthinking mass the feeling which possesses yourself. The life all round seems to stagnate, everything seems miserable and depressing. Yet you want them to realise that there is great hope for the future — that there is something

231

worth working for, if the workers will only rouse themselves. You plead with them to cast their eyes upward to the stars, instead of grovelling in the slime of their own degradation; point out to them life's promised fullness and joy if they would only seek it. You appeal to their manhood, their love of their little ones, their race instinct, but all these appeals seem to fall on deaf ears: they turn away apparently utterly apathetic, and one tramps on to the next town or meeting, feeling it was hopeless to try and move them. You then creep into a hedgerow, pull out a cheap copy of Morris's *News from Nowhere, The Dream of John Ball, Franciscan Friar, Dante's Inferno,* John Mitchel's *Jail Journal* or last but not least, *Fugitive Essays* by Fintan Lalor, then forgetting the world 'and by the world forgot', one lives.

And then suddenly when things seem blackest and dark night enshrouds abroad, lo! the Sun, and lo! thereunder rises wrath and hope and wonder, and the worker comes marching on. Friends, there is great hope for the future. The worker is beginning to feel his limbs are free."

— From an editorial by Jim Larkin, *Irish Worker*, 12 August, 1911.

Bibliography

BOOKS

Boyd, Andrew — *The Rise of The Irish Trade Unions* (Anvil Books, 1972)

Boyle, J.W. (Ed). — *Leaders & Workers* (Mercier Press/ RTE, 1966)

Cahill, Liam — *Forgotten Revolution* (The O'Brien Press, 1990)

Cain, Frank — *The Wobblies at War* (Melbourne: Spectrum Publications, 1993)

Coates, Ken/ Topham, Tony — *The Making of the T.G.W.U.* (Basil Blackwell, 1991)

D'Arcy, Fergus & Hannigan, Ken *Workers in Union* (Dublin: Stationary Office, 1988)

Gray, John — *City in Revolt* (Blackstaff Press, 1985)

Greaves, C. Desmond — *The ITGWU – 1909-1923* (Gill & Macmillan, 1982)

Holroyd, Michael — *George Bernard Shaw (Vol 1, 2 & 3)* (Chatto & Windus, 1988)

Horgan, John — *Labour – The Price of Power* (Gill & Macmillan, 1986)

Jones, Mary — *These Obstreperous Lassies* (Gill & Macmillan, 1988)

Keogh, Dermot — *The Rise of The Irish Working Class* (Appletree Press, 1982)

Kilmurray, Evanne — *Fight, Starve or Emigrate* (The Larkin Unemployed Centre, 1988)

Krause, David (Ed.) — *The Letters of Sean O'Casey* (Cassell & Co., 1975)

Larkin, Professer Emmett — *James Larkin, 1876-1947* (Routledge & Keegan Paul, 1965)

Loftus, Belinda (Comp.) — *Marching Workers* (Arts Council of Ireland, 1978)

Lysaght, Ed — *Forth The Banners Go – Reminiscences of Wm. O'Brien* (The Three Candles Ltd., 1969)

McCamley, Bill — *The Third Jim – James Fearon*

McCarthy, Charles — *The Decade of Upheaval* (Institute of Public Administration, 1973)

Marreco, Anne — *The Rebel Countess* (Weidenfeld & Nicolson, 1967)

Merrigan, Mat — *Eagle or Cuckoo?* (Matmer Publications, 1989)

Minton, Bruce & Stuart, John — *Men Who Lead Labour* (Modern Age Books, 1937)

Mitchell, Arthur — *Labour in Irish Politics 1909-1930* (Irish University Press, 1974)

Nevin, Donal — *1913, Jim Larkin & The Dublin Lock-Out* (Workers' Union of Ireland, 1964)

Nevin, Donal (Ed.) — *Trade Union Century* (ICTU/RTE/Mercier Press, 1995)

O'Casey, Sean — *The Story of the Irish Citizen Army* (Maunsel, 1919)

Ó Ciosáin, Éamon — *An t-Éireannach* (An Chéad Chló, 1993)

O'Connor, Emmet — *A Labour History of Ireland 1824-1960* (Gill & Macmillan, 1992)

O'Connor, Garry — *Seán O'Casey* (Hodder & Stoughton Ltd., 1988)

O'Leary, Jer — *Banners of Unity* (North Inner City Folklore Project, 1994)

Ryan, Desmond (Ed.) — *The Workers' Republic* (The Sign of the 3 Candles, 1951)

Ryan, W.P. — *The Irish Labour Movement* (Talbot Press)

Swift, John P. — *John Swift – An Irish Dissident* (Gill & Macmillan, 1992)

Tressell, Robert — *The Ragged Trousered Philanthropists* (Grant Richards, 1914)

Turner, Ian — *Sydney's Burning*

Williams, Francis — *Magnificent Journey – The Rise of the Trade Unions* (Odhanes Press Ltd., 1954)

Wolfe, Bertrand — *Strange Communists I Have Known* (George Allen & Union, 1966)

50 Years of Liberty Hall 1909-1959 (Sign of the 3 Candles)

JOURNALS

Workers' Union of Ireland Reports'

'Workers' Union of Ireland GEC Reports'

'Saothair' – *Journal of ILHS*

Index

A

Abraham, Wt. 63
Adamson, W. 63
Ahern, Sergeant M. 55
Asquith, Herbert 62
Aston, E.A 56
Attley, Billy 107, 206, 207

B

Barber, Bill 211
Barber, Marilyn 211
Barnes, George (M.P) 61, 63, 73
Barr, Emily 192, 193
Barry, Gerry 146
Beere, Dr Tecla 192
Behan, Francis 201
Bermingham, Willie 219
Bird, Stephen 70, 211
Birthill, Tony 213, 221
Birrell, Mr 73
Blaney, Neil 143
Bowerman, C.W. 63
Bowers, Fred 79
Brace, William (M.P.) 57, 61, 63,
    70, 73, 76
Bray, Vincent 142
Brennan, Jim 86
Brennan, Ned 140
Breslin, Sean 134
Briscoe, Ben 139
Briscoe, Robert 125, 126
Brown, Bernard 203
Brown, Elizabeth (Larkin) 7, 11,
    12, 24, 213
Brown, Robert 11
Butler, Alderman 110
Byrne, Alfred 108, 125
Byrne, Bernadette 128, 139
Byrne, Gay 203, 204, 206–208
Byrne, James 31, 35, 128

Byrne, James Patrick 128
Byrne, May 48,

C

Campbell, Inspector 49
Cardiff, Breda 148
Cardiff, Paddy 145
Carlin, Terry 222, 228
Carney, Jack 83, 86
Carney, Mina 81, 83
Carroll, Fiona 201
Carroll, Mark 201
Carruth, Michael 201
Carton, Patrick 49
Chaplin, Charlie 87
Chaplin, Ralph 128
Clarke, Tom 81
Clarkin, Senator 125,   126
Cluskey, Frank 108, 222
Clynes, J.R. 63
Coates, Christine 212
Coates, Ken 211
Coleman, Sheila 213
Cohalan, Pat 82
Colgan, Pat 101
Collins, Michael 88
Comerford, Lily 177
Connolly, James 52, 53, 55, 66,
    200, 227
Connolly, Michael 87
Connolly, Ross 200, 226, 227
Conway, Barney 108, 109, 110,
    205
Conway, Bernard 87
Corish, Brendan 179
Corish, Dick 24,
Coward, Noel 177
Cowan, Councillor 125
Cox, Michael 155
Crean, Tom 107, 134, 144, 203,

205
Croasdell, Gerald 180
Cullen, Tom 172
Cuzack, Father Ronan 127

D
Dale, Henry 87
Daly, Damian 210
Daly, Pat 226, 227
Daly, P.T. 227
Davitt, Michael 10
Deasy, Joe, 106, 110
de Coeur, Bob 81
de Courcey Ireland, John 107, 109, 128
De Valera, Eamon 84
Devine, Francis 107, 205, 207
Devoy, John 81, 82
Doherty, Susan 201
Domingo, Placido 215
Donlon, Eileen 173
Donlon, Patricia 214, 213
Donlon, Phelim 172, 173
Donlon, Sheila 173
Doolin, Dermot 134
Doolin, Maura 196
Dougherty, Sir J. 73
Doyle, Teresa 213
Doyle, Tommy 179
Duffy, Joe 203–207
Duffy, Luke 132
Duncan, Charles 63
Dunne, Tony 199

F
Fagan, Sergeant 52
Fay, John 210
Fearon, James 22
Ferguson, Sir Samuel 156, 157
Fitzpatrick, Catherine 202
Fitzpatrick, John 80, 83, 86
Flanagan, Constable Myles 54, 55
Fleming, Eric 203

Fogarty, Alex 196
Foran, Thomas 88
Forrest, R. 55
Fortune, Joan 199
Freeland, Mr 61

G
Garry, Tom 154, 210
Gibson, Leo 188, 189
Gifford, Miss 54,
Gill, A.H. 63
Glackin, Eddie 200
Glynn, Thomas 91
Gogarty, Michael 199
Goldstone, F.W. 63
Gore-Booth, Aideen 104
Gosling, Harry 61, 70, 73, 76
Gray, John 23
Griffin, Eamonn 188, 189
Guinness, Lady Mary 157

H
Hall, Fred 63
Hamilton, John 91
Hancock, J.G. 63
Handel-Booth, Mr 35
Hardie, J. Keir 63
Harding, Dave 162
Harding, Warren 97
Harris, Frank 97
Harte, Jack 203
Harvey, W.E. 63
Hastings, Stephen 87
Hatton, Seamie 168
Haughey, Charlie 141, 142
Hayes, Ann 21
Hayes, Brendan 107, 145, 199, 210, 211
Hayward, Bill 66
Hedderman, Carmencita 140
Helmand, Mary VAN 213
Henderson, Arthur (M.P.) 61, 63, 73, 119

Hepburn, Audrey 215
Hill, Joe 80
Hill, John 61, 70, 73, 76
Hillery, President 152,   220, 222
Hodge, John 63
Hudson, Walter 63

J
Jameson, Joe 227, 228
Johnson, Brian 227, 28
Johnson, Patricia 227, 28
Johnson, Tom 132
Johnson, W. 63
Johnstad, Errol L. 190
Jones, Jack 61, 70, 73, 76, 224, 225

K
Kavanagh, Bishop 152
Kavanagh, Paul 193
Kavanagh, Tammy 152
Kaye, Danny 215
Keenan, Peter A. 209
Kelly, Oisin 207, 220
Kenny, Roland 65
Kerrigan, Pauline 199
Kiely, Catherine 201
Kiernan, Superintendent 51,
King, Martin 106
King, Patricia 199, 200

L
Lalor, Fintan 231
Lanza, Mario 168
Larkin, Agnes 7
Larkin, Anne 115, 116, 127, 134, 152, 154, 155
Larkin, Annie 98
Larkin, Barney (Snr)3, 9, 16
Larkin, Barney (Jnr)3, 102
Larkin, Barney 24, 105, 113, 114, 220, 222
Larkin, Brian 114,

Larkin, Brenda (Riding)104, 163, 173, 183–185, 196, 210, 211
Larkin, Delia 7, 9, 10, 22, 87, 98, 100, 101, 104, 152, 164
Larkin, Denis 18, 22, 24, 105, 106, 113–117, 120, 123–127, 134, 139, 145–147, 149–155, 160, 162, 174, 179, 194, 197, 204, 205, 210, 218, 220–222
Larkin, Edie 114,
Larkin, Elizabeth (Brown) 104, 105, 113, 114, 151
Larkin, Professor Emmet 23,
Larkin, Esther (Russell) 98, 99
Larkin, Evelyn 114,
Larkin, Finton 24, 105, 113, 114, 123, 220, 222
Larkin, Hilda 134
Larkin, Hugh (Snr)3, 102
Larkin, Hugh 6, 10,
Larkin, James (Snr)3, 5, 9, 10, 229
Larkin, (Big) Jim 6, 7–13, 15–19, 21–27, 31–36, 38–41, 43, 46, 51–54, 57, 58, 60, 62–66, 68, 69, 71, 72, 74, 77–92, 96–98, 100, 101,103–111, 114, 118–120, 124, 129, 130, 132, 133, 146, 148, 149, 152, 153, 162, 164, 179, 194, 204, 205, 210, 219, 220, 222, 224–227, 231
Larkin, Jim (Jnr) 6, 7, 17, 24, 88, 105, 106, 113, 114, 117, 118, 120, 122–125, 131–136, 140, 141, 145, 147, 149, 179, 180, 188, 194, 204, 205, 210, 218, 222, 227
Larkin, Jim 134, 151, 155, 159, 161, 162, 164–189, 191–231
Larkin, Margaret 7, 10, 102
Larkin, Miriam 210
Larkin, Patrick 3, 102

Larkin, Peter 7, 9, 10, 77, 88, 90, 91, 92, 98, 99, 102, 104, 105, 152
Larkin, Sheila 114,
Larkin, Stella 6, 128, 151, 155, 160, 161, 163–165, 174, 175
Larkin, Vivian 152, 161
Lemass, Sean 147, 205, 206
Lennon, Margaret 20, 21
Lennox, Hugh 197
Lowry, William (Esq) 44, 46
Lynd, J.L. 45
Lynn, Dr Chris 4
Lyth, J. Harold 45

M
McAnulty, Bridget 5
McAnulty, Catherine 4, 7, 8
McAnulty, Frank 4
McAnulty, Mary 1, 5, 7, 9, 10, 90, 229
McCaig, Inspector Alex 48
McCann, Alderman 125, 126
McCarthy, Charlie 147
McConnell, Winifred 176
McConnon, Eoin 154
McConnon, Michael 174
McCormack, Tony 188, 189
MacCrae, Eoin 168
MacDonald, Ramsay 63
McGowan, Seamus 87
McGrane, Jean 213, 214
McGrane, Joe 186
McGrath, Joe 88
McKeon, Ex-councillor 52, 53
McMullen, Charles 20, 21
McNally, Margaret 162, 163
MacNeill, J. (Esq) 119, 120
McSweeney, Imelda 173
McSweeny, Olive 173
McSweeny, Paddy 173
McSweeny, Sean 173
Maguire, Andrea 212, 213

Maguire, Kelly 212, 213
Maguire, Tammy 212, 213
Major, John 218
Maloney, Helena 32, 54, 55 65
Mandela, Nelson 141, 142, 217
Mansfield, Nicholas 70, 212
Markievicz, Countess Constance 18, 32, 40, 43, 44, 46, 47, 54, 55, 65, 81, 83, 104
Markievicz, Count D. 54
Maxwell, Jack 176
Mealy, Gene 199, 200
Merrigan, Matt (Snr) 107, 133, 145
Mitchel, John 231,
Mongey, Annette 199
Montgomery, Hugh 144
Molloy, Jimmy 207
Moore, Annie 157–159, 204
Moore, James 157, 159, 160
Moore, Noreen 227, 228
Moore, Roger 215
Morris, William 231
Moses 27
Mouskouri, Nana 215
Mulcahy, General 110
Mullen, Michael 222
Murphy, Alfie 200
Murphy, J.T. 201
Murphy, Margaret 50
Murphy, Michael J. 7
Murphy, Nicholas 50
Murphy, William Martin 25, 32, 33, 38, 56, 58, 71, 72, 128, 173
Myles, Constable Patrick J. 55

N
Neligan, Colonel 119,
Nettleton, John 213
Nevin, Donal 107, 132, 142, 145, 227
Nicholls, Henry (Esq) 47, 48,
Ní Mhurchu, Padraigin 199

Nolan, Elizabeth 128
Nolan, James 31, 33, 35, 49, 128
Nolan, Mary 199
Nolan, Patrick 88
Nolan, Sean 168
Nowakovski, Marion 165

O
Oberon, Merle 87
O'Brien, Nell 199
O'Brien, William 104, 128
O'Callaghan, Con 168
O'Casey, Sean 128
O'Ceallaig, Sean 134
O'Connor, Ulick, 168
O'Friel, H. 120
O'Halloran, Michael 140, 141
O'Keefe, James 126
O'Keefe, Shirley 213
O'Leary, Jer 65, 200, 226
O'Lehane, Con 80
O'Maolain, Michael 87
O'Regan, Mrs 55,
O'Reilly, Dr Tony 169, 173
O'Sullivan, Donal 134
O'Riordan, Mrs 192
Orpen, Sir William 173
Owen, Robert 34

P
Parker, James 63
Parry, Robert 213
Partridge, William P. 52, 53, 55
Pearse, Patrick 123
Pearse, Willie 123
Perdisatt, Elsie 199
Plouvier, Peter 180
Plunkett Kelly, James 7, 107, 203
Pointer, Joseph 63
Pope Pius XII 127
Power, Charles S. 36
Prendergast, Tony 172
Priestley, J.B. 175

Pring, Justice 91

Q
Quinn, Superintendent Fergus 52

R
Rafter, Peggy 199
Redmond, James 199
Reeve, Charles 91
Richards, Thomas 63
Richardson, T. 63
Ridge, Lola 78
Riding, Brenda (Larkin), 104, 163, 173, 183–185, 196, 211
Riding, Elizabeth 184
Riding, Thomas 160, 184
Rien, Bertram W. 189, 191
Roberts, E.J. 213
Roberts, G.H. (M.P.) 61, 63, 73
Roberts, Ruairi 144
Robeson, Paul 87
Robinson, Lennox 42, 43,
Robinson, Mary 227
Rose, E.C. 61
Roseman, Jeff 181
Ross, Colonel Sir John 72
Russell, George (A.E.) 27, 28, 30
Russell, George 98, 99
Russell, Esther (Larkin) 98, 99
Ryan, W.P. 6, 17

S
Sargeant, Jack 11
Seddon, J.A. 61, 70, 73, 76
Sexton, James 15, 18, 22, 224
Shakespeare, William 175
Shankman, Leslie 141
Shaw, George Bernard 110
Sheehy-Skeffington, Francis 36, 37, 41, 54, 65
Sheridan, Pat 47
Shewin, Councillor 125

Shortt, Margaret 199
Sister Carmel 163
Smith, Florence 184
Smith, Governor Al 88, 91
Smith, Albert 63
Snowden, Philip 63
Somers, James 188, 189
Spring, Dick 221
Stanley, Albert 63
Sutton, J.E. 63
Sweetman, Jane 199
Sweetman, Larry 199
Sweetman, Thomas 199
Swift, John 18,
Swifte, E.G. 31, 52, 53

T
Tambo, Oliver 142
Taplin, Eric 213
Thatcher, Margaret 227
Thewlis, Patrick 188, 189, 191
Thomas, J.H. 63
Thorne, Will 63
Tillet, Ben 67, 68
Timmons, Eugene 206
Tracey, Stephen 188, 189
Treanor, Thomas 3, 4, 7
Trehy, Paddy 199
Turner, Ian 90

V
Vale, Peter 172
Vaughan, Joseph M. 46

W
Wadsworth, John 63
Walsh, Stephen 63
Walshe, Archbishop Dr 67
Ward, John (M.P.) 57, 61, 70, 73, 76,
Wardle, George J. 63
White, Eileen 80, 193
Whitter, Dick 179

Wilkie, Alex 63
Willie, Jim 141
Williams, John 63
Wolfe, Bertrand 79